French Light Infantry 1784-1815

From the Chasseurs of Louis XVI to Napoleon's Grande Armée

Terry Crowdy

Helion & Company

Helion & Company Limited
Unit 8 Amherst Business Centre
Budbrooke Road
Warwick
CV34 5WE
England
Tel. 01926 499619
Email: info@helion.co.uk
Website: www.helion.co.uk
Twitter: @helionbooks
Visit our blog at http://blog.helion.co.uk/

Published by Helion & Company 2021
Designed and typeset by Mach 3 Solutions Ltd (www.mach3solutions.co.uk)
Cover designed by Paul Hewitt, Battlefield Design (www.battlefield-design.co.uk)

Text © Terry Crowdy 2021
Colour uniform plates by Patrice Courcelle © Helion and Company 2021; flag art by Anderson Subtil © Helion and Company 2021. Other images as credited.

Cover: Detail from Wilhelm von Kobell's 'French cavalry and infantry on march' (1800). (Anne S.K. Brown Military Collection)

Every reasonable effort has been made to trace copyright holders and to obtain their permission for the use of copyright material. The author and publisher apologise for any errors or omissions in this work, and would be grateful if notified of any corrections that should be incorporated in future reprints or editions of this book.

ISBN 978-1-914059-78-0

British Library Cataloguing-in-Publication Data.
A catalogue record for this book is available from the British Library.

All rights reserved. No part of this publication may be reproduced, stored in a retrieval system, or transmitted, in any form, or by any means, electronic, mechanical, photocopying, recording or otherwise, without the express written consent of Helion & Company Limited.

For details of other military history titles published by Helion & Company Limited, contact the above address, or visit our website: http://www.helion.co.uk

We always welcome receiving book proposals from prospective authors.

Contents

Acknowledgements		iv
Introduction		v
Glossary of French and Technical Terms		viii
Chronologies		x
1	In the King's Army	13
2	Light Infantry in the Wars of the French Revolution	33
3	Light Infantry in the First Empire	61
4	Light Infantry Tactics	90
5	Uniforms and Equipment	138
6	Lilies and Eagles – Light Infantry Colours	161
7	Notes for Re-enactors and Wargamers	169
Bibliography and Further Reading		173

Acknowledgements

At the age of 14 I was a volunteer tunnel guide at Fort Amherst in Chatham, Kent. There were frequent re-enactments at the fort, and I first fired a Baker rifle courtesy of Richard Moore, who went on to become the technical adviser and appear in the popular 'Sharpe' TV series. My head was soon turned by a small 'French' group, representing the 9e Légère. They were rude, arrogant, and impossibly cool. Now aged 51, I have spent much of my life studying and writing about Napoleon's soldiers, all because I plucked up the courage to talk to those scoundrels. For sparking my interest in French light infantry, plaudits then to Martin Lancaster, Ian Edwards, Graeme Harrison-Jones (RIP), Gerd 'Bocagère' Hoad, Million, l'Étang, and all members, worldwide, before and since.

I want also to recognise the time and generosity of my colleague in Paris, Yves Martin. An author, researcher and collector, Yves Martin has something of a cult status among the Napoleonic cognizanti. Jakub Samek is a brilliant foil for any discussion on infantry tactics. Paul Dawson has been extremely helpful discussing the findings of his monumental research in French military archives. Paul is pushing the boundaries of what is really 'known' about the uniforms of Napoleon's armies. Another steadfast colleague is Pierre-Yves Chauvin, with whom I spend hours engaged in a veritable ping-pong of messages on our latest research. My understanding of the Napoleonic world was greatly influenced by the late Bernard Coppens who passed away in 2020 while I was writing this book, and whose mortal remains are now scattered over the field at Waterloo. Bernard introduced me to works of Bardin, which are incredible and an endless source of fascination. He also advised me to delve further back into French history to better understand the Napoleonic era. Lastly, I must thank my wife, Sarah, for the loving support bubble which allows my work to be done, even through a global pandemic.

Introduction

The existence of light infantry can be traced back to the beginnings of military history. Battles in the ancient world typically comprised of a shock action between tightly packed masses of foot soldiers, or phalanxes. The earliest light troops were those who fought outside of the phalanx, in open order, primarily using missile weapons rather than *armes blanches* (literally 'white arms)', or more figuratively, 'cold steel' (pikes and swords). Their principal role was to scout ahead and screen the phalanx while it marched and camped. On the battlefield, the light infantry would disconcert enemy formations before the main shock action began. They were lightly armoured, if at all, relying on speed of movement for protection and never standing their ground when charged.

In a great many respects, the light infantry of the Revolution and Napoleonic eras were little different from their ancient counterparts, the ancient Greek psiloi or Roman velites. Perhaps the key difference between the ancient and eighteenth-century light infantry was in the nature of the phalanx behind them. With the move from *armes blanches* to *armes à feu* (firearms), the phalanx was transformed. Given the relative inaccuracy and slow rate of fire of muskets, soldiers had to be massed to deliver an effective weight of fire; but the phalanx began to reduce in depth to maximise its firepower potential. At the time of Gustavus Adolphus (1594-1632) the phalanx had reduced to six ranks, the maximum number that could bring their arms to bear. Following the adoption of the socket bayonet at the beginning of the eighteenth century, the phalanx reduced to four and then to three ranks by the reign of Frederick the Great (1740-1786); but the formation was still, in essence, a phalanx, with men packed into ranks and files and operating in close concert. This was particularly true when the phalanx (or battalion as the principal tactical unit became known) was formed in a column formation for ease of manoeuvre, or for shock action. As was the case in ancient times, some troops were required to operate outside this formation, protecting the flanks, screening its deployment, advance and retreat. In the French army of the Napoleonic period, these troops were best known as tirailleurs (literally 'shooters', or skirmishers).

After the introduction of reliable, breach-loading, rifled firearms, smokeless gunpowder, and the machinegun, the battlefield was transformed. The infantry phalanx was finished except as a training tool, or as part of

FRENCH LIGHT INFANTRY 1784-1815

A light infantry bivouac (1808) by Benjamin Zix (1772-1811). One drawback on the advanced guard was that one often overtook the supply wagons. The boon was that their marauders usually had first pickings. (Anne S.K. Brown Military Collection)

military pageant. With the final demise of the battlefield phalanx there was no longer any requirement for light infantry in the traditional sense. All infantry soldiers operated in open order and in much smaller tactical groups. Even then, there was still a requirement for troops to operate ahead of the main body, to scout, to seize ground, to make tactical strikes. As the traditional role of light infantry declined, we see the development of Special Forces, particularly commandos and airborne troops with the ability to raid or quickly seize ground ahead of motorised infantry and armour. The bold spirit once associated with light infantry therefore continues to this day.

As we delve deeper into the subject, we find the initial purpose of light troops in the eighteenth century was not as battlefield skirmishers, but as troops of the advanced guard operating in front of the main body of an army or corps. In many respects, the role of light infantry was most important in this area. In the days of the phalanx, armies required large, open spaces to deploy and fight. This ground had to be seized and their deployment protected. Mountainous and heavily wooded terrain do not lend themselves to pitched battles, nor are they suitable for cavalry. Such terrain required lightly equipped troops who could exploit such difficult terrain for attack or defence. We should also consider the experiences of warfare in the New World – particularly the bush fighting techniques which were a feature of the French and Indian War (Seven Years War) in America. Regular, formed troops were simply unable to respond to rapid hit-and-run attacks. They could only be countered by troops fighting outside the constraints of the line.

The French experience with light infantry is particularly interesting. At first glance, we think of the French as pioneers of the mass use of skirmishers.

INTRODUCTION

It is difficult to imagine a French infantry column if not preceded by a swarm of voltigeurs. Yet, in the last years of the ancien régime, we find French military theorists in the midst of a debate on the utility of light infantry. Some argued that light infantry were essential and required specialist training; yet others believed all soldiers ought to know how to perform this function. This debate continued through the period and was still in full flow after Waterloo, with many believing light infantry were no different to the line, except in the cut of their uniform.[1] In this case, why did the French massively increase the number of light infantry battalions, and why, when the entire army was reorganised on successive occasions, did the French perpetuate having two types of infantry? Advocates of light infantry knew why. While all infantrymen could serve in the outposts and skirmish, light infantry did it better. In return, they needed special training and an entirely different mindset to the line.

In 2012 my book *Incomparable* was published. A regimental history of the 9e Légère (9th Light Infantry), the book focuses on the Napoleonic period, telling the story of the men of one regiment from Marengo to Waterloo. As a narrative history this is an exciting story reflecting the dramatic character arc of Napoleon's career as head of state. In my research I spent significant time looking at the early, formative years of this regiment before the revolution and during the 1790s. After *Incomparable* I wanted to explore the early period in more detail and understand why French light infantry developed as they did. I also wanted to explore in more detail the key contemporary work on the subject by *Général de Division* Guillaume Philibert Duhesme, who wrote two books on light infantry during the Napoleonic Wars. The first, *Précis historique de l'infanterie légère*, appeared in 1806 and, as the title suggests, is a historical survey of light infantry, into which he added some interesting anecdotes and observations. The second book is more important. Published in 1814, the *Essai historique de l'infanterie légère* was written to serve as a training manual for French officers.

Readers will hopefully forgive something of bias towards the 9e Légère in this book. For those who have read *Incomparable*, this book will complement it with a far broader survey of the organisation, tactics, and uniform of this arm. Readers may also be surprised at the detailed focus on the period before the outbreak of war in 1792; but understanding what went on before is the key to understanding Napoleon's army. The subject cannot properly be studied in isolation. This mantra (and an introduction to the works of Bardin) was taught to me by the Belgian historian, author and illustrator, Bernard Coppens (1949-2020). It is in respectful memory of our colleague Bernard that this work is dedicated.

---

1   See Colonel Marcellin Marbot's criticism of the 1816 work by Général Rogniat for many examples of this debate: *Remarques critiques sur l'ouvrage de M. le lieutenant-général Rogniat, intitulé: Considérations sur l'art de la guerre* (Paris: Anselin & Pochard, 1820), p.319.

Glossary of French and Technical Terms

The text is interspersed with French and archaic English technical terms and ranks.

… *à cheval,* on horseback, i.e. cavalry.
… *à pied,* on foot, i.e. infantry.
Ancien regime, the feudal period in French history before the revolution of 1789.
Arquebus (plural harquebuses), a long-barrelled, firearm, forerunner to the flintlock musket; typically with a matchlock mechanism and fired from a rest.
Artificer, a skilled military workman manufacturing/ repairing uniforms and equipment.
Avant-garde/advanced-guard, the body of troops scouting and protecting the march and camps of an army.
Carabine, short-barrelled, rifled, flintlock firearm. Often confused with *mousqueton.*
Carabinier, properly rifleman, an infantryman equipped with rifled carbine. The term became synonymous for the grenadier company in light infantry battalion.
Chasseur, literally 'hunter'. A French light infantryman: the term was analogous with the German *Jäger/Jaeger.*
Corps francs/franches, literally, 'free corps' (German *Frei Korps*), a unit of irregular volunteer soldiers, outside the normal military establishment, typically raised for duration of a war.
Demi-brigade, literally 'half-brigade'. French term from the 1790s, for an infantry formation of three battalions.
Dragon/dragoon, a type of mounted infantry, armed with muskets and swords.
Éclaireurs, scouts, or an unofficial light company between 1791-1805.
Enfants perdus, literally 'lost children'. The name given to light troops in the XVII and XVIII centuries who formed advanced guards and undertook perilous mission.

GLOSSARY OF FRENCH AND TECHNICAL TERMS

Flanquer, (flanker), a skirmisher protecting the flanks of a battalion or formation.

Fourrier, a quartermaster *caporal* managing the company books.

Fusilier, a soldier armed with a flintlock musket (*fusil*); a soldier of the centre companies.

Grenadier, originally a grenade-armed, assault soldier, grenadiers were elite companies or battalions formed of the strongest, tallest men.

Habit, a soldier's frock coat with lapels and turnbacks. Replaced by a short-tailed *habit-veste* (coatee).

Hussard/hussar, a type of light cavalry of Hungarian origin.

Jäger/Jaeger, German language term for 'hunter', a type of light troop.

Légère/léger, 'light' a reference to light cavalry, infantry or artillery.

Légion, a regiment-sized, mixed corps of infantry, cavalry, and specialist troops.

Mousqueton, a short-barrelled, flintlock musket, typically carried by cavalry.

Partisan, eighteenth century term for soldiers engaged in *petite guerre* operations, but latterly applying to irregular, insurrectional forces.

Peloton, French tactical sub-division of a battalion; prior to 1791, formed of a half company, and afterwards a single company of infantrymen.

Petite guerre, literally petty, or little, war. Eighteenth century term for the military operations which occurred outside pitched battles, including actions of the forward posts, reconnoitring, explorations, and raids.

Sous-lieutenant, literally 'under- or sub-lieutenant'. Subaltern officer equivalent to a second lieutenant (in French a *lieutenant en second* is a grade higher).

Surtout, an upper-coat, worn as a form of undress, principally by officers and cavalry troopers.

Tirailleur, literally 'shooter' (German *Schützen*). A soldier deployed as a skirmisher in open order (*en tirailleur*), able to fire at will, at individual targets.

Troupes légères, generic French term for light troops, mounted or foot.

Voltigeur, literally 'vaulter'. Member of a battalion light infantry company after 1804.

Chronologies

Political Chronology

1654, 7 June. Accession of Louis XIV (1643-1715).
1715, 1 September. Accession of Louis XV (1710-1774).
1774, 10 May. Accession of Louis XVI (1754-1793).
1789, 17 June. French National Assembly formed.
1789, 14 July. Storming of the Bastille in Paris.
1791, 3 September. The Constitution of 1791 is proclaimed.
1791, 1 October. The Legislative Assembly first meets.
1792, 20 September. National Convention formed.
1792, 21 September. Abolition of monarchy, France declared a Republic.
1793, 21 January. Louis XVI executed.
1793, 24 June. Constitution of 1793.
1795, 2 November. Five-man executive 'Directorate' government formed.
1799, 9 November. 'Brumaire Coup'. Beginning of the Consulate.
1799, 24 December. Constitution of Year VIII, Napoleon is First Consul.
1802, 4 August. Constitution of Year X, Napoleon First Consul for life.
1804, 18 May. Constitution of Year XII, Napoleon proclaimed Emperor.
1804, 2 December. Coronation of Napoleon I.
1814, 6 April. Napoleon I abdicates.
1814, 6 April. First restoration of Louis XVIII (1755-1824).
1815, 20 March. Napoleon I arrives in Paris, start of 100 Days.
1815, 22 June. Second abdication of Napoleon I.
1815, 8 July. Second restoration of Louis XVIII.

Military Chronology 1700-1815

1701-1714 War of Spanish Succession.
1740-1748 War of Austrian Succession.
1756-1763 Seven Years War.
1769 French conquest of Corsica.
1775-1783 American Revolutionary War.
1792-1797 War of the First Coalition.
1793-1796 War in the Vendée.

CHRONOLOGIES

1798-1802 War of the Second Coalition.
1803-1806 War of the Third Coalition.
1806-1807 War of the Fourth Coalition.
1807-1814 Peninsular War.
1809 War of the Fifth Coalition.
1812 Russian Campaign.
1813-1814 War of the Sixth Coalition.
1815 War of the Seventh Coalition (100 Days).

Excellent contemporary study by Christian Gottfried Heinrich Geissler, (1770-1844) showing youths escorting French soldiers to their billets in Leipzig, circa-1808. A light infantry carabinier (in bearskin) can be seen, with a chasseur drummer in greatcoat to his right. (Anne S.K. Brown Military Collection)

1

In the King's Army

The subject of this study is France's light infantry in the late eighteenth century and Napoleonic Wars, with a particular focus on the years from 1784-1815. As with all studies of the military arts during this period, it would be negligent not to appreciate some of what occurred before the French Revolution and the advent of the First Empire. While many owed their careers to the opportunities created by the French Revolution, professional soldiers like Napoleon Bonaparte were schooled in the art of war by the tutors of the *ancien régime* and had a good knowledge of their own recent history. The lessons of past conflicts helped inform their own careers. What might appear to be innovative at first glance may in fact have been an age-old approach, particularly at moments of great crisis such as 1792-1793 and 1814-1815. To understand the subject to its fullest extent, we must know something about the centuries and decades that came before Napoleon, with the *enfants perdus*, partisans and legions of the armies of the kings of France.

Enfants Perdus

France's first true light troops appeared with the invention of handheld firearms and the creation of *arquebusiers* and musketeers. These soldiers were interspersed with the pike corps in the sixteenth and seventeenth centuries. They were a throwback to the missile troops protecting the phalanxes of the ancients. According to Colin's excellent study of tactics in the eighteenth century, the pikemen formed a battalion mass of 2,000 men, arranged in 20-24 ranks.[1] The *arquebusiers* were arranged in groups of twenty along the front of the pikemen and with two *manches* (sleeves) of 200 men each, in five ranks, formed on the wings of the battalion, and a few held in reserve. In these early incarnations of *troupes légères* we find some references to what we might call their genetic makeup. For instance, during the Wars of Religion (1562-1598) Henri I de Guise 'Balafré' (1550-1588) wished to raise bands of light troops who were drawn from the south of France: mountain dwellers, light in frame,

---

1 Jean Colin, *L'infanterie au XVIIIe siècle: la tactique* (Paris: Berger-Levrault, 1907), p.17

FRENCH LIGHT INFANTRY 1784-1815

Mountain arquebusiers from 1715. Horns were a more practical form of signal for light troops than drums. (New York Public Library)

agile of leg and armed with light harquebuses and daggers (we will find the chasseurs of Louis XVI similarly raised in France's mountainous regions, and Napoleon's *voltigeurs* issued with short-barrelled muskets).[2]

The light troops of this earlier era are perhaps better known by the soubriquet *enfants perdus* (literally, lost children). The use of the word children had nothing to do with the age of the combatants, but instead was similar in usage to the word 'infantry' – the root of which is the same as 'infant' – a reference to those footmen too low in rank or experience to qualify for, or afford, service in the cavalry. The *enfants perdus* were soldiers who volunteered for the most dangerous missions in return for prize money. The competition for places was sometimes so strong they were selected by the drawing of lots. Dangerous missions included skirmishing ahead of the phalanx (thus being trapped between two advancing sets of pikemen) or seizing and holding key positions on the battlefield. According to Bardin's dictionary, the *enfants perdus* were formed into bands 800 to 1,600 strong, often went unarmoured, and were armed with culverins (hand cannon, not to be confused with the later use of the same word to signify a full-size cannon) and harquebuses, knives, long daggers, and clubs. For signals they used horns rather than drums (Napoleon's voltigeur cornets were nothing new). During the reign of Louis XIV the *enfants perdus* were frequently used in offensive sieges where the weapon of choice was the hand grenade. The *enfants perdus* were therefore the forerunner of the grenadiers, who in turn were associated with courage and being selected for the most dangerous and therefore honourable missions. The prize money given to *enfants perdus* seemingly evolved into the high pay of the grenadiers. Some were given small horses to go raiding with, and these mounted *enfants perdus* became the forerunner of France's dragoon regiments. This mounted infantry often fought on foot, forming themselves into great bands of skirmishers.[3] As pike warfare became less prevalent, the habit of forming bands of *enfants perdus* became less frequent, and so their role was fulfilled by more formalised corps of *troupes légères*. Over time, the term *enfants perdus* became more associated with the first wave of attackers against fortifications. They are better known to us in the anglophone world as the 'Forlorn Hope', which in modern parlance we would describe as a 'suicide mission' – that is, one from which there was little hope of survival. Our expression is an Anglicisation

---

2　Étienne-Alexandre Bardin, *Dictionnaire de l'armée de terre, ou Recherches historiques sur l'art et les usages militaires des anciens et des modernes* (Paris: J. Corréard, 1849), p.2917.

3　Colin, *L'infanterie au XVIIIe siècle: la tactique*, p.20.

of the Dutch term, *verloren hoop* (literally, lost troop) which was analogous with the original French term.

Partisans and *Petite Guerre*

There is a species of warfare known in French as *petite guerre* (literally, petty, or little war). Today we know this form of warfare better by its Spanish translation – guerrilla. Usage of the latter suggests the example of the Spanish or Peninsular War, or of popular uprisings, but it was already well-known aspect of conflict even by the end of the seventeenth century. The following passage attributed to the Napoleonic veteran Friedrich Wilhelm von Bismarck (1786-1860) summarises the subject neatly:

> The strategical object of war is the defeat of the enemy. War is divided into great and petty. The object of the former is the enemy's army – that of the latter his lines of communication. Great war consists in the operations of contending armies; petty war is conducted by partisans, and its object is the *matériel* – the military stores and provisions.[4]

As Bismarck states, this petty war was usually conducted by partisans. The word 'partisan' ultimately derives from the word 'party'. In the eighteenth century it referred to ad hoc detachments of troops sent on special missions, rather than formal military formations, such as a brigade, or division. Only after the emergence of the guerrilla fighters of the Napoleonic Peninsular War (and perhaps the Chouans in the Vendean civil war of the 1790s) did the term become associated with a civilian population waging insurrectionary war against a state party.

In the eighteenth century, partisan bands were typically made up of *compagnies franches* (free companies) or legions of mixed troops (usually dragoons, hussars, and infantry grenadiers and fusiliers). They typically existed only during wartime and were often recruited from foreigners and even deserters, semi-funding themselves from the proceeds of pillage. Their chiefs were given carte blanche to wreak havoc, waging a war of attrition by reconnoitring and attacking the enemy's advanced posts and convoys, their escorts, seizing baggage, planting ambushes, raiding deep into enemy territory as they saw fit. If nothing else, the ceaseless harassment of partisans tied up enemy soldiers as guards and escorts, thus weakening the main field army.

This was not a gentlemanly form of warfare by any stretch of the imagination, but it was considered legal. During the War of the Austrian Succession (1740-1748) the belligerents signed up to a code of conduct which forbade the use of poisoned ammunition, corrupting water supplies and called for fair treatment of prisoners of war. The convention specifically forbade the

---

4 North Ludlow Beamish, *On the Uses and Application of Cavalry in War from the Text of Bismark* (London: T&W Boone, 1855), p.299.

FRENCH LIGHT INFANTRY 1784-1815

Officer of the Volontaires Étrangers de Clermont-Prince in 1758, after Alfred de Marbot, 1830. (New York Public Library)

use of *Partis Bleus* (literally, Blue Parties).[5] The latter were independent gangs of brigands, little better than highwaymen, sometimes dressed in blue blouses or without any recognised uniform. These gangs were effectively 'land pirates' who might switch allegiances or have none. They were considered outside the law and could expect to be hanged if captured. Partisans, on the other hand, were recognised as official combatants, or *partis de guerre* (war parties). They were 'irregular' only in the sense they existed and operated outside of the regular regiments of the line. They were closely akin to the *corsairs* (privateers) on the high seas.

According the Grandmaison's 1756 work (the author was a *lieutenant-colonel* in the Volontaires de Flandre whose works were recommended by Frederick the Great), light troops and irregulars became essential because the 'Queen of Hungary' (the Hapsburg empress, Maria Theresa) had inundated Bohemia, Bavaria, and Alsace with this type of troop during the War of the Austrian Succession.[6] Irregular troops were exceedingly difficult to combat using conventional military tactics, so France found itself having to raise its own irregulars to fight like-with-like. At the beginning of the conflict, France had nothing but a few free companies and two regiments of hussars (Grandmaison writes the latter were ruined by desertion). Against them was a veritable horde of Hapsburg soldiers drawn principally from the Balkans and well-schooled in irregular warfare against the Turks.

As it happened, when the French began raising partisan corps of their own, they found they were rather good at this type of fighting. Louis Susane (author of a multi-volume history of the French Army) correctly fixes the official creation of French light infantry chasseurs to the defence of Prague in 1742.[7] Faced with incessant attacks by Croats, Pandurs and hussars, a unit of chasseurs (hunters) was formed to combat them by Jean-Chrétien Fischer (1713-1762). This irregular corps was integrated into the army and included 400 foot and 200 horse chasseurs. It served as the model for all the other irregular corps to come. Most of these were disbanded at the end of the war in 1749, but the Chasseurs de Fischer, the Volontaires Royaux

---

5   Bardin, *Dictionnaire de l'armée de terre*, Part 11, p.4302.
6   Thomas Auguste Le Roy de Grandmaison, *La Petite Guerre, ou traite du service des troupes légères en campagne* (Francfort & Leipsic: Knoch & Esslinger, 1758), pp.1-2
7   Louis Susane, *Histoire de l'ancienne infanterie française* (Paris: Corréard, 1853), Vol.7, pp.374-375.

and the Volontaires de Geschray were conserved, while the remainder were formed into two new mixed corps called the Volontaires de Dauphiné and the Volontaires de Flandre.

Fischer is such an important figure in the development of the chasseurs he merits a few words of introduction. Every Frenchman who has since worn the green epaulettes of a chasseur ought to look upon Fischer as a Godfather figure. He was a native German, born in Stuttgart, and started his military career at the very bottom of the ladder, employed as a groom or domestic servant to the colonel of the infantry Régiment d'Anjou. During the siege of Prague in 1742, he developed a reputation for bravery by taking the officers' horses out to graze despite the risk of enemy attack. While doing this, he organised the other domestics into something of a volunteer corps known for cunning and bravery. On 1 November 1743, *Maréchal* de Belle-Isle authorised Fischer to raise a free corps of foot and mounted chasseurs and made him their captain. From groom to captain in little more than a year was an almost unparalleled piece of social mobility (certainly before the emigration crisis in the 1790s), and for a foreigner too. Four years later, on 15 September 1747, he was commissioned as a *lieutenant-colonel*. Louis XV signed the brevet for this promotion, citing Fischer's excellent service in the Low Countries; or was it because Fischer brazenly kidnapped the editor of the *Frankfurt Gazette*, a noted critic of the French king? While no doubt seen as something of an upstart by the noble French officers, Fischer served as a model for future leaders of *troupes légères*.[8]

The officers commanding these partisan bands required a great deal of energy, elan and dash, and it was generally recognised this type of service was the most fatiguing and the most dangerous around. The wonderful 1759 book *Le Partisan* by Jeney gives the qualities of a good chief of light troops:

1. A lively imagination for plans, and ruses & resources.
2. A penetrating mind, capable of immediately combining all the circumstances of an action.
3. An intrepid heart against all appearance of danger.
4. Steadfast countenance, always assured, & no sign of concern nor change.
5. A fortunate memory, to call everyone by their name.
6. An alert, robust & indefatigable temperament, to go through everything, & give one's soul to everything.
7. A just & rapid coup d'œil; that he immediately grasps the faults & the conveniences, the obstacles & the dangers of terrain & all the objects, which he traverses.
8. Such feelings with which he secures the respect, trust, & dedication of the whole corps.[9]

---

8   Susane, *Histoire de l'ancienne infanterie française*, Vol.7, pp.375-378; Jean Maximilien Lamarque and François Nicolas, Baron Fririon (eds), *Le Spectateur militaire: Recueil de science, d'art et d'histoire militaires* (Paris: Spectateur Militaire, 1952), 10th Series, 27th Year, Vol.3, pp.452-453; for a general biography also see Édouard de Ribaucourt, *La vie militaire et les exploits de J.-C. Fischer* (Paris: Librarie Universelle, 1929).
9   Louis Michel de Jeney, *Le Partisan ou l'art de faire la petite-guerre avec succès* (La Haye: Constapel, 1759), pp.6-7.

Compare these qualities to the line infantry regiments of the Royal Army, where the object of their drills and brutal discipline was to produce men who thought of nothing but immobility while under heavy fire.

In the Seven Years War, France entered the conflict better prepared for *petite guerre* than the previous European war. The 1753 the *État Militaire* (military states of France) records the following units of *troupes légères* in the French army:

- Volontaires de Flandre: This mixed corps of infantry and cavalry was composed of three regiments: the Arquebusiers de Grassin created 1 January 1744; the Fusiliers de la Morlière, created 16 October 1745; the Volontaires-Bretons created 30 October 1746.
- Volontaires Royaux: mixed corps formed of the free compagnies created by the ordinance of 15 August 1745.
- Volontaires de Dauphiné: mixed corps formed from the Corps des Volontaires de Gantes created 30 January 1746 and various free companies of chasseurs and volunteers.
- Corps des Chasseurs de Fischer: mixed corps formed from a free company created 1 November 1743.
- Régiment Étranger de Geschray: mixed corps created 31 July 1747.
- Fusiliers de Montagne: Three foot companies. Raised in Roussillon the 12 February 1744: originally two battalions, but reduced to a battalion on 20 April 1747, then three companies 10 November 1748.
- Cantabres Volontaires: created 15 December 1745, reduced to four independent companies 1 August 1749.

The formations listed above were classed as foreign regiments and the soldiers were paid the same as the German regiments in French service. Additional *troupes légères* were raised during the Seven Years War, again often using foreign volunteers. This conflict was something of a disaster for France. At its conclusion, the Minister of War, the Duc de Choiseul, embarked on a succession of much needed reforms to, as his critics might put it, Prussianize the French army. Light troops did not fare well in these reforms. The irregular nature of the *troupes légères* meant they were uncomfortable auxiliaries in peacetime, when there was no plunder, and the dubious status of its soldiery might be better scrutinised.

An ordinance of 1 March 1763 reorganised the *troupes légères* into seven legions, each composed of eight companies of dragoons, a company of grenadiers and eight of fusiliers. The mixed corps were titled:

- Légion Royale (ex-Volontaires Royaux, formed 1745)
- Légion de Flandre (ex-Volontaires de Flandre, formed 1749)
- Légion de Hainaut (ex-Volontaires de Hainaut, formed 1757)
- Légion de Lorraine (ex-Volontaires de Hainaut, formed 1757)
- Légion de Condé (ex-Volontaires de Clérmont-Prince, formed 1758)
- Légion de Soubise (ex-Volontaires de Soubise, formed 1762)
- Légion de Conflans (ex-Chasseurs de Fischer, formed 1743)

These legions were eventually disbanded by the royal ordinance of 25 March 1776. The dragoons of the legions were transformed in 24 squadrons of chasseurs à cheval, one of which was attached to each of the 24 dragoon regiments, forming a fifth squadron. The infantry units were broken up, some transferring into the chasseurs à cheval to make up the numbers, and the remainder being assigned to other regiments. This reform proved to be a temporary measure. Three years later, on 29 January 1779, the chasseur à cheval squadrons were regrouped, creating six new regiments of chasseurs, each four squadrons strong. In 1784 a foot battalion of chasseurs was added to each of these six regiments (see below).

The Chasseur Companies

Before elaborating further on the dissolution and reformation of the legions, we must return to the Seven Years War and discuss the development of another species of light infantry. While on the one hand we had the freewheeling, partisan irregulars out in the advanced guard, at the same time we see the first development of light companies within the regular infantry regiments. The forerunners of Napoleon's voltigeurs are found in the army of the Duc de Broglie during the Seven Year's War.

Prior to the Seven Years War, outpost duties and skirmishing were assigned to a 'piquet'. In the most basic meaning of the word, a piquet was a piece of wood – like a tent peg. However, through the passage of time, it came to represent troops engaged in various works, from pegging-out camps, sentry duty, to fortification works, and then even to punishments and tactical roles, including sentry work and advanced-guards. By the middle of the eighteenth century this piquet manifested itself in a detachment of 50 fusiliers per battalion. On active duty the piquet would be joined to the grenadier companies. These would be employed forward of the line, or on the flanks and would fight dispersed, taking use of natural cover.[10]

Taking the piquets to one side, with the proliferation of partisan warfare and bush fighting techniques, some regimental colonels began to form ad-hoc companies of chasseurs.[11] There was a selection process. Each company of fusiliers chose its best three marksmen. These chasseurs were used for protecting the battalion on the march and in battle. *Maréchal* de Broglie approved of this measure and took the innovation a step further. In his correspondence we find an instruction from April 1759 to the general officers in his army. Each infantry brigade was to form a battalion of grenadiers and one of chasseurs – an interesting pairing which calls to mind the *enfants perdus* of the previous century. The 'troupe' of chasseurs would be ranged in the same order as the battalions they were drawn from. Each of these grenadier or chasseur battalions would be commanded by a *lieutenant-colonel* or *chef de bataillon*, seconded by an officer who would fulfil the functions of *major*. Two chasseur companies would form a peloton (a tactical sub-unit of a battalion) and the chasseur

---

10 Colin, *L'infanterie au XVIIIe siècle: la tactique*, p.47.
11 Susane, *Histoire de l'ancienne infanterie française*, Vol.7. p.377.

FRENCH LIGHT INFANTRY 1784-1815

Victor François, Duc de Broglie created battalion chasseur companies in his infantry regiments during the Seven Years War. (Anne S.K. Brown Military Collection)

battalion would camp to the left of the brigade (the left of the line was considered the second post of honour – grenadiers occupied the right). A cannon was assigned to the grenadiers and chasseurs, with a further divisional artillery reserve assigned to this 'advanced-guard'.[12] In a further account, Broglie speaks of uniting three battalions of grenadiers and chasseurs from three different brigades, supplemented by some artillery and the reserve of his Saxon grenadiers to create a powerful advanced guard force 3,600 men strong.[13] This model of brigading elite companies was still common 50 years later in the First Empire. Broglie's arrangement was copied by the other army generals, but alas the chasseur companies were disbanded at the end of the conflict.

This regression was challenged. In 1774 François-Jean de Mesnil-Durand (1736 -1799) published his *Fragments de tactique; ou six mémoires*. There is an excellent chapter on the utility of infantry chasseurs in the book, strongly advocating the restoration of these companies to the army because, he writes: 'Experience has sufficiently proved that the chasseurs, established in the infantry during the last war, were infinitely better and served better than the piquets'.[14]

Chasseurs were much more than sentries; they had a different role to the line infantry required to deliver and press home a charge and they required different skills to perform this role. Mesnil-Durand recognised there were objections to creating full-time chasseur companies. There was the question of higher pay. Service with the chasseurs was more tiring and there was a greater rate of attrition associated. Mesnil-Durand thought the men could be paid a small bonus to compensate them on campaign, but otherwise higher pay was unnecessary, because they wanted men who took pleasure in this form of service, rather than those who saw it as a way of obtaining extra pay. They would serve better still if already accustomed to their officers, rather than if they were picked at the beginning of a campaign. Another important point, those whose health deteriorated or weakened, or became slow or sluggish would be sent back to their battalion. The post of chasseur was therefore best served if it was one of emulation. Responding to the observation that these companies could be raised on an ad hoc basis each summer for four months, Mesnil-Durand conceded such an arrangement would be better than nothing; but if their service were

---

12   Jules Vernier, *Correspondance inédite de Victor-François, duc de Broglie, maréchal de France, avec le prince Xavier de Saxe, comte de Lusace, lieutenant général: pour servir à l'histoire de la guerre de Sept and campagnes de 1759 à 1761* (Paris: Albin Michel, 1903), Vol.1, pp.9-24.
13   Vernier, *Correspondance inédite de Victor-François, duc de Broglie*, Vol.3, pp.47-48.
14   François Jean de Graindorge d'Orgeville de Mesnil-Durand, *Fragments de tactique, ou six mémoires précédés d'un discours préliminaire* (Paris: Ant. Jombert, 1774), p.1

recognised as useful, why not give them all possible consistency? Concluding his argument, he made a particularly good point. No one at the time would have considered disbanding the grenadier companies, or making them a parttime appointment, or one only raised in wartime. Why do the same to the chasseurs?

Mesnil-Durand's arguments must have had an effect. When the legions were dissolved, the government ordered the formal creation of chasseur companies in every infantry regiment by the royal ordinance of 25 March 1776 (*Ordonnance du roi, concernant l'Infanterie Françoise & Etrangère*). The main purpose of this ordinance was to regularise the composition of infantry regiments. Henceforth infantry battalions would be composed of four companies of fusiliers, with each regiment having a company of grenadiers and a company of chasseurs. (the four-battalion Régiment du Roi had two companies of grenadiers and two of chasseurs). The chasseur company would be composed of a *capitaine*, a *capitaine en second*, a *premier lieutenant*, a *lieutenant en second*, and two *sous-lieutenants*; a *sergent-major*, a *fourrier-écrivan* (quartermaster-scribe), five *sergens* (the earlier spelling often omits the 't'), ten *caporaux*, a *cadet-gentilhomme* (cadet gentleman), a *frater* (barber), and 144 chasseurs, with two *tambours* or other instrumentalists. Chasseurs were paid the same basic pay as fusiliers.

The chasseurs were chosen from the fusilier companies by the officers from 'the nimblest, the most vigorous and most proper for this type of service without any regard for their height'.[15] While grenadier companies were required to draw their men from the fusilier companies, the chasseur companies were also allowed to take new recruits directly, if they appeared suitable (this perhaps recognised the energies required by chasseurs were better provided by younger men). The captains of the chasseur companies would be chosen from among those who appeared most suitable. These foot chasseurs were armed with the same musket as fusiliers and were given a grenadier sabre. Their uniform was the same as the rest of the regiment except for the epaulette and the fringeless counter-epaulette which were made from green cloth lined in white. Their coattail turnbacks were adorned with a hunting horn symbol rather than the standard fleur de lys badge.

Although the chasseurs received the same basic rate of pay as fusiliers, an element of elitism crept in. After all, they had been specifically selected for their service, they had distinctive elements to their uniform, and wore a grenadier sabre. As had been the case at the time of Broglie's army, the chasseur companies were viewed much the same as grenadier companies and were initially exempted fatigue duties. Not everyone accepted the elite status of chasseurs, and so the Minister of War was asked to make a determination on this. The reply on 15 February 1777 was that 'the pretentions of chasseurs are absolutely poorly founded; chasseurs are no more than fusiliers, and consequently held to make the service without distinction in times of peace.' The only prerogative they enjoyed was to alternate with the grenadiers to parade the colours.[16]

---

15 *Ordonnance du roi, concernant l'Infanterie Françoise & Etrangère du 25 mars 1776* (Paris: L'Imperimerie Royale, 1776), p.15.
16 Kéralio, et al, *Encyclopédie Méthodique: Art militaire*, 1784, p.586.

As mentioned above, in 1779 the chasseur à cheval squadrons formerly of the legions, were reconstituted into regiments. At the time this occurred, some of the former-legionary infantry officers were still without appointments. Perhaps the old infantry of the legions would be recreated? The officers commanding the new chasseur companies also looked on with interest. If permanent units of light infantry were formed, there would be promotion opportunities, as the new battalions or regiments would require staffs of senior officers.

Watching on with evident dismay was the author of an article which appeared in the *Encyclopédie Méthodique: Art Militaire* in 1784. Probably appearing too late to influence what happened next, the article argued against the creation of independent corps of foot chasseurs. Firstly, creating additional independent corps would require the creation of regimental staffs, which would be an additional burden to the military treasury (France had nearly bankrupted itself supporting the rebellion in Britain's American colonies). More damaging still would be the removal from each infantry regiment some of its best officers, NCOs, and men. In the long term, the author of the encyclopaedia article thought, the creation of independent chasseur companies was likely to be detrimental to chasseurs themselves. Rather than having their pick of the best recruits and from seasoned fusiliers, independent chasseur corps would be forced to recruit at random, in direct competition with the line regiments. The quality of recruit would likely suffer because of this.

Equally, there would be less object of emulation. Chasseurs would have nothing to aspire to. In wartime, the author of the encyclopaedia thought it better to reunite 20 companies of chasseurs from the regiments in an army (as de Broglie had done), rather than have two permanent regiments of chasseurs. The formation of special units would enjoy a better esprit de corps than a regiment in which the type of service was ordinary.

At the same time, the author recognised it was harmful not to recognise the chasseurs as being elite soldiers. If they were elite, they should not take new recruits, only men who had proved their service. One solution might be to choose them from men of the third rank, from those with more than three years of service. A higher pay, perhaps half of that of grenadiers would hardly be noticeable to the treasury and the benefit would be that since, 'French soldiers put a great price on everything that distinguishes them from their comrades' their attitude was 'since one pays me better than the rest of the soldiers, I must be worth more'.[17] This idea of superiority would be very quick to catch on. The hunting horn would become a distinctive mark worn only by irreproachable subjects and would provide those of mediocre height something to aspire to. The reform would also prevent complacency setting in among the grenadiers, who would no doubt respond to the competition.

Reflecting on this debate, one can see the utility of embedding a light company within each regiment and having this pool of chosen men, expert in the qualities required for light troops. One can also imagine the effect of

---

17 Kéralio, et al, *Encyclopédie Méthodique: Art militaire*, 1784, p.587.

creating special units of combined light companies in the field as de Broglie had done. In the short term, such debate proved largely academic. In 1784, the year of publication of this encyclopaedia, the Ministry of War enacted its next reform.

The Legions Resurrected, 1784

In peacetime, cavalry and infantry were uncomfortable bedfellows. They had such different requirements in terms of supply and drill, and so on. However, in wartime, light infantry and cavalry were indispensable comrades. In open territory, light horsemen could scour far into the distance and reconnoitre; but men on horses were next to useless in a forest, or in mountainous terrain. Although armed with firearms, the cavalry lacked the staying power of infantry in terms of holding a position or piece of ground. If there was a need for light horse and light infantry, why not embody a spirit of cooperation in the very structure of that arm? Such was the prevailing argument.

In 1779 six regiments of chasseurs à cheval had been created from the chasseur squadrons found in the dragoon regiments. The provisional royal ordinance of 8 August 1784 (*la formation & la solde des régimens de Chasseurs*) ordered the creation of a battalion of chasseurs à pied in each of these regiments. According to the opening article of this ordinance it was 'judged to be to the good of His Majesty's service to bring back the regiments of chasseurs à cheval to their primitive institution'. Keen-eyed observers will note this was true in spirit, but the new chasseur regiments were not called legions and were not composed of dragoons, grenadiers, and fusiliers. Our encyclopaedia author ought not have been too concerned either, because there was no dissolution of the light companies in the infantry regiments, so no weakening of resources there. It should also be noted France did not exist in a vacuum, and this 1784 reform may have been influenced by Frederick the Great's decision to unite his *jäger* (hunter) companies into a regiment in the Prussian army. It may have been no coincidence that the ordinance followed the end of the American Revolutionary War (1775-1783), where the British Army had been constantly harried by a relatively untrained militia, using the tactics of backwoodsmen, although this comparison should perhaps not be overplayed. French officers saw the revolutionary war through European prisms. Lafayette was somewhat dismissive of militiamen in comparison to professional soldiers. In a 1781 letter, Lafayette described how with only relatively small armies operating in extremely rugged terrain 'all the battalions of the line were obliged to serve as advance-guards and light troops … As to the militia, they are only armed peasants, who have occasionally fought, and who are not deficient in ardour and discipline, but whose services would be most useful in the labours of a siege.'[18] He was much more impressed with American riflemen who were drawn from 'parts of the country on the frontiers of the savage tribes, and from amongst men

---

18 Lafayette, *Memoirs, Correspondence and Manuscripts of General Lafayette*, Vol.1, p.376.

FRENCH LIGHT INFANTRY 1784-1815

Chasseur à pied des Vosges in 1784. The regimental distinction was lemon coloured lapels and cuffs. Watercolour by Charles Lyall, 1899. (Anne S.K. Brown Military Collection)

whose mode of life, and skill in firing their long carbines, rendered them peculiarly useful in that service'.[19]

Returning to the composition of the new chasseur regiments, each of the six were named after one of France's mountain regions. In order of rank, the regiments were:

- Régiment de Chasseurs des Alpes
- Régiment de Chasseurs des Pyrénées
- Régiment de Chasseurs des Vosges
- Régiment de Chasseurs des Cévennes
- Régiment de Chasseurs du Gévaudan
- Régiment de Chasseurs des Ardennes

Each regiment was composed of four squadrons of horse and a battalion of foot chasseurs. The squadrons were composed of a company, and each battalion four companies. The regiment was commanded by a *colonel commandant*, deputised by a *colonel en second*. There were two *lieutenant-colonels* and two *majors*, one each for the cavalry squadron and infantry battalion. There was a single *quartier-maître-trésorier* (quartermaster-treasurer) to handle the regimental accounts. The *majors* had a particular responsibility for the discipline and training of their respective troops. The *majors* were seconded by two *adjudants* for the chasseurs à cheval and one for the chasseurs à pied. The regimental staff was completed by a *chirgurgien-major* (surgeon-major), an *aumônier* (chaplain), one *maître maréchal* (master farrier), one *maître sellier* (master saddler), and an *armurier* (armourer) for the chasseurs à pied.

Table 1. Company/Squadron Structure 1784

Chasseurs à cheval	Peace	War	Chasseurs à pied	Peace	War
Capitaine Commandant	1	1	*Capitaine Commandant*	1	1
Capitaine en second	1	1	*Capitaine en second*	1	1
Lieutenant en premier	1	1	*Lieutenant en premier*	1	1
Lieutenant en second	1	1	*Lieutenant en second*	1	1
Sous-lieutenants	2	2	*Sous-lieutenants*	2	2
Maréchal-des-logis en chef	1	1	*Sergent-major*	1	1
Fourrier	1	1	*Fourrier*	1	1
Maréchal-des-logis	4	4	*Sergents*	4	4
Brigadiers	8	8	*Caporaux*	8	8
Appointés	8	8	*Appointés*	8	8
Chasseurs à cheval	64	128	*Chasseurs à pied*	56	104
Trompettes	2	3	*Tambour* (coys 1 & 2)	1	2
			Tambours (coys 3 & 4)	1	1

---

19 Lafayette, *Memoirs, Correspondence and Manuscripts of General Lafayette*, Vol.1. p.33

The officers staffing these new battalions included former legionary officers who had yet to find fulltime appointments in the infantry regiments. Take for example the Chasseurs des Cévennes. Of the battalion's 21 officers, 16 had been drawn from the 4e Chasseurs or the Légion de Condé. Of the others, at least two were related to serving, or former officers in these corps. If any further proof of a link with the old legion is required, we need look no further than the regimental masonic lodge, the *Saint-Louis de l'Union*. This had originally been established on 15 June 1771 by the Légion de Condé (ex-Volontaires de Clermont-Prince/Légion de Clermont-Prince). The lodge was re-established on 19 August 1784 – the Chasseurs de Cévennes was recognised as the fourth name of the regiment. Incidentally, we also find the Pyrénées-Chasseurs forming a Lodge in 1785 called 'La Réunion Parfaite' in its garrison at Philippeville.[20]

The Battalions of Chasseurs à Pied, 1788

In 1788, the Minister of War decided to reform the regiments of chasseurs once again, creating 12 independent battalions of chasseurs à pied and doubling the number of regiments of chasseurs à cheval to 12. Clearly the 1784 provisional recreation of the mixed-corps legions failed to have the desired effect. The French wanted additional light infantry and cavalry, but they did not want the two arms to be structurally linked. The reason for this, as explained in the *Ordonnance du Roi, portant règlement sur la formation & la solde de douze bataillons d'Infanterie Légère* (17 March 1788), was they wanted the infantry battalions to have enough consistency or stability to stand alone and support themselves, knowing they were likely to be detached in wartime. In other words, if an infantry battalion was required to serve in a different location to the cavalry squadrons, would the regimental command structure and depot be able to support the needs of both parties? Evidently not. If there was a need for the two arms to cooperate in the field, it took no structural or administrative changes to achieve this. A general might simply brigade, or otherwise unify, the two arms into one force as required, under the command of a senior officer or general.

The ordinance stated these new battalions of light infantry should profit from the current era of peace and be able to be trained in the 'services external and in advance' of the King's armies. Another consideration was the age-old one of recruiting 'mountain men' for service in the light infantry. The ordinance states: 'His Majesty, having also thought, that to extract part of the spirit & of the inclination of the inhabitants of some regions of its kingdom, such that these of frontiers of the Pyrenees, Alps & of the island of Corsica, it would be advantageous to open to them an outlet of a type of service that they have the aptitude for'.

---

20   Gustav Bord, *La franc-maçonnerie en France des origines à 1815* (Paris: Nouvelle Librarie Nationale, 1908), Vol.I, p.504.

Six battalions already existed. The others would be raised from existing regiments of the line. The ordinance explained the composition of each battalion:

1. A battalion of Chasseurs Royaux du Dauphiné
2. A battalion of Chasseurs Royaux de Provence

These first two battalions would be formed from the regiment Royal-Italien and would be eventually made up of officers and soldiers from the titular provinces.

3. A battalion called Chasseurs Royaux Corses (Royal Corsicans)
4. A battalion called Chasseurs Corses

These two battalions would be formed from the infantry Régiment Royal-Corse, and be entirely Corsican in officers and soldiers.

5. A battalion of Chasseurs Cantabres, formed from the Corps de Montréal, and then from Cantabrians and Basques
6. A battalion of Chasseurs d'Auvergne, formed from the Bataillon de Chasseurs du Régiment des Pyrénées
7. A battalion of Chasseurs Bretons, formed from the battalion of Chasseurs du Régiment des Alpes
8. A battalion of Chasseurs des Vôges [Sic Vosges]
9. A battalion of Chasseurs des Cévennes
10. A battalion of Chasseurs du Gévaudan
11. A battalion of Chasseurs des Ardennes

The last four of these battalions were each to formed from the battalions of chasseurs from the regiments of the same name. Recruitment for these battalions had no regional restrictions.

12. A battalion of Chasseurs du Roussillon.

This last battalion was to be formed from the surplus of the Royal-Italien and Royal-Corse regiments, after which it was to be recruited from men from the province of Roussillon.

Each battalion had a staff formed of a *lieutenant-colonel* commandant (who exercised the authority in his battalion as a colonel), a *major*, a *quartier-maître*, an *adjudant*, a *chirurgien-major*, a *tambour-major*, four *musiciens* (with hunting horns or trumpets), an *armurier*, a *maître tailleur*, and a *maître cordonnier* (master cordwainer). The four companies each had six officers and 102 men, including: 1 *capitaine-commandant*, 1 *capitaine en second*, 1 *lieutenant en premier*, 1 *lieutenant en second*, 2 *sous-lieutenants*, 1 *sergent-major*, 1 *fourrier*, 4 *sergens*, 8 *caporaux*, 8 *appointés* (chosen men), 78 chasseurs and 2 *tambours*.

The ordinance was quite specific on the type of recruits it wanted for the new battalions: 'The service of light infantry battalions particularly demands

Chasseurs à pied in 1787 with their distinctive colours: (L-R) Alpes (scarlet), Cévennes (buff), Ardennes (white). (New York Public Library)

robust men and good marchers, the commanders of these battalions will take care to procure recruits of this type, not prizing them by the greatness of height'.

There was an exciting provision in the new battalions. A criticism of the chasseur battalions was the lack of promotional opportunities for common soldiers with no grenadier company and no flag to carry. The ordinance therefore allowed for four NCOs to be raised up to the officer corps with the rank *of sous-lieutenant* or *lieutenant*. At a time when the officer corps was the almost exclusive preserve of the nobility, this was an excellent opportunity for long-serving soldiers.

The 1788 ordinance also created the new post of *chasseur-carabinier*. Each company would have 12 of these marksmen, the first six of whom would receive a high pay of an additional daily *sou* (shilling), the other six would only receive an additional 6 *deniers* (pence). Unlike grenadiers in the line regiments, these *chasseur-carabiniers* would be chosen 'without a single regard for their height, from among the best soldiers in the battalion, giving equal preference to the most skilful shooters and never admitting recruits'. The title suggests these soldiers would be armed with rifled carbines, but there was nothing in the regulation requiring battalions to purchase carbines. We should not therefore automatically consider these troops as riflemen, as their title suggests, but rather as marksmen.

Another boon was the allowance of male, child soldiers. 'His majesty would like to admit in addition, for each company of chasseurs, two children of NCOs or soldiers, who would receive a soldiers' pay'. They would not be eligible for this pay until reaching the age of six to eight years old, or if they had any infirmity that would prevent them from becoming soldiers. At the age of 16, the children were to be offered an eight-year enlistment, which if accepted, would warrant them the enlistment bounty of 100 *livres* (French pounds). As part of their military apprenticeship, the children would be taught by the battalion's master craftsmen, 'to learn the trades useful to the troop'. Finally, in case of war, 'those of the child-soldiers who were not ready to follow the battalion, will be left in the auxiliary depot'. We might also note at this point it was common for four women to be permitted as part of the battalion. These were usually the wives of NCOs. Two of them would have been laundresses, while the other two would have been married to the *vivandiers*, the soldier-sutlers authorised to sell non-rationed goods to the battalion. Although tolerated, at this time sutler-women had no formal recognition of their own (this came in 1792).

The eight drummers in the battalion would form a squad led by an *appointé-tambour* under the direction of the drum-major, who held the rank of *sergent*. The latter also commanded the four musicians, who the ordonnance stipulated would have '*cors de chasse* [hunting horns] or trumpets' as their instruments. The musicians could be supplemented by some of the battalion's children, 'with fifes or other similar instruments'.

The inspection reports of 1788 provide some interesting information on the first formation of independent battalions.[21] The idea they were somehow formed of mountain men from the wilder provinces really has taken hold over the centuries. In fact, of the five battalions which were permitted flexibility of recruitment, their composition was quite diverse. The Chasseurs des Cévennes did have their largest number of men from the Languedoc, but Ardennes had many men from Provence. The Chasseurs de Roussillon had just four natives of that region. We should not therefore think of these battalions are having a regional composition (see Table 2). Of the 1,536 men recorded, we can conclude that the largest contributors to chasseurs in 1788 were the provinces of Languedoc (10.9 percent), Alsace (10.9 percent), Lorraine (French and German) (10.8 percent). The Chasseurs de Roussillon skew the statistics somewhat because 139 of their 232 men (60 percent) were foreign nationals. The next most represented French provinces are Franche-Compté (8.8 percent) and Burgundy at 6.7 percent.

We are also able to dispel the notion these men were huntsmen or poachers in any great number. In the 1788 inspections, the trades of 1,302 men are recorded (See Table 3). The majority (56 percent) described themselves as having a skilled trade or as townsfolk (including

---

21   The Inspection Reports (*Livret de revue d'inspection*) are found at the Service Historique de la Défense, Vincennes. The code for the dossier containing the documents cited in this section is Xb/124 (1788–1790).

manufacturers of luxury goods). While agricultural labourers make up the largest single occupation represented, they were as a group statistically in the minority. It is interesting to note the number of cordwainers (manufacturers of shoes) and tailors in the battalions (11 percent); these skilled soldiers may have found additional work manufacturing uniforms and would have been prized as recruits.

The majority (66 percent) had less than four years' service in 1788 (see Table 4); but there is a good blend of experience through the battalions. The Chasseurs des Cévennes had the largest number of men with a double service chevron or veteran status (38 men), but in all, 35 percent of the men in these battalions were on their second term of engagement or more. In terms of the height of the men (see Table 5), 52 percent were under 5 *pieds* 3 *pouces* (1.705 metres). The majority of the men (58 percent) ranged from 5 *pieds* 2 *pouces* to 5 *pieds* 4 *pouces* (1.679-1.732 metres) Just nine men (0.5 percent) might be classed as 'six-footers', in the Anglo-Saxon sense of the term. From these statistics combined, we can perhaps describe the average chasseur of 1788 as measuring between 5 *pieds* 4 *pouces* (1.70-1.73 metres), in his early to mid-twenties, still in his first term of engagement, originating from Alsace or Lorraine in the east of France, or the Languedoc in the southwest; having undergone an apprenticeship in a skilled trade, rather than an agricultural labourer.

Table 2. Recruitment by Province, 1788

(Vosges, Cévennes, Gevaudan, Ardennes, Roussillon)

Provinces of France	Vos	Cev	Gev	Ard	Rou	All
Alsace	42	32	25	7	62	168
Anjou & Maine	3	1	3	12	-	19
Auvergne	3	3	3	4	-	13
Avignon (county of)	1	-	-	1	-	2
Berry	-	1	6	-	-	7
Bourbonnais	8	1	1	5	-	15
Burgundy	16	20	57	9	2	104
Brittany	-	12	3	2	-	17
Champagne	36	29	14	15	-	94
Corsica	-	-	-	1	1	2
Dauphiné	3	3	29	16	2	53
Evêchés	10	-	1	7	-	18
Flanders	2	3	27	5	3	40
Franche-Compté	6	36	44	44	5	135
Guyenne	7	9	-	27	-	43
Isle-de-France	7	7	-	5	1	20
La Marche		-	1		-	1
Languedoc	17	71	51	27	2	168
Limousin	19	-	-	10	-	29
Lorraine (German)	19	8	3	6	9	45
Lorraine (French)	73	2	9	38	-	122
Lyonnais	8	3	9	2	-	22
Navarre or Bearn	1	-	2	25	-	28
Nivernois	-	8	-	-	-	8

FRENCH LIGHT INFANTRY 1784-1815

Provinces of France	Vos	Cev	Gev	Ard	Rou	All
Normandy	13	14	13	20	-	60
Orléannois	-	4	1	-	-	5
Paris	23	12	6	3	-	44
Picardy	4	5	25	-	-	34
Provence	6	1	-	49	2	58
Poitou, Aunis, Saintonge	-	5	3	2	-	10
Roussillon	-	-	-	3	4	7
Touraine	-	2	1	2	-	5
Country of Liege	-	1		-	-	1
Foreigners of all nations	-	-	-	-	139	139

Table 3. Professions of Soldiers, 1788

(Vosges, Cévennes, Gevaudan, Ardennes, Roussillon)

Trade	Vos	Cev	Gev	Ard	Rou	All
Bakers	7	5	4	5	-	21
Blacksmiths	-	1	-	-	-	1
Carpenters	3	4	5	6	-	18
Cordwainers	15	10	15	17	20	77
Labourers and pioneers	102	127	173	124	45	571
Veterinary surgeons	-	-	5	1	1	7
Masons	7	9	9	18	6	49
Millers	5	4	11	9	3	32
Wigmakers	8	5	8	14	3	38
Saddlers	6	-	5	1	3	15
Surgeons	3	1	1	7	-	12
Locksmiths/ toolmakers	4	4	4	7	7	26
Tailors	11	14	13	11	14	63
Tanners	1	2	4	6	-	13
Townsfolk	146	7	80	126	-	359
						1302

Table 4. Length of Service, 1788

(Vosges, Cévennes, Gevaudan, Ardennes, Roussillon)

Length of Service	Vos	Cev	Gev	Ard	Rou	All
Veterans 24+ yrs	2	3	4	4	4	17
Double service chevron 16-23 yrs	27	35	12	20	11	122
Single service chevron 8-15 yrs	49	27	44	40	22	182
4 – 8 years' service	25	40	40	22	89	216
Less than 4 years' service	215	195	237	260	106	1,013
Total men	318	300	337	346	232	1,533

Table 5. Height of the men, 1788

(Vosges, Cévennes, Gevaudan, Ardennes, Roussillon)

French feet and inches	Metric (in metres)	Vos	Cev	Gev	Ard	Rou	All
5'1 or less	1.651 or less	14	10	17	10	36	87
5'1–5'2	1.652–1.678	48	26	34	35	90	233
5'2–5'3	1.679–1.705	107	90	114	119	60	490
5'3–5'4	1.706–1.733	86	104	99	90	23	402

5'4–5'5	1.734–1.760	38	47	48	55	11	199
5'5–5'6	1.761–1.787	18	21	17	22	12	90
5'6–5'7	1.788–1.814	4	1	6	12	-	23
5'7 or above	1.815–1.841	3	1	2	3	-	9
Total men		318	300	337	346	232	1,533

(1.6242 m = 5 pieds; 0.0272 m = 1 pouce)

Alas, not everyone agreed with the 1788 restructure. An argument against independent corps was penned for a fourth, supplementary volume of the *Encyclopédie méthodique – Art Militaire*. This volume was not published until 1797, but the work was begun in 1789 by Jean-Gérard Lacuée de Cessac, then a captain in the infantry Régiment du Dauphin. He argued strongly against separating the two arms, for financial and tactical reasons. His central argument was that the two arms would naturally serve together and would therefore perform better if they trained together and shared the same command. Twelve legions of light troops, he argued, each composed tactically of four 'divisions' formed from a company each of foot and horse, would create an excellent advanced-guard force. Each of these divisions would be commanded by the most senior captain, and light infantry companies would only to have two officers. This would produce a saving of more than three million *livres*, at a time when the national debt was 'difficult to conceive'.[22] Alas for de Cessac the reform had already taken place and events were about to overtake academic discussions.

At this point we might summarise the period up to 1788 as one of experimentation. The utility of light infantry was by this point well understood, and France had turned its irregular mixed corps into professional squadrons and battalions of light troops. Experience had shown that one ought not to wait for a war to commence before raising these troops, and that professional light troops benefitted from the training afforded by peacetime. Although the light infantry and cavalry had a shared role, the French had also concluded the two arms should be separate in their administration and command. While 12 battalions might appear modest in number, one must also remember that every regiment then had a company of chasseurs, formed of the best marksmen, and these could be detached to form ad hoc battalions as had occurred in the Seven Years War. On paper at least this was a very strong force of light infantry. The French had even begun to consider the possibility of a portion of their light infantry of being armed with rifled carbines, as was common among the light infantry of German states. Everything was progressing in a methodical and well-structured manner. Then came 1789, the year which saw everything thrown up in the air.

---

22   Kéralio, et al, *Encyclopédie Méthodique: Art de Guerre*, Vol.4, pp.423-424.

FRENCH LIGHT INFANTRY 1784-1815

Table 6. Company Structure 1788

	FIRST DIVISION				SECOND DIVISION			
	Capitaine-commandant				*Capitaine en second*			
	Formation of Subdivisions							
	FIRST SUBDIVISION		THIRD SUBDIVISION		SECOND SUBDIVISION		FOURTH SUBDIVISION	
	Lieutenant en premier		*Premier S-Lieut.*		*Lieutenant en second*		*Second S-Lieut.*	
	1st *Sergent*		3rd *Sergent*		2nd *Sergent*		4th *Sergent*	
	Formation of the Squads							
Different FOOTINGS	1st squad	5th squad	3rd squad	7th squad	2nd squad	6th squad	4th squad	8th squad
	1st Cpl & App.	5th Cpl & App.	3rd Cpl & App.	7th Cpl & App.	2nd Cpl & App.	6th Cpl & App.	4th Cpl & App.	8th Cpl & App.
Peace	12	12	12	11	12	12	12	11
War	15	14	15	14	15	14	15	14
Great war	18	17	18	17	18	17	18	17

	FORCE							
Different FOOTINGS	Squads inc. *caporal & appointé*	Coy inc. NCOs & drums	Coy inc. officers					
Peace	94	102	108					
War	115	123	129					
Great war	140	148	154					

2

Light Infantry in the Wars of the French Revolution

The 1789 revolution saw the end of the feudal regime in France. The legal class of nobility was abolished on 4 August and all citizens declared equal regardless of birth. The following summer, on 19 June 1790, all titles of nobility were formally abolished. There was a wave of mutinies across France as the army wrestled with the realities of what 'liberty and equality' meant in the context of submission to military discipline. Some enlightened nobles embraced the reforms, but a growing number emigrated from France out of fear, particularly after the declaration of war in 1792. The emigration of officers created opportunity for commoners (or fellow citizens, in the new parlance), who since 1781 had not qualified for the officer corps, unless their father had been an officer awarded the Cross of St Louis. The result of this was an increased number of NCOs gained officer rank. The general result of this was the new officer class had no formal military instruction at anything beyond platoon command. The army also had to contend with the formation and expansion of the National Guard. Politically in-tune with the new order, the National Guard presented amazing opportunities for fast promotion and better pay.

France declared war on Austria and Prussia on 20 April 1792. The initial focus was an attack on the Austrian Netherlands. Things did not start well. By 11 July 1792 the French National Assembly was obliged to make the famous declaration *la patrie est en danger* (the fatherland is in danger) and make a mass appeal for recruits. On 25 July 1792, the infamous Brunswick Declaration announced the coalition would restore Louis XVI's powers and reverse the revolutionary reforms. Any Frenchmen opposing the allied army would be met with harsh justice. When news of this declaration reached Paris, there was uproar. The Tuileries Palaces was stormed on 10 August and Louis XVI was arrested. The Prussian invasion of France was halted on 20 September at the Battle of Valmy. On 21 September a National Convention replaced the Legislative Assembly, and the monarchy was abolished. The following day, 22 September 1792, was the first day of the French Republic. After the Battle of Jemappes on 6 November, the French government began planning to export the revolution beyond France's frontiers. Louis XVI met his fate with the guillotine on 21 January 1793, an event which turned the remainder of Europe against France. With this brief overview of events in mind, let us consider the impact of these momentous events on the light infantry.

The National Army, 1791

The year 1791 saw important changes to France's infantry regiments and chasseur battalions. On 1 January 1791 the line infantry regiments were reorganised. The chasseur companies attached to each regiment were disbanded. On 1 August 1791 a new drill regulation was published (*Réglement concernant l'exercice et les manoeuvres de l'infanterie*). This document would remain in force throughout the 1790s and the First Empire – in fact, it was only superseded in 1831. The new regulation saw a reorganisation of the battalion structure. Previously, as set out in the instructions of 1776 and 1788 respectively, each battalion was formed of two half battalions. Each half-battalion was formed of two divisions. Each division was composed of two pelotons, each of which was divided into two sections. Each peloton was formed in three ranks in 16 files in peace, or 20 files in wartime. Any surplus soldiers were formed into a reserve peloton behind the centre of the battalion. The grenadier company stood to the right of the first battalion, while the chasseur company stood to the left of the second battalion (on active service, both these companies were usually detached). The front rank was composed of the tallest men, the second rank the shortest, with the middling men in the third. There was a one-*pied* gap between the back or haversack of one man, and the chest of the man behind him.

Table 7. Battalion tactical structure, 1776

Second								Premier								Demi-bns
Quatrième				Troisième				Second				Premier				Divisions
8e		7e		6e		5e		4e		3e		2e		1er		Pelotons
2e	1er	2e	1er	2e	1er	2e	1er	2e	1er	2e	1er	2e	1er	2e	1er	Sections

The 1791 regulation copied some of the earlier tactical structure, except that previously a company of soldiers in the administrative sense, equated to a division of two pelotons. In 1791 the company was said to form only a single peloton. This saw the end of the classification of premier and second subaltern officers and doubled the number of *sergent-major* and *caporal-fourrier* positions within each battalion.

To facilitate the new structure a reorganisation of the chasseur battalions took place *on 1 April 1791 in the Règlement sur la formation, les appointements et la solde de l'infanterie légère*. In the new structure each light infantry battalion was composed of eight companies and a staff totalling 457 officers and men. The staff included: 2 *lieutenant-colonels*; 1 *quartier-maître-trésorier*; 1 *adjudant-major*; 1 *chirurgien-major*; 1 *adjudant*; 1 *tambour-major*; 1 *maître tailleur*; 1 *maître armurier*; 1 *maître cordonnier* (shoemaker). The former post of *major* was replaced by a second *lieutenant-colonel*. The senior *lieutenant-colonel* exercised command over the battalion and had a particular responsibility for the instruction of the officer corps. The second *lieutenant-colonel* was to supervise all details of battalion service, policing, discipline, training, and accounting.

Each company was composed of 1 *capitaine*, 1 *lieutenant*, 1 *sous-lieutenant*, 1 *sergent-major*, 2 *sergents*, 1 *caporal-fourrier*, 4 *caporaux*, 4 *appointés*, 40 chasseurs, 1 *tambour* (drummer). The companies were designated by the names of the captains commanding them and were listed according to their seniority. When the companies were placed in the battalion, they were be paired in such a way that the four most senior captains were paired with one of the junior ones: 1st – 5th; 2nd – 6th; 3rd – 7th; 4th – 8th.

Perhaps the most interesting thing about this reform is the omission of the 12 chasseur-carabinier riflemen previously allowed. Article 29 of the regulation clearly states: 'His Majesty abolishes all posts, offices and ranks which have not been included in this regulation'. An instruction to the commanders of the light infantry regiments stated the first six carabiniers were allowed to keep their high-pay until such time as they were promoted to *appointé* or *caporal*. France's short experiment with riflemen was seemingly at an end.

Under the same regulation the twelve chasseur battalions lost their provincial titles and were henceforth (officially) known by the number indicating their rank. This reform had already occurred in the line infantry following the regulation of 1 January 1791.

- Chasseurs Royaux de Provence became the 1er Bataillon de Chasseurs
- Chasseurs Royaux du Dauphiné became the 2e Bataillon de Chasseurs
- Chasseurs Royaux Corse became the 3e Bataillon de Chasseurs
- Chasseurs Corses became the 4e Bataillon de Chasseurs
- Chasseurs Cantabres became the 5e Bataillon de Chasseurs
- Chasseurs Bretons became the 6e Bataillon de Chasseurs
- Chasseurs d'Auvergne became the 7e Bataillon de Chasseurs
- Chasseurs des Vosges became the 8e Bataillon de Chasseurs
- Chasseurs des Cévennes became the 9e Bataillon de Chasseurs
- Chasseurs du Gévaudan became the 10e Bataillon de Chasseurs
- Chasseurs des Ardennes became the 11e Bataillon de Chasseurs
- Chasseurs du Roussillon became the 12e Bataillon de Chasseurs

Soldiers are creatures of habit. Rather than forgetting their provincial names, they added the prefix *ci-devant* (formerly or ex), for example 7e Bataillon de Chasseurs *ci-devant* Auvergne.

Later in 1791, two new battalions were created – the 13e and 14e Bataillon d'Infanterie Légère. These battalions were formed from the dissolution of the famous Gardes Françaises, the Paris regiment which sided with the protestors and took part in the attack on the Bastille fortress on 14 July 1789. Although the decree dissolving the Gardes Françaises was dated 3 August 1791, the new battalions were not created until the October of that year.

The omission of provincial titles was one of many social changes that were beginning to affect the army. The revolution saw the end of noble privileges.

FRENCH LIGHT INFANTRY 1784-1815

Carabinier of the 6e Chasseurs and chasseur of the 13e Chasseurs (ex-Gardes Françaises) in 1792 by Boisselier. The carabinier is equipped with a rifled carbine extra-long bayonet. Also note the powder horn and ramrod, in addition to a mallet attached to his cartridge pouch. His bearskin cap follows the regulation of 1 April 1791. (Collection Yves Martin)

Officers renounced their former titles and even changed the spelling of their names, (for example, incorporating the prepositions du / de/des, le, and la into their surname). Many noble officers began to emigrate from France, and this created promotional opportunities, particularly for senior NCOs. The remaining officers were promoted, sometimes into the regiments of the line; others moved between battalions. Already the officer corps was much changed before the effects of enemy fire were felt.

Each year France published an *État Militaire*. These books record the names of every officer then serving. If we analyse the 12 chasseur battalions formed in 1788, we can make some startling conclusions. Of the original *lieutenant-colonels* and *majors* at the formation of the chasseur battalions in 1788, 17 of them were still present in 1791, but just six remained serving in those battalions in 1792. None of the senior officers listed in 1788 were present in 1793. Of the 24 available lieutenant-colonelcies available in 1793, five are listed as vacant. Fourteen posts were filled by officers who had not been listed as *lieutenant-colonels* the year before. Of the remaining five, none of these officers had held the rank of *lieutenant-colonel* in 1791, in other words they had held command for 18 months of less. To conclude, 100 percent of the senior officers from 1788 had gone by the time of the next great reform in the French army – the amalgamation of volunteer and regular corps.

The Regular Battalions, 1792

At the beginning of the war in April 1792 the French found themselves with just 14 independent battalions of chasseurs. According to the *État Militaire* (military states) of 1792, these battalions were dispersed around the country in the following manner:

- 1er *ci-devant* Royaux de Provence at Monaco.
- 2e *ci-devant* Royaux du Dauphiné at Romans
- 3e *ci-devant* Royaux Corses at Grenoble
- 4e *ci-devant* Corses at Tournon.
- 5e *ci-devant* Cantabres at Saint-Jean-Pied-de-Port.
- 6e *ci-devant* Bretons at Strasbourg.
- 7e *ci-devant* d'Auvergne at Strasbourg.
- 8e *ci-devant* Vôsges at Montpellier.
- 9e *ci-devant* Cévennes at Metz.

- 10e *ci-devant* Gévaudan at Maubeuge.
- 11e *ci-devant* Ardennes at Lorgues.
- 12e *ci-devant* Roussillon at Perpignan.
- 13e and 14e at Paris.

Of these fourteen battalions just four (6e, 7e, 9e, and 10e) were stationed along France's north-eastern border, from Strasbourg to the Channel coast. The remainder were concentrated near to the Alps, the Pyrenees and along the south coast. With the regimental chasseur companies disbanded the year before, France entered the war with perilously few light infantrymen available to the army commanders. According to Roche-Aymon's *Des Troupes Légères* the Austrians employed a large amount of light infantry in 1792. In the early stages of the war, there were many preliminary skirmishers and outpost clashes. The French soldiers sent out to the pickets found themselves completely outmatched by the skill of special units such the Tyrolean Jaegers, the Chasseurs de Leloup, the Free Corps of Michalowitz, and so forth. Mostly without experienced officers because of the emigration, they became the victims of, in Roche-Aymon's words, their 'reckless and misguided bravery'.[1]

When news of these setbacks arrived back in Paris the response was somewhat predictable. In the previous two major European wars, the French had successfully employed legions of mixed corps in the advanced guard and that solution was proposed again. The *Décret relative à la formation des légions* of 27-29 April 1792 legislated for the urgent creation of six new legions (numbered 1-6), each would be composed of two battalions of light infantry, one regiment of horse chasseurs and a division of *ouvriers* (workers) composed of 2 *sergents*, 2 *caporaux*, 2 *appointés* with 12 woodworkers and 12 metalworkers, all of whom had previously served in the companies of miners and sappers. The commanding general of each army would allocate each legion with foot or horse artillery as he saw fit.

These legions were supposed to be formed from the original 12 battalions of light infantry and from six of the regiments of chasseurs à cheval. The light battalions and cavalry would remain administratively independent and maintain their own command structures. The army commander-in-chief would appoint a commander for each legion. The senior *lieutenant-colonel* in the two battalions of chasseurs would be promoted to the rank of *colonel*. To bring the legions up to full strength, servicemen from the colonies and other 'arbitrarily deposed soldiers' would be provided with cartridges, or certificates of civility by their municipalities and sent to front, where they would be incorporated at their former rank. Foreigners were also invited to join the legions.

An interesting footnote to the decree was the resurgence of specialist marksmen. Each of the eight companies of the light infantry battalions would provide men to form a company of carabiniers (riflemen). They were not allowed to augment the number of men in each battalion to provide for

---

1 Antoine Charles Etienne Paul de la Roche-Aymon, *Des Troupes légères, ou réflexions sur l'organisation, l'instruction et la tactique de l'Infanterie et de la Cavalerie légères* (Paris: Magimel, Anselin & Pochard, 1817), p.61.

these, nor employ additional officers. The carabiniers were to be 'the best marksmen, the most vigorous and the nimblest'. They were armed with carbines and 'equipped and exercised in the manner analogous with this service'. With the Austrians employing specialist, rifle-armed light infantry, someone at the Ministry of War clearly saw the error in disbanding the chasseur-carabiniers in 1791.

As with many wartime reforms, events appear to have overtaken deliberations in Paris. It is debatable to what degree, if any, this reform took place with some battalions already committed to battle and others much further afield. What the armies needed was more chasseurs at the frontiers. A month after the decree creating the legions, on 28 May 1792, the National Assembly heard a report from Claude Hugau (deputy for l'Eure) of the *Comité Militaire*. Promising to report back on the progress of creating the six legions, Hugau instead lobbied the National Assembly for the urgent formation of entirely new light infantry free companies.[2] This appeal would result in a veritable explosion in the recruitment of chasseurs over the coming year.

The Free Legions and Companies

The *Décret relatif à la création de cinquante-quatre compagnies franches* of 28-31 May 1792 led to the raising of 54 free companies. Each company had a paper strength of 200 men strong, officers included. Service was for the duration of the present war only, and they were intended to supplement the second light infantry battalions in the new legions.

In addition, *Lieutenant-général* François Christophe Kellermann was authorised to raise a légion franche (free legion) composed of 18 companies of light infantry and eight companies of horse, of which the Hussars *ci-devant* Saxe and the *ci-devant* Royal-Allemand would form the nucleus (these two regiments had suffered heavily from emigration, and only a squadron of each remained). *Lieutenants-généraux* Luckner and La Fayette were authorised to raise free legions for their armies on 28 May 1792, each with 18 infantry companies and eight companies on horseback. Each company was formed of 108 men, including three officers. The staff of these legions included three *lieutenants-colonels*, a *quartier-maître-trésorier*, three *adjudants*, a *chirurgien-major*, a *tambour-maître* and of four *maîtres ouvriers* (master workers) (2,821 men each). A voluntary registration would be opened in all the municipalities of the 83 departments of the kingdom, where all men, from the age of 18, able-bodied, at least five *pieds* and well formed, were allowed to serve in the said legions and free companies. Registration would close on 1 October 1792. Enlistment was for three years, or less if peace was made. Ex-soldiers were told they could retain their pensions in full if they enlisted. Officers and NCOs would be chosen by the commanders-in-chief and commissions would be granted by the King. There was an enlistment bounty of 5 *livres* (pounds) for the first month, and 1 *livre* 10 for each month

---

2   Jérôme Mavidal, and Émile Laurent (Founders), *Archives Parlementaires de 1787 à 1860: Première Serie 1789 à 1799* (Paris: Paul Dupont, 1894), Vol.XLIV, pp.234-235.

served afterwards, on top of their pay. They were even to be provided modest travel expenses to join the army.

A fourth légion franche was ordered for the Armée du Midi on 7-21 July 1792 (*Décret portant création d'une quatrième légion franche*). This legion was to be composed of 18 companies of light infantry and four companies of horsemen. The details were exactly the same as the decree of 28-31 May 1792 regarding the first three legions.

Also in July, Jean-Pierre Lacombe-Saint-Michael of the *Comité Militaire* presented a project to redeploy all the soldiers in the colonial regiments stationed in the Department of Morbihan (Brittany) into the free companies and legions thus far raised. A decree of 23-25 July 1792 saw these troops sent to the eastern frontier as fast as possible but instructed the artillery to be left behind in Morbihan, presumably because it was useful in the defence of the coast and ports. Then followed the decree of 26 July – 1 August 1792 forming a foreign legion – the Légion Franche Étrangère, assembling at Dunkerque. As its title suggests, only foreigners were permitted to serve, except for those French citizens who had obtained their letters of naturalisation since 1 January 1789. This legion was to be composed of 2,822 men, including 500 on horseback.

National Guard and Volunteer Chasseurs

While the line regiments had supressed them, some National Guard battalions preserved their chasseur companies. In the first months of 1792 the National Assembly debated their future (*Décret relatif aux compagnies de chasseurs conservées en divers endroits dans les bataillons de la garde nationale* 11 February – 2 March 1792). It was decided that all National Guard battalions and legions would be organised as per the decree of 29 September 1791. The chasseur companies would be formed into battalions of grenadiers and chasseurs, with men drawn from the same or nearest municipalities. Two field pieces were attached to each of the battalions of grenadiers or chasseurs created by this decree.

Under the law of 14 October 1791, the National Guard could be mobilised in the event of the invasion of French territory. These battalions were therefore mobilised by the decree of 24-25 July 1792 and sent to 'defend the empire' (France classed itself as an empire before the First Empire). The 83 departments of the kingdom were divided between France's four field armies, so that each of the generals could requisition men from the departments proportionate to the importance and the size and extent of the borders he was responsible for defending.

- Armée du Rhin: Haut-Rhin, Bas-Rhin, Doubs, Jura, Vosges, Haute-Saône, Haute-Marne, Côte-d'Or, Saône-et-Loire, Aube, Yonne, Nièvre, Creuse, Allier, Puy-de-Dôme, Cher, Indre, Indre-et-Loire, Paris. Total 19.
- Armée du Centre: Ardennes, Moselle, Meurthe, Marne, Meuse, Vienne, Haute-Vienne, Charente, Charente-Inférieure, Deux-Sèvres, Vendée, Loir-et-Cher, Loiret, Eure-et-Loire, Sarthé, Seine-et-Oise , Seine-et-Marne, Loire-Inférieure. Total 18.

FRENCH LIGHT INFANTRY 1784-1815

- Armée du Nord: Pas-de-Calais, Aisne, Nord, Somme, Oise, Seine-Inferieur, Eure, Calvados, Orne, Manche, Mayenne, Maine-et-Loire, Ille-et-Vilaine, Côtes-du-Nord, Morbihan, Finistère. Total 16.
- Armée du Midi: Ain, Isère, Rhône-et-Loire, Haute Loire, Drôme, Ardèche, Hautes-Alpes, Basses-Alpes, Var, Corsica, Bouches-du Rhône, Lozère, Hérault, Gers, Aude, Pyrénées-Orientales, Hautes - Pyrénées , Basses Pyrénées, Ariège, Aveyron, Haute-Garonne, Gard, Landes, Lot, Lot-et-Garonne, Girond, Dordogne, Cantal, Corrèze, Tarn. Total 30.

A further decree of 17 July 1792 (*Décret relatif à la formation de plusieurs compagnies de chasseurs nationaux*) sought to recruit light troops from volunteers who had recently attended the national ceremony marking the storming of the Bastille. Mathieu Dumas's speech to the Assembly proposing this decree is interesting, because it shows service in the light infantry was seen as particularly exciting:[3]

National Guard chasseur bids farewell. Notice the light infantry cut gaiters with red trim and green tassels. His tricolour sash holds a brace of pistols and he has green epaulettes. The rest of the uniform is in the standard national colours. (Collection Yves Martin)

The National Assembly, wishing to support the zeal of the volunteers who, impatient to fulfil the oath which they renewed in the Field of the Federation want to make our freedom triumph or to die gloriously with weapon in hand; considering that it is necessary and very urgent to oppose to the numerous light troops of our enemies with the sort of troop whose composition and particular organization make it possible to take advantage of the aptitude and the impulse of the national character for that kind of service; considering that it is right to give to the citizens who hastened to fly to the aid of the fatherland in danger the choice of the post where the danger presses more, the choice of the weapons with which they will prefer to fight, finally the honour and the advantage of being the first to meet the enemy.

---

3   Mavidal and Laurent, *Archives Parlementaires*, Vol.XLVI, pp.578-579.

In those politically turbocharged times, service in one of these chasseur companies was billed as the most honourable, because it placed volunteers in the vanguard of the army where they were most likely to get to grips with the enemy. The National Assembly therefore invited all the National Guards registered with the municipality of Paris to go to the frontier to serve in the companies of National Chasseurs in the vanguards of the various armies.

Each company of National Volunteer Chasseurs would be formed of 150 volunteers. A *captaine-en-premier*, a *capitaine-en-deuxième*, three *sous-lieutenants*, a *sergent-major*, four *sergents*, eleven *caporaux*, four *cornets*, 124 *chasseurs*. Of the latter, the 90 best educated, strongest and most agile would be sent on campaign. The remaining 34 would form a depot near to the front. The officers would be elected by the chasseurs. The company would be named after the department which contributed the most men to it. If more than five companies were gathered in an army, the general might decide to form them into a battalion, and this would lead to the elections of *lieutenant-colonels* and *adjudants*.

The Volunteer Legions

From July 1792 we see another escalation in the formation of light infantry corps. The Brunswick Manifesto of 25 July and the subsequent invasion of France by the Prussian Army resulted in an outpouring of patriotic and revolutionary spirit. The storming of the Tuileries on 10 August, and subsequent declaration of the French Republic only added to the popularity of soldiering. Reading the French *Archives Parliamentaires* (the record of legislative and political debates in the French chambers from 1787-1860) we can see some extremely moving displays of patriotism. At a more prosaic level, the parliamentary archives provide a useful chronology for the creation of a myriad of light infantry units and mixed corps.

For example, on 30 July a group of petitioners from Savoy were admitted to the bar. Their spokesperson said: 'Gentlemen, the cause of the French is that of all men; so we do not want to limit ourselves to patriotic offerings. We ask to serve as a legion which will bear the name of Légion des Allobroges'.[4] This led to the decree of 8-13 August 1792 which instructed the commander of Grenoble to raise a Légion Franche Allobroge to defend the Alps (Allobroge was the name of a Gallic tribe which lived between the Rhône and the Alps in Roman times). This legion was to be composed of 14 companies of light infantry of 120 men each, including officers, of which seven companies were rifled-armed, the other seven with muskets and bayonets.

The legion included three companies of light dragoons, each of 100 men, including officers, doing service on foot and on horseback, and a company of light artillery, 160, officers included. The staff included a *colonel commandant*, two *lieutenant-colonels*, a *quartier-maître-trésorier*, three *adjudants-majors*, three *adjudants particulaires*, a *chirurgien-major*, an *aide chirurgien*, a

---

4   Mavidal and Laurent, *Archives Parlementaires*, Vol.XLVII, p.291.

tambour-maître, a *maître maréchal* (farrier), a *maître sellier*, a maître tailleur, and a *maître bottier-cordonnier* (boot and shoe maker). Each infantry company was composed of a captain, a *lieutenant*, a *sous-lieutenant*, a *sergent-major*, four *sergents*, eight *caporaux*, one of whom was a *caporal-fourrier*, a *tambour* and 103 carabiniers or chasseurs. The companies of dragoons were commanded by the same number of officers and non-commissioned officers; there was a *trompette* (trumpeter) in each company in place of a *tambour*. The artillery company had a *capitaine commandant*, a *capitaine en second*, a lieutenant, a sous-lieutenant, a *sergent-major*, four *sergents*, eight *caporaux*, a *caporal*-fourrier, eight *appointés*, four *artificiers*, four *ouvriers en bois* (woodworkers), four *ouvriers en fer* (ironworkers), 60 *cannoniers* (gunners) of the 1st class, sixty *cannoniers* of the 2nd, and two tambours. There would be attached to this *légion* four cannon (mounted on sleigh carriages, such as those used in the Corsican War) or two six-inch howitzers.[5]

On 24-26 August there was another scheme, this time to incorporate loyal Swiss soldiers into the original 14 light infantry battalions. The decree even allowed for these battalions to become regiments, with the same composition as a line regiment, but retaining the uniform and name of the light infantry. On 27 August M. Lasource pointed out Belgians and Sardinians willing to fight tyranny were classed as French citizens. He asked for the favour to be extended to Prussians and called for the formation of a Légion des Vandales. The Assembly adopted the proposition and called on the War Committee to draw up an organisation for the force.[6]

On 2 September, a free company of volunteers from the Oratory Section in Paris came to the bar. The commanding captain took an oath on behalf of his comrades, to serve equality until death. To great applause he asked the National Assembly for weapons. That same day Capitaine Duhesme of the 2e Bataillon du Département de Saône-et-Loire was admitted to the bar. After taking the oath to maintain liberty and equality, and to defend his homeland to the death, he paid homage to the free company he commanded, which he was authorised to raise by the commander of the Armée du Nord (Dumouriez). Already 100 men strong, he petitioned the Assembly for uniforms and arms to be provided to his citizen soldiers without delay. Noting

Légion des Allobroges (1792) by Marbot. The uniform is green with red piping. (New York Public Library)

---

5   Mavidal and Laurent, *Archives Parlementaires*, Vol.XLVII, pp.557-559.
6   Mavidal and Laurent, *Archives Parlementaires*, Vol.XLIX, p.49.

the zeal of Duhesme, the president referred the petition to the provisional Executive Council. This excerpt in the parliamentary archives stands out, for this is the same Guillaume Philibert Duhesme who later rose to *Général de Division*, and was mortally wounded at Plancenoit on 18 June 1815, commanding Napoleon's Young Guard. Having raised his own free company of chasseurs, and commanded numerous advanced-guard operations, one can understand why he is such an important source on this subject.[7]

Following Duhesme, on 3 September the student surgeons presented themselves at the bar, offering to form a free company, offering their services either as soldiers or surgeons. They presented the National Assembly with a sum of 2,644 livres, 2 sous for military expenses. The President thanked the petitioners and allowed them to parade into the chamber.

Miquelets were traditionally a form of Catalonian irregulars. These French troops were raised in 1793. (New York Public Library)

In response to the earlier instruction to raise a Légion des Vandales, on 3 September a decree was presented to form a foreign legion under the name of Légion des Germains. This was to be composed of free volunteers, not enlisted men, and was not allowed to recruit deserters from the French army. This legion was composed of four squadrons of light cuirassiers, four squadrons of piqueurs (pikemen) à cheval, two battalions of chasseurs à pied, a battalion of arquebusiers, and an artillery company; in total 3,000 men, of which 1,000 were on horseback and 2,000 on foot. The decree was debated further on 4 September. A number of Prussian and German *federées* (federates; that is, supporters of the revolution) were admitted to the bar. They demanded the order to leave for the front. One of these *vandals* placed the sum of six golden Louis coins on the desk so other citizens might be armed, then asked for his donation to remain anonymous. To great applause and cries of *vive la nation!* the President granted the petitioners the right to parade in the chamber.[8]

Also on that day, a delegation of citizens from Paris's Louvre Section came to the bar. One of them addressed the Assembly: 'We are gathered in a company of a hundred voluntarily enlisted men, all armed and equipped, who ask to leave [for the front]. We ask you nothing but the road that leads to the enemy. We assure you that this pathway will be one of glory'.[9] These words were met with loud applause. Then came a free company from the Pont-Neuf Section, asking for permission to parade in the chamber. The assembly granted permission and the company passed through in good order amid the applause and took the oath. They were followed by the Tuileries Section, who

---

7 A Lievyns, Jean Maurice Verdot, and Pierre Bégat, *Fastes de la Légion-d'honneur* (Paris: Bureau de l'Administration, 1844), Vol.3, pp.191-194.
8 Mavidal and Laurent, *Archives Parlementaires*, Vol.XLVIX, p.348.
9 Mavidal and Laurent, *Archives Parlementaires*, Vol.XLVIX, p.336.

asked for the same authorisation and permission to march to the frontier. The volunteers swore to come back victorious and paraded to the loudest applause. A letter was read from a Sire Carrière in Marseille asking for authorisation to raise a free company in the Bouches-du-Rhône Department. The Assembly agreed. In what must have been an extraordinary day, a Sire Schrecken was admitted to the bar. He offered a rifled carbine as a patriotic gift and asked permission to raise a company of Tyrolean chasseurs. The Assembly accepted the offer with more applause and referred the petition to its *Comité Militaire*.[10]

On 6 September a free company from the Gironde department presented itself at the bar. Before leaving for the front, they came to bid farewell to the Assembly and to ask for arms. In something like the ancient Spartan pledge to return home carrying their shields, or be laid out dead upon them, they said of the weapons: 'We'll bring them back to you, or you won't see us again'. To continued applause, one of the officers cried out: 'Lawmakers, we swear to win or to die'; his soldiers responded 'Yes, yes!'. They marched in good order through the chamber with cries of *vive la liberté! vive l'égalité!* They were followed by a great number of volunteers from the Observatoire Section. Taking the oath, they asked for the favour of parading before the Assembly. The President applauded their zeal and granted their request. Again the chamber rang out to cries of *vive la liberté! vive l'égalité!*[11]

Two days later, Mathieu Dumas of the *comité militaire* presented a project to raise a Légion Nationale du Midi (National Legion of the South). The decree was passed with the following endorsement:

> The National Assembly considering the usefulness of the light troops, and the increase of this species of troops, to cover the marches and the movements of our armies; after hearing the report of its *Comité Militaire* and the proposals of the Minister of War, decrees that it is urgent.[12]

This new corps would be raised and commanded by *Capitaine* Jean Prast of the 83e Régiment d'Infanterie. It was to be composed of 800 chasseurs à pied and 200 chasseurs à cheval. Each light infantry company would be 100 strong, with a *capitaine, lieutenant, sous-lieutenant*, 1 *sergent-major*, 3 *sergents*, one *caporal-fourrier*, 2 *tambours* and 84 chasseurs. Prast would receive 200 livres for every infantryman he equipped and 700 livres for every horseman. The staff of the legion was composed of a *colonel commandant-légionnaire*; a *lieutenant-colonel*, an *adjudant-major d'infanterie*, an *adjudant-major de cavalerie*, two *adjudants*, a *chirurgien-major*, a *chirurgien aide-major* (assistant surgeon), a *trésorier quartier-maître*, an *armurier*, a *maréchal-expert* (veterinary surgeon), a *tambour-major*, and a *trompette-major* (trumpet-major).[13]

---

10   Mavidal and Laurent, *Archives Parlementaires*, Vol.XLVIX, p.341.
11   Mavidal and Laurent, *Archives Parlementaires*, Vol.XLVIX, pp.395-396.
12   Mavidal and Laurent, *Archives Parlementaires*, Vol.XLVIX, p.471.
13   Mavidal and Laurent, *Archives Parlementaires*, Vol.XLVIX, pp.471-472

There is an interesting decree of 9-14 September about the raising of the free company of the Observatoire Section. The commander and several of his companions took the stand and explained how the Section had tried to raise a chasseur company. Three hundred men registered, so two companies of chasseurs had been formed. However, no funds had been provided for the second company, so for the last eight days these chasseurs had lived at the expense of a few individuals in the Section. They were ready to fight, but money was required. Matthieu Dumas explained there had been a misunderstanding and only that morning it had been agreed to make funds available. He asked for a decree to be made allowing for the pay and equipment of the company. The decree was issued to more applause in the chamber.[14]

This last episode had an important effect. A further decree was issued determining the conditions under which corps of light troops could be formed in future. Only those free corps raised by decree would be permitted. Anyone who wished to raise a company would be required to display for three days in his section or in his municipality, his name, the details of his services or his civic titles, and his proposal, and to bring back a certificate, either to the Assembly, if he presented a petition, or to the Executive Power, if he addressed it directly. Anyone wishing to serve in such a corps would be required to produce a certificate of civility and to prove he had made an active and personal service in the National Guard.

Proposals continued to follow. On 10 September it was proposed to raise a free company at Rosenthal called the Compagnie Franche de la Liberté. This proposal came back to the Assembly on 12 September and was granted. Also on 10 September, a decree was made for the formation of free company known as the chasseurs *bons tireurs* (literally, good shooters). This unit was specifically raised to combat the enemy Tyrolean Jägers. Formed in the Departments of Oise and Somme, the company would be 150 strong, with 1 *capitaine commandant*, 1 *capitaine en seconde*, 2 lieutenants, 1 *sergent-major* and 2 *sergents*, who will all be chosen by election. The chasseurs would be obliged to provide their own uniform and armaments (an advance was available for this), and they would not receive tents or any other camping equipment.[15]

Then came the Compagnie Franche des Chasseurs de la Mort (Death Chasseurs) who presented themselves at the bar on 11 September. The commander promised not to recognize any other sovereign on earth than the people, any other idol than freedom and equality and he expressed the desire, after having offered a sum of 300 livres, to parade in the enclosure of the legislative body. The President applauded this zeal and granted the request. The company paraded in good order, crossed the chamber exhibiting a 'formidable demeanour' earned it unanimous applause from the Assembly and the galleries.[16]

---

14   Mavidal and Laurent, *Archives Parlementaires*, Vol.XLVIX, p.512.
15   Mavidal and Laurent, *Archives Parlementaires*, Vol.XLVIX, p.515.
16   Mavidal and Laurent, *Archives Parlementaires*, Vol.XLVIX, p.565.

The last big decree of the summer came on 16 September with the Légion Nationale des Pyrénées. This legion was to be formed of 1,600 chasseurs à pied, 600 chasseurs à cheval, 200 artillerymen, and 100 workers – a grand total of 2,500 men. The chasseurs à pied were formed into two battalions and organised like the regular infantry battalions. The horsemen were organised into four squadrons. The staff were composed of a *colonel commandant légionnaire*, 3 infantry *lieutenants-colonels*, 2 cavalry *lieutenants-colonels*, 2 infantry *adjudants-majors*, 2 cavalry *adjudants-majors*, 2 infantry *adjudant* NCOs, 2 cavalry *adjudant* NCOs, a surgeon-major, a *quartier-maître-trésorier*, an *armurier*, *maître sellier*, a *tambour-major*, a *trompette-major*.[17]

There was then something of a pause in the creation of new units of light troops. In October France's armies began something of an offensive, seizing Frankfurt, Basle, and invading the Austrian Netherlands. In November they seized Brussels and annexed the County of Nice and Savoy to France. This resurgence in the fighting gave impetus to new decrees by the National Convention. On 6 December a Légion Franche des Américains was ordered, composed entirely of chasseurs à cheval. The National Treasury also made a payment of 40,000 livres to Lieutenant-Général Kellermann for the light troops he had assembled under the name Éclaireurs Républicains (Republican Scouts). On 10 December there was confirmation of the status of the Légion des Ardennes, which had actually been formed by Dumouriez in July 1792 under the command of the Polish-born *Maréchal de Camp* Joseph de Miaczynski. It was composed of two battalions of light infantry and four squadrons of light cavalry. A decree of 26 January 1793 (*Décret relatif aux trois légions belges et liégeoises*) saw the incorporation of three Belgian and Liege legions into the army.[18] On other fronts, on 30 December there was a request from *Général de Division* Joseph Servan to raise a corps of Miquelets in the Pyrenees (Miquelets were an irregular Catalan militia).[19] On 29 January a decree created the Légion des Montagnes des Pyrénées;[20] on 5 February a decree to raise four battalions of light infantry on Corsica.[21]

We must pause here and take stock. France had begun the war with 14 battalions of light infantry. In the first 10 months of the war the government decreed 13 legions of newly raised mixed-corps troops (containing 26 battalions of chasseurs à pied; four additional Corsican battalions of chasseurs à pied; 58 free companies ranging from 100-200 men each (although there appear to have been far more companies raised). Nor should the number of National Guardsmen be underestimated, approximately 300,000 men were conscripted into service with the armies in April 1792. A portion of these were allocated to light infantry service. This was an enormous increase in manpower.

---

17   Mavidal and Laurent, *Archives Parlementaires*, Vol.L, pp.60-61.
18   *Collection complète des lois, décrets, ordonnances, règlements et avis du conseil-d'état* (Paris: A. Guyot, 1825), Vol.5, p.159.
19   *Collection complète des lois*, Vol.5, p.125.
20   *Collection complète des lois*, Vol.5, p.164.
21   *Collection complète des lois*, Vol.5, p.178.

LIGHT INFANTRY IN THE WARS OF THE FRENCH REVOLUTION

The Demi-Brigades (First Formation)

The companies, battalions and legions recorded in previous sections are the ones the government knew about. We saw from the example of the Légion des Ardennes that it had existed for six months before it was officially recognised. Although there was a national crisis, with the King's head in basket, this ad-hoc, spontaneous method of building an army was anarchy, not a sustainable system for supplying and maintaining troops in the field. Urgent reform and reorganisation were required.

One of the great architects of the French army was Edmond Louis Alexis Dubois-Crancé (1747-1814). A soldier from the minor nobility, Dubois-Crancé was elected deputy to the Estates General in 1789 and was one of those who took the famous Tennis Court Oath not to be disbanded until France had a constitution. Later that year he proposed national conscription (something not adopted until 1798) and was a prominent voice in the anti-slavery movement. His great mission at the beginning of 1793 was reorganising France's military, creating a single national army from the remains of the old regular army and the enormous number of National Guard volunteers now in uniform.

On 7 February 1793 Dubois-Crancé made a report to the National Assembly on behalf of the *Comité de la Guerre*. He proposed reforming the army, uniting regular and volunteer battalions to form demi-brigades of line and light infantry. Focusing here exclusively on the light infantry component, Dubois-Crancé's report set out the existing composition of light troops. There were the 14 battalions of chasseurs, each with a paper strength of 700 men, providing 9,800 troops. On paper, the infantry of the various legions and free corps had a theoretical strength of 35,000 men. Dubois-Crancé reported the actual returns provided to the Minister of War from the various units indicated their effective strength was less than a quarter of the official establishment. In addition to these, there were about 50 small corps of 100-150 men dotted around the various *Départements*.

It was vital France retained a strong force of light infantry. Dubois-Crancé described them as the class of men which war consumes the most, because they are always active and always under

Infanterie légère, 1795 by Auguste Raffet, Auguste (1830). This depicts a carabinier wearing a mirliton style shako. (Anne S.K. Brown Military Collection)

fire. 'An army cannot be surrounded by too many scouts,' he said. 'Your enemies have clouds of them, and your committee has thought it advisable to oppose them with a force of this type, equal to that which they can put in the field'.[22] By combining the 14 battalions of light infantry with the infantry of the legions and free corps, Dubois-Crancé believed France could have 30,000 well organised troops. The full text of his proposition read as follows:

> Light infantry.
> Art. 1st. The fourteen light infantry battalions will receive the same formation as the line infantry; as a result, the Minister of War will form into battalions the free corps and the infantry troops of the legions and incorporate two of these battalions with a battalion of chasseurs, in numerical order. Three battalions thus assembled will form a light infantry demi-brigade, which will have the same organisation and pay as the line infantry. After the formation of these demi-brigades, they will enjoy the same mode of promotion as the line infantry.
> Art. 2. The Minister of War is authorized to use, in the formation of light infantry half-brigades, those existing battalions of volunteers, who would wish to do this service in the absence of the battalions of the legions.
> Art. 3. If corps that have not found a place in the new organization of the armies remain to be used, the Minister will report back to the Convention to advise the means of rendering useful services to the Republic.[23]

With the benefit of hindsight, one can see the obvious and pressing necessity of the proposed reforms, but at the time, politicians objected. Even before he finished reading his lengthy proposal, Dubois-Crancé was interrupted by several complainants, one of whom loudly declared this was not the time for complex reorganisations – the enemy was at the gates. The session was therefore adjourned until 12 February. On that day, Dubois-Crancé made a formidable defence of the proposal. His analysis is extremely interesting and gives an insight into the deliberations of the *Comité Militaire*. Critics of the amalgamation of regulars and volunteers complained it was imprudent to disorganise the army when it was in front of the enemy. Dubois-Crancé pointed out the army was already disorganised – physically and morally. The invasion of France by the Duke of Brunswick the previous summer caused the regular infantry regiments to be divided. Regulars were needed to bolster the outposts of volunteers. This meant regimental administration was impractical. One regiment might have its first battalion in the army of Miranda with the second in that of Custine, while its grenadiers were in the army of Dumouriez, and its depot was in Metz or Strasbourg. None of these parts of the regiment were linked, they were unable to offer mutual aid to one another, and the officers barely knew each other. On top of this, soldiers were daily deserting the regular regiments to join volunteer units, their service actively solicited by the captains and lieutenant-colonels of the latter. 'You want to keep the army of the line, and I say that you will kill it', Dubois-

---

22 Mavidal and Laurent, *Archives Parlementaires*, Vol.LVIII, pp.363.
23 Mavidal and Laurent, *Archives Parlementaires*, Vol.LVIII, pp.368.

Crancé added forcibly to his critics[24]. With better conditions of service in the volunteer units, the line regiments would not receive a single recruit, and because of desertion, by the month of July he predicted regular units would be down to 100 men per battalion. By then the government would have lost all the benefits provided by regular soldiers in terms of tactics, discipline and administration. The enemy would be able to triumph without any effort. This is why such a major reform was needed.

The proposal was adopted by law on 21 February, but its enactment was adjourned on 31 March 1793 because of the military situation. On 12 August 1793 an instruction was produced (*Mode d'amalgame pour l'infanterie de la république*) by Citizen Merlino, Deputy for the Ain. This important document set out the method of *embrigadement* (the amalgamation of the various corps) and the staff requirements of each demi-brigade (see Table 8). A law of *2 Frimaire II* (22 November 1793) further clarified the composition of the companies (see Table 9).

Good rendition of a light infantry subaltern officer of the demi-brigades, circa.1795. (New York Public Library)

Table 8. Staff of demi-brigades, 12 August 1793

Chef de Brigade	1
Chef de Bataillon	3
Quartiers-maîtres-trésoriers	1
Adjudant-major	1
Chirurgien-major	1
Adjudants-sous-officiers	3
Tambour-major	1
Caporal tambour	1
Musiciens (including a chef)	8
Maître tailleur	1
Maîtres armuriers	3
Maître cordonnier	1

---

24   Mavidal and Laurent, *Archives Parlementaires*, Vol.LVIII, p.482.

Table 9. Composition of companies, 22 November 1793

Grade	Fus.	Gren.
Capitaine	1	1
Lieutenant	1	1
Sous-lieutenant	1	1
Sergent major	1	1
Sergents	4	4
Corporal-fourrier	1	1
Caporaux	6	8
Hommes	104	64
Tambours	2	2
Total	123	83

The decree of 9 Pluviôse Year II (January 1794) enacted the reform, officially disbanded all the legions and free corps which had been raised previously. The existing 22 battalions of chasseurs kept their identifying number and gave it to the demi-brigades they were to take form part of. The remainder of the demi-brigades were issued a number drawn by lottery by the government's *comité militaire*. The first stage of the *embrigadement* was to form all the free companies into battalions. These battalions were then grouped with the existing battalions. Historians and researchers have been attempting to understand and document what happened next for the best part of two centuries; but because of the irregular nature of the corps, because they were often known by different names, and because there was duplication in the numbering of the demi-brigades, clarifying exactly what happened is difficult. Table 10 is largely based on Avril's 1824 *Essai historique*. (Note: where the same number was assigned more than once *bis* means repeat; *ter* means tertiary).

Table 10. Demi-Brigades Légères (First Formation)

No.	Corps of which composed
1er	1er Bataillon de Chasseurs (ex-Royal-Italien) 8e Bataillon de Volontaires de la Gironde 1er Bataillon des Vengeurs du Midi
2e	2e Bataillon de Chasseurs (ex-Royal de Dauphiné) 2e des Chasseurs Pyrénées-Orientales
3e	3e Bataillon de Chasseurs (ex-Royaux-Corses) 4e Bataillon de Chasseurs des Hautes-Alpes 9e Bataillon de Volontaires de l'Isère
4e	4e Bataillon de Chasseurs (ex-Corses) 5e Bataillon de Volontaires de l'Ain 1er Bataillon de Volontaires de la Creuse
5e	5e Bataillon de Chasseurs (ex-Cantabres) 1er Bataillon Chasseurs Pyrénées-Orientales
6e	6e Bataillon de Chasseurs (ex-Bretagne) 8e Bataillon de Volontaires du Calvados 4e Bataillon de Volontaires de Saône-et-Loire
7e	7e Bataillon de Chasseurs (ex-Auvergne) 1er Bataillon de Volontaires de la Corrèze 2e Bataillon de Volontaires de la Dordogne
8e	8e Bataillon de Chasseurs (ex-Vosges) 1er Bataillon de Volontaires du Cantal 2e Bataillon de la Légion de la Moselle

LIGHT INFANTRY IN THE WARS OF THE FRENCH REVOLUTION

No.	Corps of which composed
9e	9e Bataillon de Chasseurs (ex-Cévennes) Bataillon d'éclaireurs de la Meuse 28e bis Bataillon de Chasseurs
10e	10e Bataillon de Chasseurs (ex-Gévaudan) Légion du Centre 1er Bataillon de la Légion de la Moselle
11e	11e Bataillon de Chasseurs (ex-Ardennes) 5e Bataillon de Volontaires du Doubs 6e Bataillon de Volontaires de la Drôme
12e	12e Bataillon de Chasseurs (ex-Roussillon) 2e Bataillon de Volontaires de Lot-et-Garonne 3e Bataillon de Volontaires de la Haute-Saône
13e	13e Bataillon de Chasseurs 8e Bataillon de Chasseurs de Rheims
14e	14e Bataillon de Chasseurs Bataillon de Chasseurs de Mont Cassel 5e Bataillon de Tirailleurs
14e (bis)	3e Bataillon de Volontaires du Cher 1er Bataillon de Volontaires de la Dordogne
15e	1er Bataillon de la Légion des Allobroges 2e Bataillon de la Légion des Allobroges 2e Bataillon de Volontaires des Bouches-du-Rhône 9e Bataillon de Volontaires du district de Lille
15e (bis)	8e Bataillon de Volontaires de la Drôme 4e Bataillon de Volontaires des Vosges Six compagnies franches
16e	1er Bataillon de Volontaires de l'Aveyron 8e Bataillon de Volontaires de l'Isère
16e (bis)	6e Bataillon bis Chasseurs du Nord Bataillon de Chasseurs du Bas-Rhin
17e	Formed of men from new levies from different departments.
17e (bis)	1er Bataillon de la Légion des Alpes 2e Bataillon de Volontaires de l'Allier 9e Bataillon de Volontaires de l'Ain
18e	3e Bataillon de Volontaires de Vaucluse 3e Bataillon de Volontaires du Mont-Blanc
18e (bis)	2e Bataillon de la Légion des Alpes 5e Bataillon de Volontaires des Côtes maritimes 6e Bataillon de Volontaires du Doubs
19e	8e Bataillon de Volontaires des Vosges 2e Bataillon de Tirailleurs des Alpes 1er Bataillon de la Légion du Nord 2e Bataillon de la Légion du Nord
20e	20e Bataillon de chasseurs 3e Bataillon de Paris (part only) 9e Bataillon de Volontaires de la Haute-Garonne 10e Bataillon de Volontaires de la Haute-Garonne
20e (bis)	4e bis Bataillon de Volontaires de la Charente 11e Bataillon de Volontaires du Doubs
20e (ter)	Formed of men from new levies from different departments.
21e	1er Bataillon Franc de Muller 10e Bataillon des Fédérés Nationaux 17e Bataillon des Fédérés Nationaux

No.	Corps of which composed
21e (bis)	1er Bataillon de Volontaires du Rhône 1er Bataillon de Volontaires de Villefranche 11e Bataillon de Volontaires de la Côte-d'Or
22e	Légion de Rosenthal 1er Bataillon Chasseurs de la Nèthe 2e Bataillon de Volontaires d'Argelès
23e	1er Bataillon de la Légion des Ardennes 2e Bataillon de la Légion des Ardennes 16e Bataillon des Chasseurs, Sédan
24e	Not formed.
25e	Formed of men from new levies from different departments.
26e	Formed of men from new levies from different departments.
27e	Not formed.
28e	Formed of men from new levies from different departments.
29e	1er Bataillon de la Légion des Pyrénées 2e Bataillon de la Légion des Pyrénées 9e de la Dordogne 4e de Vaucluse
30e	Légion Franche étrangère
31e	Formed of men from new levies from different departments.
32e	Bataillon de Chasseurs du Hainault 4e Bataillon de Chasseurs francs du Nord

Two final remarks on the decree of 9 Pluviôse Year II ought to be made. The company of carabiniers was formed the same strength as the grenadier companies in the line and they received the same pay as grenadiers. However, unlike grenadiers, carabiniers were to be chosen 'from among the most skilful marksmen'. Another interesting qualification was confirmation the light infantry demi-brigades would not receive an artillery complement.

The Demi-Brigades (Second Formation)

We have seen how it took France a year to agree the composition of the demi-brigades and to begin the process of *embrigadement*. Such was the complexity of the task it should be no surprise to find the first attempt only partially succeeded. At the end of 1795 the infantry element of the French army consisted of 652,000 men organised as follows:[25]

- 252 demi-brigades of the line (including 47 vacant numbers) 410,000 men
- 40 demi-brigades of light infantry (including 2 vacant numbers) 76,000
- 11 Free legions (many of which were incomplete) 22,000
- 227 battalions of unincorporated volunteers 136,200
- 152 distinct companies 7,800

---

25   Avril, *Essai Avantages d'une bonne discipline*, p.337.

On 18 Nivôse Year IV (8 January 1796), the Directory government ordered a new reorganisation which would complete the *embrigadement*. This decree stated there would be 109 line and 30 demi-brigades (the number of line demi-brigades was raised to 110 soon after). These demi-brigades of the second formation were subsequently reinforced by a third amalgamation of sorts. The law of 4 Fructidor Year XI (21 August 1798) saw the establishment of a system of conscription in France. The subsequent law of 10 Messidor Year VII (28 June 1799) saw the conscripts of years 5, 6 and 7 mobilised and organised into *bataillons auxiliaires* (auxiliary battalions) or companies of chasseurs. The battalions were comprised of eight companies of fusiliers and one of grenadiers, and the chasseur company was attached as a tenth company. On 14 Pluviôse Year VIII, the auxiliaries were incorporated into the demi-brigades, with the chasseur companies sent to reinforce the light infantry demi-brigades.

Table 11. Demi-Brigades Légères (Second Formation, 1796-1803)

1re	14e Demi-Brigade Légère Chasseurs Aux. of 1er Aux., Côte-d'Or, Doubs, and Jura.
2e	21e Demi-Brigade Légère
3e	15e bis Demi-Brigade Légère 7e Demi-Brigade Légère 1er Bon, Chasseurs Réunis Remains of 107e Inf. Régt. ex-Bourbon and 108e Inf. Régt. ex-Ile-de-France
4e	8e Demi-Brigade Légère 52e Demi-Brigade de Ligne (part) 1er Aux. des Hautes-Alpes. 1° Bon de la Charente. Bon de Nyons, Drôme 1er Aux. de la Haute-Garonne 5e de l'Isère.
5e	6e Demi-Brigade Légère 22e Demi-Brigade Légère 55e Demi-Brigade de bataille (part) 3e Provisoire (part)
6e	19e Demi-Brigade Légère (part) Chasseurs de la Charente Comp. franches de Grenadiers et Chasseurs des Côtes-du-Nord Chasseurs d'Évreux, Eure Bon Aux. du Gard (part) 2e du Morbihan 9e de Paris 11e de Paris Chasseurs Républicains de Paris 6e de Paris Chasseurs de Saône-et-Loire 5e Batailllon formé à Orléans 2e des Chasseurs Réunis

FRENCH LIGHT INFANTRY 1784-1815

7e	20e Demi-Brigade Légère Demi-Brigade des Aurois Demi-Brigade du Jura et de l'Hèrault (part) Demi-Brigade de la Sarthe Fédérés de Marseille 1er Bon de Jemmapes Chasseurs du 1er Aux. de l'Isère 3e des Chasseurs de la Nèthe 1er de Saint-Amand, Nord 2e de Paris Bon des Chasseurs du Midi
8e	30e Demi-Brigade Légère 11e Bon de Volontaires de la Seine-Inférieure (Égalité) 8e Bon de Volontaires des Réserves Chasseurs Corses
9e	9e Demi-Brigade Légère Chasseurs Aux. de l'Aisne, Eure-et-Loir, de la Moselle, Seine-et-Oise, Seine-et-Marne, 1er Aux. De l'Eure, two companies of chasseurs from Paris auxiliary battalions
10e	11e Demi-Brigade Légère 20e bis Demi-Brigade Légère 154e Demi-Brigade de Ligne 3e Bon de la Demi-Brigade des Landes 5e bis Bon de Chasseurs à pied 1er Bon de Volontaires de l'Aube 1er Bon Franc Chasseurs Aux. du Cher, Loir-et-Cher, de la Meuse.
11e	3e Demi-Brigade Légère 4e Bon de Chasseurs des Hautes-Alpes 9e de l'Isère Chasseurs Aux. du Bas Rhin (2 bons) Chasseurs Révolutionnaires Chasseurs des Haute Alpes
12e	2e Demi-Brigade Légère 2e des Chasseurs des Pyrénées-Orientales Chasseurs Aux. de la Corrèze, de la Haute-Marne, de la Nièvre, du Pas de Calais, 1er Aux de la Somme, des Vosges, de l'Yonne 3e Bon Franc
13e	Demi-Brigade de Paris et Vosges 1er et 2e Bons, 84e Rohan 6e de la Côte-d'Or 5e de Paris 2e et 5e des Fédérés Nationaux 3e et 11e Bataillons (formed at Orléans) Légion Germanique 17e des Chasseurs, Haute-Garonne 23e de Chasseurs de Bardon 2e Bon de Tirailleurs
14e	108e Demi-Brigade de Ligne (part) 139e Demi-Brigade de Ligne (part) Chasseurs Aux. de l'Ain, de Allier, de l'Aube, 2e Aux de la Côte-d'Or, du 1er Aux de la Dordogne, de la Haute-Saône. 11e Légion des Francs (Légion Noire)
15e	Demi-Brigade de Tirailleurs Demi-Brigade Basques Bon Auxiliaire du Mont-Blanc

LIGHT INFANTRY IN THE WARS OF THE FRENCH REVOLUTION

16e	12e Demi-Brigade Légère 204e Demi-Brigade de Ligne (part) 23e Demi-Brigade Légère 26d Demi-Brigade Légère
17e	1er Demi-Brigade Légère 32e Demi-Brigade Légère Chasseurs Aux. de l'Ardèche, de la Haute-Loire, du Puy-de-Dôme, du Var Chasseurs de l'Armée d'Italie 1er & 2e Chasseurs Francs du Nord
18e	180e Demi-Brigade de Ligne (part) 200e bis Demi-Brigade de Ligne 12e Demi-Brigade Provisoire 20e ter Demi-Brigade Légère
19e	31e Division de Gendarmerie à Pied (part) Demi-Brigade formed 24 Ventôse Year VII from detachments of the 3e and 6e Demi-Brigade Légère, the 141e Demi-Brigade de Ligne, 2e Bon de l'Aisne (part), Régiment de Ferdat (part)
20e	10e Demi-Brigade Légère Chasseurs Aux from the departments of Arriège, Aude, Aveyron, Lozère, Tarn
21e	4e Demi-Brigade Légère 14e bis Demi-Brigade Légère 21e bis Demi-Brigade Légère
22e	16e Demi-Brigade Légère 52e Demi-Brigade de Ligne (part) 11e Bon de l'Ain 5e des Basses-Alpes
23e	18e bis Demi-Brigade Légère 7e Demi-Brigade Provisoire (part) 4e Bon de Volontaires de l'Hérault Bon de Saint-Denis Bon Aux. De Saône-et-Loire 2e Bon de Volontaires de Seine-et-Oise
24e	5e Demi-Brigade Légère (part) 169e Demi-Brigade de Ligne 3e Bon de Volontaires des Ardennes Bon de Chasseurs du Mont-des-Chats Demi-Brigade de Chasseurs de montagnes Légion des Francs, Mayence Légion des Monts Légion Nantaise 4e Bon Franc
25e	13e Demi-Brigade Légère 17e Demi-Brigade Légère
26e	16e bis Demi-Brigade Légère 17e bis Demi-Brigade Légère Chasseurs Aux. from the Departments of Creuse and Meuse 32e Auxiliaire de la Somme
27e	15e Demi-Brigade Légère 52e Demi Brigade de ligne (part) 11e Demi-Brigade Provisoire 1er Bon de Volontaires des Gravilliers (part) 1er Bon de Tirailleurs des Alpes

28e	Demi-Brigade de l'Ardèche Demi-Brigade de Gers et Gironde Demi-Brigade de Gers et Bayonne Demi-Brigade de Gironde et Lot-et-Garonne 5e Bon de la Charente-Inférieure 14e Bon de la formation d'Orléans 4e Bon de Volontaires de la Dordogne 12e Bon de Volontaires de la Haute-Saône 31e Bon de Volontaires des réserves 10e bis de la Gironde 1er Bon d'infanterie Légère (Ouest) 2e Bon d'infanterie Légère (Ouest) Bon de Volontaires de Chinon 4e Bon de Maynne-et-Loire 2e Bon de Volontaires de Saint-Amand 1er Bon de Paris (second formation)
29e	6e Demi-Brigade Légère (part only) 18e Demi-Brigade Légère Demi-Brigade de la Haute-Saône 25e Demi-Brigade Légère 1er Auxiliaire des Ardennes Bon de Volontaires d'Apt
30e	Demi-Brigade de la Dordogne 1er Bon, Volontaires du Nord 3e Bon, Volontaires de la Charente-Inférieure 3e Bon, Volontaires de Lot-et-Garonne 3e Bon, Volontaires de la Nièvre 6e ter Bon, Volontaires du Nord 2e Bon, Volontaires de la Haute-Saône 8e Bon, Volontaires de la Sarthe 8e Bon, Volontaires de la Somme 2e Auxiliaire de la Somme 3e Bon, Volontaires des Vosges 2e Bon, Légion des Ardennes
31e	Troupes Piémontaises (formed in Year IX)

In addition to the demi-brigades listed in Table 11, several ad-hoc units of light infantry were created. The law of 14 Pluviôse Year VIII (3 February 1800) ordered the formation of four battalions of light infantry under the name of Francs, numbered one to four respectively. These battalions were destined for service in the west of France where there was a resurgence in pro-royalist insurgency, or 'Chouanerie'. The battalions followed a similar model to those within the demi-brigades, with nine companies, eight of chasseurs-francs and one of carabiniers. The company included a *capitaine*, a *lieutenant*, two *sous-lieutenants*, 1 *sergent-major*, 4 *sergents*, 1 *fourrier-écrivran* (note the archaic addition of 'scribe' to the title), 8 *caporaux*, 2 *tambours* and 120 carabiniers or chasseurs-francs. The staff was composed of 1 *chef de battaillon*, an *adjudant-major*, an *adjudant sous-officier*, 1 *porte-drapeau* (standard bearer), an *officier de santé* (medical officer), 1 *tambour-major*, and four *maître ouvriers* (an armourer, tailor, cordwainer, gaiter maker). The carabiniers were to be armed with rifled carbines and the whole uniformed and equipped like the line infantry.

Once completed, these battalions were incorporated into the Légion de la Loire, the existence of which was decreed on the 22 Brumaire Year IX (13

LIGHT INFANTRY IN THE WARS OF THE FRENCH REVOLUTION

November 1802). This force included various isolated companies and battalions, including a Légion Nantaise which had been raised on 14 Messidor Year VII (2 July 1799). The new legion would be composed of two battalions of infantry, each of eight companies, including, one of carabiniers, one of sapeurs, and six of fusiliers, and a squadron of light cavalry. Clearly the old mixed corps formular proved itself useful for counter-insurgency warfare.[26]

On 28 Floréal Year 11 (18 May 1803), four new legions were created, each including a staff, five battalions of infantry and an artillery company. Three battalions were line infantry and two of light. Each battalion was composed of five companies, four centre companies and one of grenadiers or carabiniers. These legions were principally formed from officers and troops from the Alpes Maritimes department and those from the new departments created in Piedmont which was annexed by France after the battle of Marengo. These soldiers were dressed in a *gris de fer* (iron grey) coat, with white gilet and breeches. The light infantry battalions wore shakos.[27]

The Éclaireurs

We have seen how even before the Seven Years War infantry regiments created piquets to skirmish and scout, and then formed official chasseur companies, until these were formally suppressed in 1791. Given the necessity of these troops in previous wars, there is no surprise to find this same need existing in the 1790s. Duhesme confirms this, describing how, in the absence of light infantry who were often placed on the wings in battle or detached, each line infantry battalion would form detachment of 50 to 80 men, all volunteers, to skirmish ahead of the battalion, scout the march and drive off enemy skirmishers.[28] In its simplest form, the word éclaireur means 'scout' in English. A subtle difference between the Anglo-Saxon and Gallic terms: where the English 'scout' derived from the Old French scouter (to listen or heed), the term éclaireur came from éclairer – to illuminate. In the military sense, this term was a new one, according to Bardin. Earlier in the eighteenth century one spoke of découvreurs (discoverers). On the one hand the term

Light infantry carabinier purported as a veteran of Marengo. Had he been at Marengo, shakos would have been more likely than bearskins. (New York Public Library)

---

26 *Collection complète des lois*, Vol.11, p.333.
27 B.C. Gournay, *Journal militaire* (Paris: Imprimerie du Journal Militaire, Year XI), p.141.
28 Philibert-Guillaume Duhesme, *Précis historique de l'infanterie légère: de ses fonctions, et de son influence dans la tactique des différens siècles* (Lyon: Bérenger, 1806), p.273.

referred to infantry or (more commonly cavalry) sent ahead to scout a march, but it was also applied to companies of skirmishers formed during the wars of the French Revolution and Consulate.

The éclaireurs were sometimes formed on an ad hoc basis, much like a piquet, but sometimes on a more permanent basis. For instance, Guyard speaks of éclaireurs being formed by detaching a predetermined number of files from each infantry company.[29] At the command, *Éclaireurs, en avant!* (scouts, forwards!), they would advance from their parent company and form a screen in front of it. These men scouted ahead and skirmished in front of the unit. When they operated on the wings of a battalion, they were called flanquers.

Duhesme's 1806 essay describes how Marshal Massena, 'who excelled above all in mountain warfare', formed éclaireur companies in his armies in the campaigns before the empire, and had ordered his divisions to do the same in 1805 before the formation of formal voltigeur companies.[30] There are ample references to éclaireurs in Napoleon's published correspondence. The earliest dates from 25 February 1797, when he gives instruction to the formation of the Italian Légion Lombarde. In addition to a company of grenadiers, each company were required to nominate ten men for a company of éclaireurs who drew the same high pay as the grenadiers when the legion was on active service. They were united into a company only when the legion marched on the enemy, with the battalion providing a captain, lieutenant and *sous-lieutenant* to command them. During the 1799 Syrian campaign, two infantry demi-brigades had already formed éclaireur companies which proved their worth, hence the following daily order by Napoleon:

> Order of the Day
> General Headquarters, in front of Acre, 17 Floréal year VII (6 May 1799).
>
> The general-in-chief orders the formation of a company of éclaireurs in each demi-brigade; those of the 18e and of the 32e have already distinguished themselves by their bravery in the attack on the parade ground on the night of the 15th. He remembers the services rendered by these companies whenever they have been formed; he especially relies on them: a brave éclaireur never shows his back to the enemy.
>
> By order of the commander in chief.[31]

Another interesting letter dated Cairo, 15 June 1799 concerns an inspection and revue of the 69e Demi-Brigade. Napoleon wanted to inspect the three grenadier companies and would only accept grenadiers who were present at the battle of Mondovi or had been awarded a sabre or musket of honour or other award, or had been an éclaireur in the army of Italy or Syria. This clearly

---

29   Colonel Guyard, *Instruction pour le service et les manoeuvres de l'infanterie légère, en campagne* (Paris: Magimel, An XIII), p.54.
30   Duhesme, *Précis historique de l'infanterie légère*, p.275.
31   Napoleon I, *Correspondance de Napoléon Ier: Publiée Par Ordre de L'empereur Napoléon III* (Paris: H. Plon, J. Dumaine, 1860), Vol. V, p.535.

Detail from Pierre Martinet's Battle of the bridge at Arcola (1796). French tirailleurs provide covering fire for the main attack across the bridge. (Anne S.K. Brown Military Collection)

demonstrates éclaireurs were used in Italy and then resurrected in Syria in 1799. We also find references to éclaireur companies after the Marengo campaign. In his later writings, he referred to the 200 éclaireurs of the 9e Légère at Marengo, at the head of whom Desaix was mortally wounded.[32]

A decree of 13 Thermidor Year VIII (1 August 1800) instructed the grenadiers and éclaireurs of the 5e, 6e, 35e, 64e de Ligne and the 26e Légère to be assembled and form themselves into one battalion per demi-brigade, coming under the command of *Général de Division* Murat.[33] This confirms light infantry battalions were also forming éclaireur companies. On 18 July 1800 another letter, this time to Minister of War Lazare Carnot: *Général de Division* Mortier is ordered to complete the companies of grenadiers in the 12e, 45e and 64e demi-brigades and for each battalion to form a company of éclaireurs of 100 men each. These men are to be chosen from the men who are vigorous and élite, commanded by distinguished officers. The same order was to be given to the 5e, 6e and 35e de Ligne and the 26e Légère. Each demi-brigade was also to provide a *chef de bataillon*, an *adjudant-major* and an *adjudant* NCO to command these companies.[34]

---

32 Général Gourgaud, *Mémoires pour servir à l'histoire de France sous Napoléon, écrits à sainte-helene, sous la dictée de l'empereur, par les généraux qui ont partage sa captivité et publiés sur les manuscrits entièrement corrigés de sa main* (Paris: Didot & Bossange, 1823), Vol.1, p.234.
33 Napoleon I, *Correspondance de Napoléon Ier,* Vol.VI, p.431.
34 Napoleon I, *Correspondance de Napoléon Ier,* Vol.VI, pp.411–412.

Skirmisher of the Légion Italique in French service in 1800. (New York Public Library)

On 1 August 1800 Carnot was ordered to create a piquet of 300 men from the 45e Demi-Brigade and 150 men from the 24e Légère. The grenadier and éclaireur companies were exempted from this piquet. On 16 August there is another instruction to form a mobile column composed of the grenadiers and éclaireurs of the 45e de Ligne. On 20 December 1800 a corps of éclaireurs is to be raised in the department of Var and another in the Bouches-du-Rhône. The latter would be composed of the three companies of éclaireurs of the 19e Demi-Brigade de Ligne, each composed of 60 men, and three companies of éclaireurs of the 74e, each composed of 60 men. The Var corps would be composed of three companies of éclaireurs from the Naval Corps, again 60 men strong each, three companies of carabiniers and three more of éclaireurs from the 7e Légère, each 60 men strong. Each corps of éclaireurs was to be commanded by a *général de brigade*.[35] In 1802 and 1803 we see columns of éclaireurs raised from the Paris military district.[36] These were initially composed of 200 infantry, 60 horse and 30 gendarmes and were sent to pacify the rebellious departments in the west of France. By 1804 there were eight such columns active.[37] Several others were formed in the southern departments and in Italy where they fought against brigands and smugglers. After 1803, mention of éclaireur companies becomes increasingly rare, because their role was assumed by the newly created voltigeur companies formed in 1804 and 1805.

---

35 Napoleon I, *Correspondance de Napoléon Ier*, Vol. VI, pp.430, 444, 537-538.
36 Napoleon I, *Correspondance de Napoléon Ier*, Vol. VIII, p.22.
37 Napoleon I, *Correspondance de Napoléon Ier*, Vol. VIX, pp.138-139, 147, 149, 184, 189, 238.

3

Light Infantry in the First Empire

Under Napoleon, the light infantry regiments were created from the republican demi-brigades. There then followed one of the most important changes in this period: the creation of the voltigeur companies, as will be detailed below. The creation of these light companies raises many comments about the continued validity of the chasseurs in light infantry regiments. Were they really any different from their cousins in the line? Initially at least, light infantry regiments did retain a specialist role; but after the initial years of success from 1805-1807, greater emphasis was placed on the voltigeurs, who were classed as elite and received a high pay for their services.

Napoleon's Grande Armée of 1805 was much larger than the army he took to Marengo in 1800, and was composed of army corps, each comprised of multiple infantry divisions (or the reserve of cavalry) capable of a high degree of operational independence. It was common for each corps to form its own advanced guard, and the light infantry regiments formed an important component of this. The memoirs of *Maréchal* Ney provide a detailed set of instructions for his corps. Discussing the formation of an advanced guard, he wrote:

> The advanced-guard will be charged with scouting the march, and to discover by its flanqueurs the position and situation of the enemy. It will open its march with a squadron of light cavalry, a company of carabiniers, an 8 or 4-pounder gun; a light infantry battalion, three light cavalry squadrons on the flanks of this infantry; behind it, two pieces of artillery, a howitzer and an 8- or 4-pounder, a subdivision of sapeurs; the rest of the infantry will follow with the surplus of the artillery, and the march will be closed by the cavalry. The piece of cannon at the head of the column will be fired at full speed as soon as the enemy is encountered in force, to warn the Army Corps: a staff officer will be immediately detached from the general commander-in-chief, to report to him what has been noticed on the strength, position, and movements of the enemy.[1]

---

1   Bulos, *Mémoires du Maréchal Ney*, Vol.2, p.384.

This instruction pre-dates the creation of the voltigeur companies. One will note the most advanced element of the light infantry were the elite carabinier companies. By October 1806 we find a different picture emerging. In the 1891 study of light infantry by the Belgian officer, Waldor de Heusch (*Étude sur l'infanterie légères*), we find the advanced guard of Ney's army corps commanded by *Général de Brigade* Colbert. It comprised of four companies of voltigeurs, two light artillery pieces, a regiment of hussars and a regiment of chasseurs à cheval. At the head of each infantry division a regiment of light infantry was in front, and one regiment of light infantry was pushed ahead to support the advanced guard. Ney further stated that the voltigeur companies would march at the head of each regiment and would be constantly employed in the forward posts. The grenadiers would be placed at intermediate points, to support the voltigeurs. Of the remaining seven companies of each regiment, one would be required to provide the police guard of the regiment.[2]

Through this and other examples, Heusch concludes the role of light infantry regiments in First Empire was not to form the advanced-guard (that being left principally to the light cavalry and voltigeurs), but to march at the head of each infantry division and to be ready to accelerate or force its march to arrive quickly in support of the advanced-guard should it meet significant opposition. The light infantry regiment would then fulfil its traditional role of screening the deployment of the heavy infantry brigades behind it. By the end of the period, fulfilment of even this special role is debatable. The attrition of successive campaigns, then the disaster of Russia, had an extremely detrimental impact on effectiveness of light infantry in the closing years of the war. Although the carabiniers and voltigeurs were still classed as elite companies, they were for the most part composed of conscripts, the pick of whom had already been syphoned off into Napoleon's Young Guard. These guard units were increasingly used for important missions on campaign. To illustrate this point, Heusch gives an example from the 1815 Waterloo campaign where the cavalry of Pajol and that drawn from the III Corps of Vandamme were not supported by infantry and were halted by the rearguard of Ziethen. In the early years of empire, light infantry would not have been far behind this cavalry, but on this occasion, Napoleon instead sent a battalion of Young Guard to support them.[3]

A better illustration still of the deterioration in quality is found in the memoirs of *Maréchal* Marmont, illustrating a scene from the campaigns in France of 1814:

> Two conscripts were out skirmishing. … I saw one who, although very calm as the bullets whistled by, was not using his musket. I said to him, "Why don't you shoot?" He replied naively, "I would shoot as well as anybody else if I had someone to load my musket." This poor child was entirely ignorant of his profession. Another, more astute, realizing how useless he was, approached his lieutenant and said to him: "My officer, you have been doing this job for a long time; take my musket, shoot, and I will give you some cartridges." The lieutenant accepted the

---

2   Waldor de Heusch, *Étude sur l'infanterie légères* (Bruxelles: Spineux & Cie, 1891), pp.20-21.
3   Heusch, *Étude sur l'infanterie légères*, p.39.

offer, and the conscript, exposed to deadly fire, showed no fear throughout the duration of the affair.[4]

There we have it. While personally brave, at the moments of crisis in the later imperial period, many soldiers lacked even the simplest skill associated with skirmishing: the ability to load and fire. We also see a return of the partisans at the end of the empire; ex-soldiers and woodsmen, raiding behind enemy lines and paid significant bounties for capturing enemy couriers and ADCs. The subject therefore returns full circle, back to the days of the Seven Years War, with line infantry light companies, and freewheeling, irregular mixed corps.

The Regimentation of 1803

The decree of 1 Vendémiaire Year XII (24 September 1803), restored the title of regiment to the infantry and resurrected the rank of *colonel* in place of the republican *chef de brigade*. The decree created the rank of *major*, an intermediate grade between *colonel* and *chef de bataillon*, replacing the fourth *chef de bataillon* charged with details (this post had been created on 23 Fructidor VII (9 September 1799) specifically to oversee the administration of the corps). The *major* was specially charged with details, with inspections, uniform, discipline, policing the battalion and the accounts, and he commanded the regiment in the absence of the *colonel*. Other than the inclusion of the *major*, the internal structure of the regiments did not change from that of a demi-brigade. The majority of the light infantry regiments consisted of three battalions, the first two being labelled the *bataillons de guerre* (war or combat battalions), with the third initially remaining as a depot battalion responsible for training and equipping the recruits. There were 27 such regiments on paper, numbered 1-31 with four vacant numbers (see Table 12). Six further regiments of light infantry were added through the course of the First Empire (see Table 13). There is a useful recapitulation given in Avril's *Essai Historique* which shows the links between the original fourteen battalions and the Napoleonic Regiments (see Table 14). Table 15 describes the fate of the legions raised in the early part of the war.

In 1804-1805 the light infantry component of France was described in the *État Militaire*, a document providing the number of battalions in each corps, the name of its *colonel* and its location:[5]

- 1er Rég. d'Inf. Légère, 3 bns, *Col.* Bourgeois (Kingdom of Naples)
- 2e Rég. d'Inf. Légère, 3 bns, *Col.* Schramm (Cherbourg)
- 3e Rég. d'Inf. Légère, 3 bns, *Col.* Mas (Perpignan)
- 4e Rég. d'Inf. Légère, 3 bns, *Col.* Bazancourt (Paris),
- 5e Rég. d'Inf. Légère, 4 bns, Vacant, being reorganised (Pau)

---

4   Marmont, *Mémoires du Maréchal Marmont Duc de Raguse de 1792 à 1841*, Vol.6, p.51.
5   Adjudant-commandant Champeaux, *État Militaire de la République Française pour l'an douze* (Paris: Leblanc, 1804), pp.164-212

- 6e Rég. d'Inf. Légère, 3 bns, *Col.* Laplane (1er & 2e at Montreuil, 3e Givet)
- 7e Rég. d'Inf. Légère, 4 bns, *Col.* Boyer (1er & 2e at Camp of Brest, 3e & 4e at Saint-Malo)
- 8e Rég. d'Inf. Légère, 3 bns, *Col.* Bertrand (1er & 2e at Nice, 3e see Chasseurs Corses)
- 9e Rég. d'Inf. Légère, 3 bns, *Col.* Meunier (1er & 2e at Camp de Montreuil, 3e at Philippeville)
- 10e Rég. d'Inf. Légère, 3 bns, *Col.* Pouzet (1er & 2e at Camp de Saint-Omer, 3e at Evreux)
- 11e Rég. d'Inf. Légère (incorporated into 5e Légère)
- 12e Rég. d'Inf. Légère, 3 bns, *Col.* Lainé (1er at Belle-Ile-sur-Mer, 2e & 3e at Nantes)
- 13e Rég. d'Inf. Légère, 3 bns, *Col.* Cartex (1er & 2e at Camp de Bruges, 3e at Gand)
- 14e Rég. d'Inf. Légère, 3 bns, *Col.* Goris (Saint-Pierre d'Aréna, Liguria)
- 15e Rég. d'Inf. Légère, 3 bns, *Col.* Desailly (Landau)
- 16e Rég. d'Inf. Légère, 4 bns, *Col.* Harispe (1er, 2e, 3e at Camp de Brest, 4e at Belle-Ile-en-Mer)
- 17e Rég. d'Inf. Légère, 3 bns, *Col.* Védel (1er & 2e at Camp de Saint-Omer, 3e at Strasbourg)
- 18e Rég. d'Inf. Légère, 3 bns, *Col.* Balleydier (1er & 2e at Camp d'Utrecht, 3e in India)
- 19e Rég. d'Inf. Légère, 3 bns, (1er incorporated into 11e Légère, 2e & 3e inc. into 3e Légère)
- 20e Rég. d'Inf. Légère, 3 bns, (Incorporated into 7e Légère)
- 21e Rég. d'Inf. Légère, 3 bns, *Col.* Tarayre (1er & 2e at Camp de Bruges, 3e at Vanloo)
- 22e Rég. d'Inf. Légère, 3 bns, *Col.* Goguet (Beasançon)
- 23e Rég. d'Inf. Légère, 3 bns, *Col.* Abbé (Corsica)
- 24e Rég. d'Inf. Légère, 3 bns, *Col.* Marion (1er & 2e at Camp de St-Omer, 3e at Nantes)
- 25e Rég. d'Inf. Légère, 4 bns, *Col.* Godinot (1er & 2e at Camp de Montreuil, 3e & 4e at Verdun)
- 26e Rég. d'Inf. Légère, 3 bns, *Col.* Baciocchi (1er & 2e at Camp de Saint-Omer, 3e at Evreux)
- 27e Rég. d'Inf. Légère, 3 bns, *Col.* Charnotet (Hanover)
- 28e Rég. d'Inf. Légère, 3 bns, *Col.* Praefke (Granville)
- 29e Rég. d'Inf. Légère, (Incorporated into 16e Légère)
- 30e Rég. d'Inf. Légère, (Incorporated into 25e Légère)
- 31e Rég. d'Inf. Légère, 3 bns, *Col.* Mejan (1er at Fécamp, 2e Dieppe, 3e Trepport/Saint-Valery)

Table 12. Formation of the Light Infantry Regiments, 1803

Regt.	Demi-Brigades which compose this corps
1er	1e Demi-Brigade Légère
2e	2e Demi-Brigade Légère
3e	1er Bon, 3e Demi-Brigade Légère 2e & 3e Bons, 19e Demi-Brigade Légère

LIGHT INFANTRY IN THE FIRST EMPIRE

Regt.	Demi-Brigades which compose this corps
4e	4e Demi-Brigade Légère
5e	1er Bon, 5e Demi-Brigade Légère 3e Bon, 7e Demi-Brigade Légère 3e Bon, 14e Demi-Brigade Légère 2e Bon, 3e Demi-Brigade Légère
6e	6e Demi-Brigade Légère
7e	1er & 2e Bons, 7e Demi-Brigade Légère 20e Demi-Brigade Légère
8e	8e Demi-Brigade Légère
9e	9e Demi-Brigade Légère
10e	10e Demi-Brigade Légère
11e	1er & 2e Bons, 11e Demi-Brigade Légère
12e	12e Demi-Brigade Légère
13e	13e Demi-Brigade Légère
14e	2e bon, 5e Demi-Brigade Légère 1er & 2e Bons 14e Demi-Brigade Légère
15e	15e Demi-Brigade Légère
16e	16e Demi-Brigade Légère
17e	17e Demi-Brigade Légère
18e	18e Demi-Brigade Légère
19e	(Vacant number)
20e	(Vacant number)
21e	21e Demi-Brigade Légère
22e	22e Demi-Brigade Légère
23e	23e Demi-Brigade Légère
24e	24e Demi-Brigade Légère
25e	25e Demi-Brigade Légère 1er & 2e Bons 30e Demi-Brigade Légère
26e	26e Demi-Brigade Légère
27e	27e Demi-Brigade Légère
28e	28e Demi-Brigade Légère
29e	Vacant number
30e	Vacant number
31e	31e Demi-Brigade Légère 1er & 2e Bons, 112e de Ligne

Table 13. Light Infantry Regiments Formed 1808-1812

32e	29 May 1808.	Formed from troops of the Grand Duchy of Tuscany
33e	Sept. 1808	From provisional regiments in the Army of Spain, then Dutch troops.
34e	9 March 1811	From the 2e, 4e, 5e and 7e Auxiliary Battalions of the Army of Spain.
35e	1812	From 1er Régiment de la Méditerranée (formed 1810)
36e	1812	From the Régiment de Belle-Ile (formed 1811)
37e	7 Feb. 1812	From detachments of the reserve companies

To the regiments listed in Tables 12 and 13 we must mention numerous provisional demi-brigades or march battalions which coexisted with them, but which are too numerous to list here. Perhaps the most famous of these are the so-called Grenadiers of Oudinot from 1806-1809. This was a division formed from the combined elite companies of the depot battalions.

Carabinier and voltigeur companies serving in these corps came under the general appellation grenadiers. Then, in 1809, we find numerous provisional or reserve corps formed from the fourth battalions of various regiments for service with the Armée d'Allemagne and in the Armée d'Espagne. Of these, perhaps the most interesting are the four light infantry demi-brigades which saw service in the 1809 campaign against Austria. These demi-brigades were formed as follows:

II CORPS
1er Division (Tharreau), 1er Brigade (Conroux):
    1er Demi-Brigade Légère (4e Bons of 6e, 24e, 25e Légère)
    3e Demi-Brigade Légère (4e Bons of 9e, 16e, 27e Légère)

2er Division (Claparède/Frère), 1er Brigade (Coëhorn)
    2e Demi-Brigade Légère (4e Bons of 17e, 21e, 28e Légère)
    4e Demi-Brigade légère (4e Bon, 26e Légère, Tirailleurs Corses, Tirailleurs du Pô)

The remaining brigades of each division were formed out of the 4e Bataillons of line infantry regiments.

Under Napoleon's rule, there were a number of units of 'troupes auxiliaires' which were classed as light infantry. Five battalions of Corsican light infantry were raised following an initial instruction on 8 July 1802 to raise a battalion of the 3e Légère in Corsica.[6] These eventually became the Légion Corse which passed into the service of the King of Naples, Joseph Napoléon. In 1804 the battalions had the following emplacements:[7]

- 1er Bat. d'Inf. Légère Corse, at Ajaccio, *Chef de bataillon* Bonelli
- 2e Bat. d'Inf. Légère Corse, at Bastia, *Chef de bataillon* Caraffa
- 3e Bat. d'Inf. Légère Corse, Fiumorbo, *Chef de bataillon* Emanelli
- 4e Bat. d'Inf. Légère Corse, Bonifacio, *Chef de bataillon* Perretti
- 5e Bat. d'Inf. Légère Corse, Calvi, *Chef de bataillon* Gentile

There were also a large number of foreign battalions or regiments in French service which also came under the designation of light infantry, but which are outside the scope of this work. Among the most famous of these was the green-coated Légion Irlandaise (Irish Legion) which was formed in 1803 to support a potential French invasion of Ireland and remained in existence until 1815. Another well-known unit was the Tirailleurs du Po from Italy which were also created in 1803 and eventually incorporated into the 11e Légère in 1811. Worthy of note are the six regiments of Croatian 'Grenzers' which entered French service in 1809 and were known as the Chasseurs Illyriens. Unsurprisingly these Balkan troops proved to be excellent light infantry.

---

6   Napoleon I, *Correspondance de Napoléon Ier*, Vol. VII, p.658
7   Champeaux, *État Militaire de la République Française pour l'an douze*, p.80.

Table 14. Destiny of the Original 14 Battalions of Chasseurs

Provincial name	Bn	Demi-Brigade		Regt.
	1791	1794	1796	1803
Royal de Provence	1er	1er	17e	17e
Royal de Dauphiné	2e	2e	12e	12e
Royal-Corse	3e	3e	11e	/
Corse	4e	4e	21e	21e
Cantabres	5e	5e	24e	24e
Bretagne	6e	6e	5e	/
			29e	16e
Auvergne	7e	7e	3e	3e & 5e
Vosges	8e	8e	4e	4e
Cévennes	9e	9e	9e	9e
Gévaudan	10e	10e	20e	7e
Ardennes	11e	11e	10e	10e
Roussillon	12e	12e	16e	16e
(Garde Nat. de Paris)	13e	13e	25e	25e
	14e	14e	1er	1er

Table 15. Legions and the amalgamations

Légion	Demi-Brigade		Regt.
	1794	1796	1803
Allobroges (2 bns)	15e	27e	27e
Alpes (1er Bn)	17e	26e	26e
Alpes (2e Bn)	18e	23e	23e
Ardennes (1er Bn)	23e	16e	16e
Ardennes (2e Bn)	/	30e	11e
			25e
Centre	10e	20e	7e
Des Francs (Mayence)	/	24e	24e
1er des Francs	/	14e	5e
			14e
2e des Francs	/	46e*	46e*
Franche-Étranger	30e	8e	8e
Germanique	/	13e	13e
1er des Montagnes	/	24e	24e
2e des Montagnes	/	24e	24e
Des Montagnes	39e*	4e*	4e*
1er de la Moselle	10e	20e	7e
2e de la Moselle	8e	4e	4e
Nantaise	/	24e	24e
1er du Nord	19e	53e*	53e*
2e du Nord	19e	53e	53e*
1er des Pyrénées	29e	35e*	35e*
2e des Pyrénées	29e	35e*	35e*
Rosanthal	22e	5e	/
Étranger	/	8e	8e
31e de Gendarmes	/	19e	3e*
			11e
	/	7e	/

*Converted to line infantry

The Voltigeurs

From piquets, to chasseurs, to éclaireurs, the next step in the journey of battalion light companies takes us to the voltigeurs. In a military sense, this term is somewhat bizarre, and derives from the verb *'voler'* (to fly) and *'voltige'*, a form of equestrian acrobatics. This reference is better understood when one learns they were intended to be transported by cavalry, riding pillion behind the cavalier. We find the first reference to this new type of light infantry in a letter from Bonaparte to Minister of War, *Général de Division* Berthier on 30 Frimaire Year XII (22 December 1803). In it the first consul asks Berthier to draft a decree to create a company in each battalion of light infantry known as the *compagnie à cheval*, or *compagnie d'expédition*, or *compagnie de partisans*, or something of a similar ilk. This company would be ranked third in the battalion, after the carabiniers and first company of chasseurs, and be composed of:[8]

> [W]ell-formed, vigorous men, but of the smallest size. No non-commissioned officer or soldier may be more than 4 feet 11 inches; officers cannot be over 5 feet. It will be armed with guns lighter than those of the dragoons and will be practiced in shooting. Officers and NCOs will be armed with rifled carbines. The men of these companies will be trained to follow the cavalry at the trot, holding sometimes to the rider's boot and sometimes to the horse's tail, to mount nimbly and with a jump behind the rider, so as to be able to be thus quickly transported by the cavalry … All non-commissioned officers and light infantry who were less than 4 feet 11 inches would be admitted, and there would be a call of 6,000 men in the conscription of years IX, X, XI and XII. These men would be taken from those who had been exempted from conscription by default of size.

Berthier worked on the project and formulated what became the consular decree of 22 Ventôse /year XII (13 March 1804). This is an interesting document, repeated in full here:

> TITLE I. ORGANISATION OF VOLTIGEUR COMPANIES.
> Article 1. There will be, in each battalion of the light infantry regiments, a company which will bear the name of company of voltigeurs.
> Art. 2. This company will be made up of well-formed, vigorous and nimble men, but of the smallest stature. Non-commissioned-officers and soldiers who will be admitted to it must not be more than 1 meter 598 millimetres (4 pieds 11), officers no more than 1 meter 625 millimetres (5 pieds).
> Art. 3. This company will be constantly maintained at a war footing and composed as follows: 1 *capitaine*, 1 *lieutenant*, 1 *sous-lieutenant*, 1 *sergent-major*, 4 *sergents*, 1 fourrier, 8 *caporaux*, 104 voltigeurs, 2 *instruments militaires*; totalling 123.
> Instead of drums, this company will have for military instruments small hunting horns called *cornets*.

---

[8] Napoleon I, *Correspondance de Napoléon Ier*, Vol.IX, pp.212-213.

LIGHT INFANTRY IN THE FIRST EMPIRE

Art. 4. The officers of these companies will be taken from across the regiment, in their respective rank, on the presentation of three subjects made to the Minister of War by the colonel. These officers will be replaced in their original companies. Thus the number of officers will be increased, by battalion, by a *capitaine*, a *lieutenant* and a *sous-lieutenant*.

Art. 5. The number of non-commissioned officers of each battalion will likewise be increased by a *sergent-major*, four *sergents*, a *fourrier* and eight *caporaux*; but the strength of the battalion, except for three officers, will remain as fixed by the organizational decree for Year XII. For this purpose, the strength of each company of light infantry, except that of the carabiniers, will be reduced by fifteen men.

TITLE II. ARMAMENT, CLOTHING AND INSTRUCTION OF VOLTIGEURS.

Art. 6. The voltigeurs will be armed with an infantry sabre and a very light, dragoon model musket. The officers and non-commissioned officers will have, instead of musket, a rifled carbine.

Art. 7. The voltigeurs will be dressed like the light infantry; they will bear the distinctive marks of their respective corps; with a collar of *chamois* (buff) cloth.

Art. 8. The voltigeurs being specially intended to be transported quickly by troops on horseback to the places where their presence is necessary, will be trained to climb nimbly and jump onto the back of a man on horseback, and to descend lightly; to form up rapidly, and to follow on foot a rider at the trot. The voltigeurs will also be particularly trained to shoot with promptness and much accuracy.

TITLE III. FIRST FORMATION OF THE VOLTIGEUR COMPANIES.

Art. 9. The officers and non-commissioned officers of the companies of voltigeurs will be appointed immediately; the officers, as was said in Article 4. The First Consul will name their replacements, and will take them either from the corps, or without. The non-commissioned officers will be appointed by the colonel on the presentation, which will be made to him by the captain of the voltigeurs, of three subjects for each place, but always with the conditions relating to their height.

A French light infantry voltigeur lighting a pipe, by Charlet. Our voltigeur is evidently a veteran as he is wearing three service stripes on his upper arm, and a *légion d'honneur*. Evidently illiterate, because he has yet to receive a promotion of any kind. The uniform depicted must date from before the Battle of Eylau in 1807 because he still carries a sabre-briquet. (Anne S.K. Brown Military Collection)

Art. 10. It will be chosen, by each *capitaine de voltigeurs*, forty-eight soldiers from across the battalion, at the rate of six per company; they can only be taken from among the twelve smallest men of each company; they will form the nucleus and the head of the companies.

Art. 11. The companies of voltigeurs will be completed immediately with conscripts of years XI and XII, taken from among those who have been exempted from service by lack of height, but whose constitution is strong and robust. The quota of each department will be determined according to the bases fixed by the decree of 29 Fructidor Year XI.

Art. 12. In Year XIII and following, there will be designated by each department a particular contingent for the companies of voltigeurs. This contingent will be taken from the individuals of the class who will be less than 1 meter 598 millimetres. Those who are appointed will be reimbursed for the sums they have been required to pay in execution of the decree of 29 Fructidor Year XI.

TITLE IV. PAY OF VOLTIGEUR COMPANIES.

Art. 13. The pay of the companies of voltigeurs will be the same as that of the companies of carabiniers.

Art. 14. The Minister of War is responsible for the execution of this decree.

BONAPARTE.[9]

There are some remarks which must be made at this point. What was Napoleon attempting to achieve with this decree? Did he feel the centre companies of light infantry regiments were no longer suited to advanced guard operations? Did he believe dragoons were unable to act as mobile infantry? Others, more cynical, believe Napoleon invented the voltigeurs, with the lowered height requirement, simply in order to increase the pool of conscripts available (this was nothing to do with Napoleon being vertically challenged in anyway – the emperor was then the average height of a Frenchman, and far too tall to qualify for service in the voltigeurs). In which case, why not simply reduce the height requirement for military service in general? Traditionally soldiers had never been admitted if they were below 5 ft 1 (French). Duhesme perhaps offers a more practical observation for this. The shortest men were consigned to the middle rank, and found their muskets were obstructed by the taller men in front (who were meant to kneel to fire in combat, but rarely did).[10] At the time it was commonly believed that shorter men made the best light infantry. Guyard provides an explanation of this in his *Instruction pour le service et les manœuvres de l'infanterie légère en campagne*:

> Experience has shown us that a man of five feet, one, two or three inches, is wirier; that his bodily forces being better collected than in a man of seven to eight inches, are more considerable; by consequence, he is more able to resist the fatigues of war, less likely to be hit with a bullet; lastly that he enters more easily than a large man into a thicket, etc.[11]

---

9 Napoleon I, *Correspondance de Napoléon Ier*, Vol.IX, pp.365-367.
10 Duhesme, *Précis historique de l'infanterie légère*, p.274.
11 Guyard, *Instruction pour le service et les manoeuvres de l'infanterie légère, en campagne*, p.6.

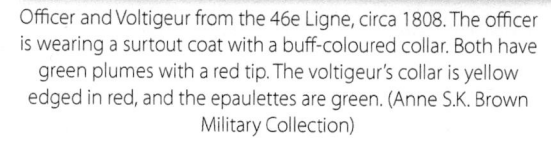

Officer and Voltigeur from the 46e Ligne, circa 1808. The officer is wearing a surtout coat with a buff-coloured collar. Both have green plumes with a red tip. The voltigeur's collar is yellow edged in red, and the epaulettes are green. (Anne S.K. Brown Military Collection)

Grenadier and Voltigeur from the 94e Ligne circa 1808. The voltigeur has a yellow collar, piped red. His plume is green with a yellow tip. Interestingly the grenadier does not have a brass plate on his bearskin. (Anne S.K. Brown Military Collection)

Whatever the reason for this innovation, by reducing the height requirement to 4 ft 9 (French) this placed an estimated 40,000 men at Napoleon's disposition. From being classed physically incapable of military service, with a stroke of a pen, these men were not only now fit for service, but were labelled as elite soldiers and given high pay like the grenadiers. Needless to say, a degree of rivalry quickly existed between the voltigeurs and grenadiers.

From reading the text of the decree it appears that an entirely new company was being raised, with new officers appointed. This would have raised the number of companies to 10 in each battalion. Instead, the voltigeurs replaced the second company of chasseurs, in other words they took the third place of seniority in the battalion after the carabiniers and first company of chasseurs. This modification to the original instruction was apparently confirmed on 25 Thermidor Year XII (13 August 1804).

We should also highlight the adoption of the cornet in place of drums. Clearly if voltigeurs were intended to leap onto the back of horses, a man carrying a drum would find himself at a distinct disadvantage. That said, the cornets were not as useful as the bugles employed by other nations. They were low in pitch and not very loud. In battlefield conditions their signals were often drowned out by the noise of gunfire and artillery or carried off on the wind. The result of this was voltigeurs sometimes misheard the signal being played, and officers and NCOs had to go in search of their skirmishers and verbally recall them. This was dangerous and slow. Unlike a drum, which could be picked up and beaten by anyone, only a trained instrumentalist could make a noise from a cornet. All that said, Bardin records a lucky incident during the passage of the Adige River on 18 October 1805, when voltigeurs went into combat for the first time. The Austrians heard the voltigeur cornets and thought they were about to be attacked by cavalry.[12]

The armament of the voltigeurs is also interesting, because we see light infantry at scale being equipped differently to those troops expected to fight in the line. The dragoon musket (model year IX) was just 4 inches (10.8 cm) shorter than the infantry musket at 1 metre 42 in length. Despite the shorter barrel and some brass fittings, the weapon only really differed from the standard infantry model by the band around the barrel called the *grenadière*. This feature allowed a sling to be attached to the weapon (in other words, in times past it allowed grenadiers to sling their weapons while throwing grenades). The voltigeur model had a double band to strengthen the fitting when the musket was slung across the shoulder while riding horses. One should point out at this early stage, this tactical innovation – an early experiment of mobilised infantry – was not widely used. In his description of the modification to the *grenadière* band, Bardin indicates it was a pointless exercise, because 'the voltigeurs only marched on foot'.[13] However, there are a few examples of voltigeurs mounted *en croupe*. A British officer, Charles Stevens remarked of the Corunna campaign of 1808-1809: 'I have frequently seen their light troops mounted behind their dragoons, so that when they came to a favourable place to make an attack, these fellows dismounted quite fresh, and our light troops, who had been always marching, had to oppose them.'[14] There is another widely quoted example where dragoons took voltigeurs across the Berezina river in 1812. However, such examples are extremely rare.

Writing in 1816, with the benefit of hindsight, *Général de Division* Rogniat on the one hand supported the idea of voltigeurs riding with cavalry, or at least running alongside them, but at the same time implied they had not done so thus far. In order to sling a musket over their backs and to leap onto the back of a horse behind the rider, Rogniat observed, the voltigeur would first need to remove his haversack and the rider would need to carry his portmantel in front of, not behind the saddle.[15] The famous soldier and memoirist, *Colonel* Marbot responded to Rogniat's suggestion with a scathing response, claiming, 'I dare to assure in advance that all these exercises are impracticable in war; and what is more, I will prove that they have never been practiced'.[16] Marbot went on to describe how leaping onto the back of a horse

---

12 Bardin, *Dictionnaire de l'armée de terre*, Vol. 17, p.5271.
13 Bardin, *Dictionnaire de l'armée de terre*, Vol. 9, p.2660.
14 Charles Stevens, *Reminiscences of my military life from 1795 to 1818* (Winchester: Warren & Sons, 1878), p.63.
15 Joseph Rogniat, *Considérations sur l'art de la guerre,* (Paris: Magimel, 1816), p.170-171.
16 Marbot, *Remarques critiques sur l'ouvrage de M. le lieutenant-général Rogniat*, p.319.

was extremely difficult and dangerous, and was something of a circus trick by performers who had practiced the stunt since childhood. Moreover it was impractical for cavalrymen to carry their portmantel forwards of the saddle because that is where they carried their forage on campaign. Marbot even rubbished the idea that light infantry could operate with cavalry by running alongside them. Marbot described the conditions faced by a voltigeur trying to keep up with cavalry, overloaded by the weight of a musket, cartridges and equipment, in wet clothes, with heavy shoes, which were already falling apart, having marched all night on dirt tracks, half-starved, exhausted by long marches. How was a man supposed to run alongside a body of cavalry, over wet, ploughed fields, churned up by the horses' hooves, or in the summer heat, with crops up to his chin and suffocating and choked by the cloud of dust cast up as the horses advanced at the full trot? Marbot's observations are difficult to ignore.[17]

Detail of a contemporary picture entitled 'Halte des grenadiers et voltigeurs'. Two line infantry voltigeurs are depicted. The seated figure has short, light-infantry style gaiters, with a yellow fringe. The standing figure has standard line infantry gaiters. Their collars are yellow, piped red and their cuff flaps are white. The epaulettes are green with yellow and red edging. Note their shirt collars protrude above the coat collar. (Collection Yves Martin)

Following the introduction of voltigeurs in the light infantry regiments, in a letter to *Général de Brigade* Lacuée on 5 August 1805, the emperor asked for a draft decree establishing a company of voltigeurs in each battalion of line infantry, composed of small men, armed with dragoon muskets, just like the light infantry. This resulted in the imperial decree of 2nd Complementary Day XIII (19 September 1805):

- Art. 1. There will be in each line battalion, a company which will bear the name of company of voltigeurs. This company will always be the third of the battalion, including that of the grenadiers, but became the number of companies shall not be increased, it replaces the second of fusiliers, which will be dissolved and shared among all the others in the battalion.
- 2. The company of voltigeurs will be made up of well-formed, vigorous and nimble men, but of the smallest stature. Non-commissioned-officers and soldiers who will be admitted to it must not be more than 1 meter 580 millimetres (4 pieds 11), officers no more than 1 meter 625 millimetres (5 pieds).
- 3. It will be constantly maintained on a war footing, and composed as follows: 1 *capitaine*, 1 *lieutenant*, 1 *sous-lieutenant*, 1 *sergent-major*, 4 *sergens*, 1 *fourrier*, 8 *caporaux*, 104 voltigeurs, 2 *instrumens militaires*; totalling 123.

---

17 Marbot, *Remarques critiques sur l'ouvrage de M. le lieutenant-général Rogniat*, p.337.

4. The officers, non-commissioned officers and soldiers of these companies will be taken from the whole regiment, in their respective ranks, by the *colonel*, among those of the size indicated above and below this size, and which will show the most aptitude for the kind of service the voltigeurs have to do.
5. The strength of this company does not augment that of the battalion, which remains composed, in the number of men, as fixed by the organizational decree for Year XII. For this purpose, the strength of each company of line infantry, except that of the grenadiers, will be reduced by fifteen men.
6. The voltigeurs will be armed with an infantry sabre and a very light, dragoon model musket. The officers and non-commissioned officers will have, instead of a musket, a rifled carbine.
7. The voltigeurs will be dressed like the line infantry, and they will bear the distinctive marks of their respective corps; but the collar of their coat and veste [jacket] shall be of chamois [buff] woollen cloth.
8. The voltigeurs being intended to do the same service as the light infantry, will be trained to mount nimbly, with a leap, onto the back of a man on horseback, to descend lightly, to form quickly, and to follow on foot a rider at the trot. They will also be particularly trained to shoot promptly and very accurately.
9. The pay of the companies of voltigeurs will be the same as that of the companies of grenadiers.[18]

The issuing of this decree came at an inopportune moment, with the Grande Armée about to embark on the campaigns of Ulm and Austerlitz. We find a letter from *Maréchal* Ney instructing Dupont's division to get on with forming these companies on 23 October while at Ulm.[19]

The wording of the voltigeur decrees must have caused some confusion. Administratively, the voltigeurs were assigned the place of the third in seniority within the battalion, replacing the second company. However, there was no instruction on how the voltigeurs ought to be tactically employed. When the battalion drilled alone, did the voltigeurs occupy the place of the second company, or did they adopt the old practise of standing to the left of the line? Duhesme pragmatically placed his on the left so they did not disrupt the rest of the battalion when they deployed or were detached. If the voltigeurs were detached from the battalion, this left just seven centre companies, which meant the battalion could only form into three-and-a-half divisions. The fourth division would have in fact been formed of a single peloton at the rear of a column. *Colonels* and *chefs de bataillon* no doubt improvised during the campaigns of the Grande Armée in 1805-1807 (Ulm, Austerlitz, Jena, Eylau and Friedland) until clarification was obtained in 1808.

A final remark on the voltigeurs can be made here and explored further in the chapter concerning tactics. Did the formation of voltigeur companies effectively spell the end of the special function of light infantry regiments? From the start voltigeurs were often removed from their parent battalion and formed into special detachments and even battalions, at regimental,

---

18 *Journal Militaire*, 16th Year, Second Part (Paris: Magimel, Year 13), pp.226-228.
19 Paul Claude Alombert-Goget, Jean Lambert Alphonse Colin, *La Campagne de 1805 en Allemagne* (Paris: Librairie militaire R. Chapelot, 1902), p.1146.

brigade and even divisional level. Roche-Aymon believed so and explained how light infantry continued to march at the head of each division, and made advanced- and rear-guards, but because it had received voltigeur companies, light infantry centre companies became increasingly seen as ordinary infantry, but with a different costume. From 1806 onwards Roche-Aymon states light infantry regiments were increasingly made to manoeuvre like line infantry and, in Roche-Aymon's opinion, the art of *petite guerre* fell into disuse and was soon forgotten.[20]

Organisation of 1808

After the Treaties of Tilsit ended the war of the Fourth Coalition in July 1807 there was an opportunity to reform the infantry regiments, increasing the number of battalions while at the same time reducing the number of companies within each. The imperial decree of 18 February 1808 applied to line and light infantry regiments alike. Each would be composed of an *état-major* (staff) and five battalions. The first four battalions would be classed as *bataillons de guerre* (war battalions), the fifth as the depot battalion. Each war battalion would be commanded by a *chef de bataillon* who had under his orders an *adjudant-major*, two *adjudant* NCOs responsible for the discipline and training of the battalion. Each battalion would be composed of six companies of equal strength: one of grenadiers or carabiniers, one of voltigeurs and four of fusiliers (there was no mention of chasseur companies, perhaps reinforcing Roche-Aymon's claim they were increasingly seen as ordinary infantry). Each company would have a strength of 140 officers and men. The fifth, or depot battalion would be composed of four fusilier companies only, each commanded by a *capitaine*. One of the company commanders would be nominated by the Minister of War to command the depot battalion, albeit under the orders of the regiment's *major*. The depot battalion would also have an *adjudant major-and* two *adjudant* sub-officers. The strength of the staff and each company is set out in Table 16.

Table 16. Organisation of 18 February 1808

État-major (staff)	The company
1 *Colonel*	1 *Capitaine*
1 *Major*	1 *Lieutenant*
4 *Chefs de bataillon*	1 *Sous-lieutenant*
5 *Adjudants-majors*	1 *Sergent-major*
1 *Quartier-maître trésorier*	4 *Sergents*
1 *Officier payeur*	1 *Caporal-fourrier*
1 *Porte-aigle*	8 *Caporaux*
1 *Chirurgien-major*	121 Grenadiers, voltigeurs, fusiliers
4 *Aides-chirurgiens*	2 *Tambours*
5 *Sous-aides*	

---

20   Roche-Aymon, *Des Troupes légères*, p.68.

Continued	
10 *Adjudants sous-officiers*	
2 *Deuxième & troisième porte-aigle*	
1 *Tambour-major*	
1 *Caporal tambour*	
8 *Musiciens* (including a *chef*)	
4 *Maîtres ouvriers*	

For the first time the requirements for service in the grenadier and carabinier companies was defined. On the part of the carabiniers there was no longer any mention of marksmanship. They were to be drawn from the tallest men in the regiment and to have served for four years, or taken part in two of the four campaigns of Ulm, Austerlitz, Jena or Friedland. As an elite company, the carabiniers were placed on the right of the battalion when it was ranged in line formation, this being the traditional place of honour for elite troops. The decree also formally recognised the elite status of voltigeurs by assigning them to the left of the line, the second place of honour. When all six companies were present, they would always march and act in divisions. Somewhat controversially the grenadier and voltigeur companies would form their divisions with the relevant centre companies, using the same principles given in the 1791 formation (see Table 17). When the grenadiers or voltigeurs were absent from the battalion, the companies would act as individual pelotons and not form divisions.

Table 17. Battalion organisation 1808

Battalion					
First division		Second division		Third division	
Carabiniers	3e Cie	1er Cie	4e Cie	2e Cie	Voltigeurs

The idea of mixing elite companies with centre ones caused great upset to Bardin. He argued (probably correctly), that the grenadiers and voltigeurs ought to be paired together, but that would mean removing the voltigeurs from their place of honour on the left. To have placed them to the left of the carabiniers would have resulted in a gap being formed in the battalion if the voltigeurs skirmished. Bardin concluded the matter was largely academic, as on active service the voltigeurs (and grenadiers) were often detached from their parent battalion.[21]

Article 12 of the decree outlined a classification for officers, with *capitaines* and *lieutenants* being classed, first, second or third, each grade being assigned different levels of pay. Henceforth a regiment would have eight first class *capitaines*, ten second class and ten third class *capitaines*; fourteen first class *lieutenants* and fourteen second class (*sous-lieutenants* were not assigned a class). The four longest serving *capitaines* would be graded first class and would command the first company of fusiliers in each battalion. The four carabinier *capitaines* would be chosen by the *colonel* and would also be graded first class.

---

21   See a summary of the problems with the *endivisionnement* of elite and centre companies in Bardin, *Dictionnaire de l'armée de terre*, Vol.3, p.1935.

The decree also made formal provision for some specialist troops. For example, each combat battalion was granted four *sapeurs* (pioneer troops) who were chosen from among the grenadier companies. There would be one *caporal* among them who would command all the pioneers in the regiment. Although regiments had these pioneer troops before 1808, they did so on an unofficial basis. They were in fact a vital component of a light infantry regiment, able to cut passageways through vineyards and hedges, and to fill in ditches.

Each regiment would have one eagle standard carried by a *porte-aigle* having the grade of *lieutenant* or *sous-lieutenant* and having at least 10 years' service; or having made the four campaigns of Ulm, Austerlitz, Jena and Friedland. He would enjoy the pay of a *lieutenant* first class. The eagle-bearer would be seconded by two old soldiers with at least 10 years' service, noted for their bravery, but who were unable to obtain promotion due to illiteracy. These escorts were titled the *second* and *troisième porte-aigle* respectively and had the rank of *sergent* with the pay of a *sergent-major*. As a further identifying mark, these escorts would wear four rank chevrons on both sleeves. Lastly, the *porte-aigle* and his escorts formed part of the regimental staff and could only be named or dismissed by the Emperor himself. They were officially armed with halberds and pistols.

According to the decree, the regiments would henceforth have a single eagle (previously each combat battalion had an eagle). This eagle would always be located where the largest number of battalions were united (in practice where the *colonel* was located). In addition, the decree of 18 February 1808 stated each of the other combat battalions would have an *enseigne* which was to be carried by a non-commissioned officer chosen by the *chef de bataillon*. Flags having a practical purpose in helping a battalion keep alignment when marching in line. It is worth remembering that since 1807 light infantry regiments were forbidden from carrying their eagles on campaign. It appears this remained Napoleon's intention because article nine of the decree stated only line infantry regiments would carry an eagle. All other corps would only have *enseignes*.[22] As it turned out, the confirmation on battalion flags was only decided much later by the circular of 25 December 1811 (see chapter 6) by which time *enseignes* were described as *fanions*.

Contemporary illustration by Zimmermann, entitled 'Soldat du 16ième Régiment de Chasseurs' (1808). He wears the early pattern shako and appears to have his hair tied in queue. (Anne S.K. Brown Military Collection)

---

22 Napoleon I, *Correspondance*, Vol.XVI, pp.398–402.

FRENCH LIGHT INFANTRY 1784-1815

Light infantry voltigeur by Martinet in *habit-veste* with yellow collar and blue cuffs. The plume is green tipped yellow. The epaulettes are yellow with green fringe. (Collection Yves Martin)

Charlet's interpretation of a light infantry *sapeur* in 1812. He wears a bearskin shako, or colpack in the style of light cavalry. His trousers are brown with a double red stripe on the outer seam. (Collection Yves Martin)

The internal structure of the battalions did not change for the remainder of the First Empire, but the staff composition and the number of battalions did. On 8 April 1811, a *major-en-second* was added to all the regiments forming the Armée d'Allemagne. These would command the regiment if the *colonel* was absent, and ordinarily would command two battalions if the regiment had four battalions present in the line and formed a brigade by itself. It was felt this would give the *major-en-second* experience of commanding a larger force than a battalion so he would be better-prepared to take over should the *colonel* become a casualty.

On 11 April 1811 a decree announced the formation of a sixth battalion for each regiment in the Armée d'Allemagne, thus bringing the total number of war battalions to five. On 19 April, an additional instruction concerned the I Corps d'Observation de l'Elbe of this army. This Corps was formed of five infantry divisions, with light infantry attached to the 1er Division (13e Léger, 5 Bns), 2e Division (15e Léger, 5 Bns), 3e Division (7e Léger, 5 Bns). Firstly, note the new abbreviated designation of 'léger' in place of 'légère'. Also note light infantry regiments were not attached to the fourth and fifth divisions of this corps. Lastly, note the following clause: 'Each regiment will have four regimental pieces [of artillery]'.[23] The instruction continued, assigning two pieces of artillery to the 24e Légère (II Corps, 1er Division, 1er Brigade), with additional regimental artillery issued to the other divisions in the Corps with 40 regimental guns in total. In a letter of 24 April 1811 to his brother Jérome Bonaparte, King of Westphalia, Napoleon describes the regimental pieces with the Armée d'Allemagne as being 3-pounder guns.[24]

We find similar remarks in Napoleon's correspondence regarding the forces in Spain. In a letter to the Minister of War, *Général de Division* Clarke on 12 June 1811 there is a reference to the artillery companies of the 5e Léger and 23e Léger which were about to travel to Spain. Napoleon advised these artillery companies not to take French artillery with them, but purchase their horses, harnesses and caissons in France, then to use Spanish 4-pounders. In a second letter that day, this time to *Général de Division* Lacuée, Napoleon explained that the 5e Léger ought to have caissons for four battalions. The 10e Léger is also mentioned as having an artillery company.[25] This is a quite remarkable development. While artillery was often assigned to the advanced guard, to ask light infantry to structurally incorporate regimental guns is another demonstration they were increasingly viewed as nothing more than regiments of the line.

Light Infantry of the Imperial Guard

The detailed composition of Napoleon's Garde Impériale is outside the scope of this work. However, it would be remis not to introduce here the significant number of 'light infantry' units which existed within this force which numbered a few thousand men at the time of Marengo in 1800, but over 100,000 by 1814. It must be remembered that the chasseurs of the Imperial Guard were among the most senior in the army and were, in Napoleon's mind at least, an object of emulation for every soldier.

Since the decree of 25 April 1792, each army was permitted a company of 'guides' to act as a mounted escort to the commanding general. Bonaparte enjoyed this prerogative too, ordering *Chef de Brigade* Lannes on 30 May 1796 to form a company of 50 Guides à Cheval to protect his headquarters (Bonaparte had been surprised by a force of Austrian cavalry that day).[26] This small force was placed under the command of *Capitaine* Bessières, formerly of the 22e Chasseurs à Cheval (and a school friend of Joachim Murat – it is always interesting to see the early and humble beginnings of the

---

23 Napoleon I, *Correspondance*, Vol.XXII, p.87.
24 Napoleon I, *Correspondance*, Vol.XXII, pp.108-109.
25 Picard & Tuetey, *Correspondance inédite de Napoléon Ier*, Vol.4, p.359.
26 Napoleon I, *Correspondance*, Vol.I, p.415.

FRENCH LIGHT INFANTRY 1784-1815

Napoleonic marshalate). This force of Guides was significantly expanded on 25 September 1796, including 161 officers and men.[27] By the following summer we find mention of a light infantry force, the Guides à Pied. In a letter of 11 August 1797 to *Adjudant-Général* Boyer, Bonaparte complains about their conduct in public places and towards women, particularly at night, and warns them he will disband the unit unless their discipline improves! The quality of a guide was 'not only his bravery, but more so by his exact discipline.' The letter goes on to instruct Boyer to form and organise two companies of guides à pied under Chef de Bataillon Caire, with the warning they would each be returned to their corps on the second complaint against them.[28] The Guides à Pied were formally united with the Guides à Cheval the following year, in an instruction to *Chef de Brigade* Bessières, dated Malta, 14 June 1798. The guides were 'to demonstrate an example to the army with excellent discipline and the most audacious bravery.'[29] The force of Guides à Pied was further reorganised on 6 July 1798 and increased to three companies.[30]

Returning to France and becoming first consul in 1799, Bonaparte reorganised the Legislative Guard in Paris to the create the Garde des Consuls with the law of 7 Frimaire an VIII (28 November 1799). To the existing guardsmen Bonaparte added a company of chasseurs. Numbering around 130 men, many of these chasseurs were former Guides à Pied who served in Italy, Egypt and Syria, and had accompanied their general back to France. This company fought at Marengo in 1800, acting as skirmishers for the Grenadiers à Pied. On 21 Fructidor Year VIII (8 September 1800), a battalion of Chasseurs à Pied was formed. The conditions of service stipulated at least three campaigns, to have obtained rewards granted for brilliant actions or to have been wounded, to be active, free from charges of misconduct, and to have a minimum height of 5 feet 3 inches French (1.705 metres). On 23 Brumaire Year X (14 November 1801) a second battalion of chasseurs was created, incorporating more Guides à Pied returning from Egypt.

In 1804 these became the 1er Régiment de Chasseurs à Pied in the newly constituted Garde Impériale, following the imperial decree of 10 Thermidor Year XII (29 July 1804). Entry requirements were amended to five years of service and two campaigns, and regiments throughout the army were asked to draw up lists of NCOs and soldiers of distinguished service who might be admitted. The regiment comprised of a staff and each battalion had eight companies (see Table 18). The two battalions of chasseurs were supplemented by a battalion of Vélites. This battalion was created by the decree of 30 Nivôse

Uniform of the Guides à Pied of the Army of the Alps, 1795-1796, by Boisselier. This figure wears a light cavalry-style mirliton, has a carbine slung over his back, and wears a Corsican-style cartridge pouch across his front. (Collection Yves Martin)

---

27 Napoleon I, *Correspondance*, Vol.II, pp.13-14.
28 Napoleon I, *Correspondance*, Vol.III, pp.230-231.
29 Napoleon I, *Correspondance*, Vol.IV, pp.151-152.
30 Napoleon I, *Correspondance*, Vol.IV, pp.221-223.

Left. Chasseur à pied of the Régiment de Dauphiné by Nicolas Hoffmann. This infantryman from a chasseur company wears a dark green coat and has hunting horn emblems on his coat tails (the paint pigment is now turning blue). Right. Hoffmann's 'Caporal de chasseurs, Régiment du Roi, 1779-80'. The badge on his left breast is a veteran's medallion. The single gold chevron on his forearms indicate he is in fact a *sergent*. His green epaulettes have a crisscross pattern embroidered onto them.
(Anne S.K. Brown Military Collection)

Top left. A chasseur des barrières de Paris from 1790. This National Guardsman wears a cartridge pouch in the style of a Corsican *carchera*, on a belt, over the stomach. Top right. Nicolas Hoffman's study of a chasseur of the Garde Nationale of Versailles (1789). (Anne S.K. Brown Military Collection)

Bottom left. A chasseur of the Garde Nationale de Paris in 1789, in a casque, with a brace of pistols, by Nicolas Hoffman. Bottom right. A second version of a chasseur from the Paris National Guard in 1789, by Hoffman. (Anne S.K. Brown Military Collection)

Detail of Wilhelm von Kobell's 'French cavalry and infantry on march' (1800). The carabinier on the right (red plume) has a four-button cuff. He is wearing a pair of trouser-gaiters, which combine the two garments and strap under the shoe. He is wearing a regulation neck stock. Notice the cutaway collar revealing it. His shako has the decorative band common to light cavalry mirliton hats. It has a black ribbon tied in a bow over the visor. The chasseur to his right has a less ornate 'flame' around the shako. His habit is open, revealing a shirt and a civilian manufacture waistcoat. He wears a simple pair of trousers with no gaiters or socks. He appears to have lost his cross straps and haversack. (Anne S.K. Brown Military Collection)

Detail of an 1808 work by Geissler. Two figures in the foreground appear to be chasseurs, with short gaiters and green epaulettes. The bicorn hats are therefore unusual. Their greatcoats are coloured light green and pale blue respectively. The figure with his hands in his pockets is wearing a red and white cravat and appears to have a pet squirrel on his shoulder. (Anne S.K. Brown Military Collection)

Top left. Classic study of a First Empire light Infantry officer. Notice the silver *hausse-col* (gorget) and shako decorations. Top right. Chasseur of the 13e Légère by Martinet. Notice the plume is completely green, and that the green epaulettes have red edgings. (Collection Yves Martin)

Bottom left. Carabinier of the 2e Légère in bearskin cap. The cords, plume and epaulettes are red. Bottom right. Carabinier in shako decorated with silver chin scales and red cords. The *dragon* (sword knot) and gaiter tassels are red. (Collection Yves Martin)

Excellent study of a chasseur *caporal* by Martinet. The stripes on his arm are white wool on a red backing. His plume is green, as are the epaulettes, but with a red border. This shako plate is brass and the piping on the gaiters is white. (Collection Yves Martin)

Grenadier et Fusilier du 9me Reg: des Chasseur à pié.

Part of a set of unsigned drawings, possibly by Weiland, known as the 'Otto Manuscript' (they were in the estate of a Major Otto of Baden-Baden), showing the uniforms of the Grande Armée in Germany between 1807–1808. This pair are a carabinier and a chasseur from the 9e Légère. Note the height difference between the men and the ornamentation on their headgear and sword knots. (Anne S.K. Brown Military Collection)

vii

Grenadier et Chasseur du 16me Reg:

The subjects in this Otto Manuscript study have been identified as a grenadier and chasseur of the 16e Légère circa 1808. This should be a carabinier and a voltigeur. The figure on the left has an unmistakable chamois (buff) collar and also cuff flaps. The tip of his plume is also coloured chamois. Note the carabinier does not wear a bearskin. (Anne S.K. Brown Military Collection)

Carabinier officer of the 9e Légère. (1808) Note the four button cuff and sabre, rather than epee. This officer has been awarded the *légion d'honneur* (red ribbon and medal on left lapel), and wears his sabre on a waistbelt rather than a shoulder belt. (Anne S.K. Brown Military Collection)

Tambour major of the 16e Légère (1808). This drum major wears a surtout. Although not permitted to wear any distinctions other than his rank markings, this *tambour major*'s collar, cuffs and his *sergent-major* stripes have been embellished with embroidered pattern which gives the effect of moonlight. Notice his shoulder straps, and that he is wearing buff-coloured gloves.
(Anne S.K. Brown Military Collection)

Sapeur from the 16e Légère from the Otto Manuscript (circa 1808). This figure has a unique style of lapels which are coloured pink. He also has a scallop-edged pink braid running down the outer seam of his pantalons. As well as the crossed-axes badge on his arm, he wears grenade badges on his collar. His shako is similarly peculiar. The peak has been detached and appears to be hanging flat against the body of the shako. The dark brown apron and gauntlets are an equally interesting touch. (Anne S.K. Brown Military Collection)

A slightly more conventional *sapeur* from the 10e Légère from the same series. This soldier is wearing a bearskin 'colpack' in the style of the elite squadrons of the chasseurs à cheval. His sword has a cockerel's head hilt, a common feature among sapeurs. Note the crossed axe badges on his arms and on his sword belt. (Anne S.K. Brown Military Collection)

The first in a set of four plates from the Otto manuscript, shown over the following pages, depicting various interpretations of line infantry voltigeurs between 1807-1808, depicting an officer and voltigeur from the 96e de Ligne. The officer wears a surtout and light infantry style blue *pantalons*. (Anne S.K. Brown Military Collection)

Officer and voltigeur from the 24e de Ligne. The officer is in a double-breasted surtout, and appears to have a fur-covered shako, or colpack. (Anne S.K. Brown Military Collection)

Officer and voltigeur from the 85e de Ligne. The officer's shako is decorated with three bold, golden chevrons along the side. The voltigeur has a buff collar, but retains the typical red cuff flaps of a fusilier. (Anne S.K. Brown Military Collection)

Officer and voltigeur from the 22e de Ligne. The voltigeur wears the white uniform which some regiments adopted from 1807. The distinctions worn follow the regulations more closely, with a chamois collar the only modification to the coat. Note the green epaulettes, sword knot and shako cords. (Anne S.K. Brown Military Collection)

Wonderful study of a Chasseur à Pied of the Imperial Guard attributed to Weiland (1807-1808). The guardsman is wearing a surtout. The reverse image shows red badges on the red turnbacks. The outer badges are a grenade, while the inner ones are hunting horns. Above the haversack, the small flat parcel in ticking cloth, on top of the blue, rolled-up capote, contains a bicorn hat. The surtout has blue, pointed cuffs. (Anne S.K. Brown Military Collection)

Officer of chasseurs of the Imperial Guard by Martinet. The cords and epaulettes are gold, with a green plume tipped red. He wears boots with a turned down cuffs. Note the pull loops on the top of the boots. (Collection Yves Martin)

Chasseur of the Imperial Guard in full dress by Martinet. Note the blue collar on the coat and the green boards on the epaulettes (fringed red). The plume has a green base (also tipped red). The chasseur bearskin does not have a brass plate. Ironically, this style lives on today with the British Guards who adopted the headgear of the French chasseur guards as a battle honour after Waterloo. (Collection Yves Martin)

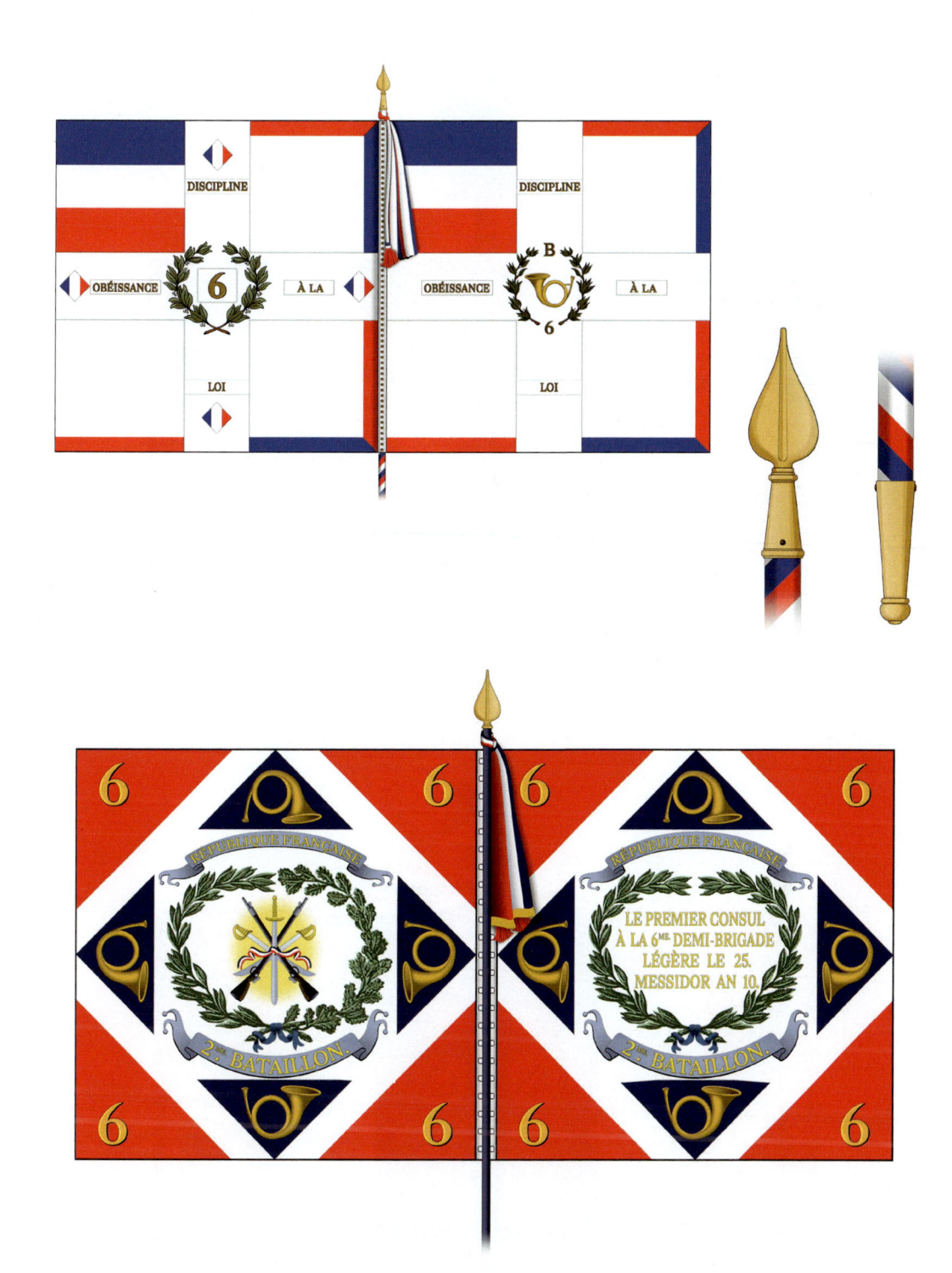

Light infantry colours, 1791 and 1802. There is no known surviving example of the 1791 flag issued to the light infantry battalions, but they were allowed to carry one. This example of the 6e Bataillon is reconstructed from the variations shown on artillery models. Instead of a set of crossed cannon barrels, the centre of the flag has a *cors de chasse* emblem and the 'B' initial indicates battalion. The original fleur-de-lys emblems have been patched over with lozenges in the national colours, and the pike head replaced. Below is a depiction of the flags awarded to light infantry demi-brigades in 1802. This time we show the 2e Bataillon, 6e Demi-Brigade Légère, which fought at Marengo. Beautifully designed, these flags are perhaps of academic interest only. In 1803 the demi-brigades were titled regiments, and these flags were handed in when swapped for 'eagles' in 1804. (Artwork by Anderson Subtil © Helion and Company 2021)

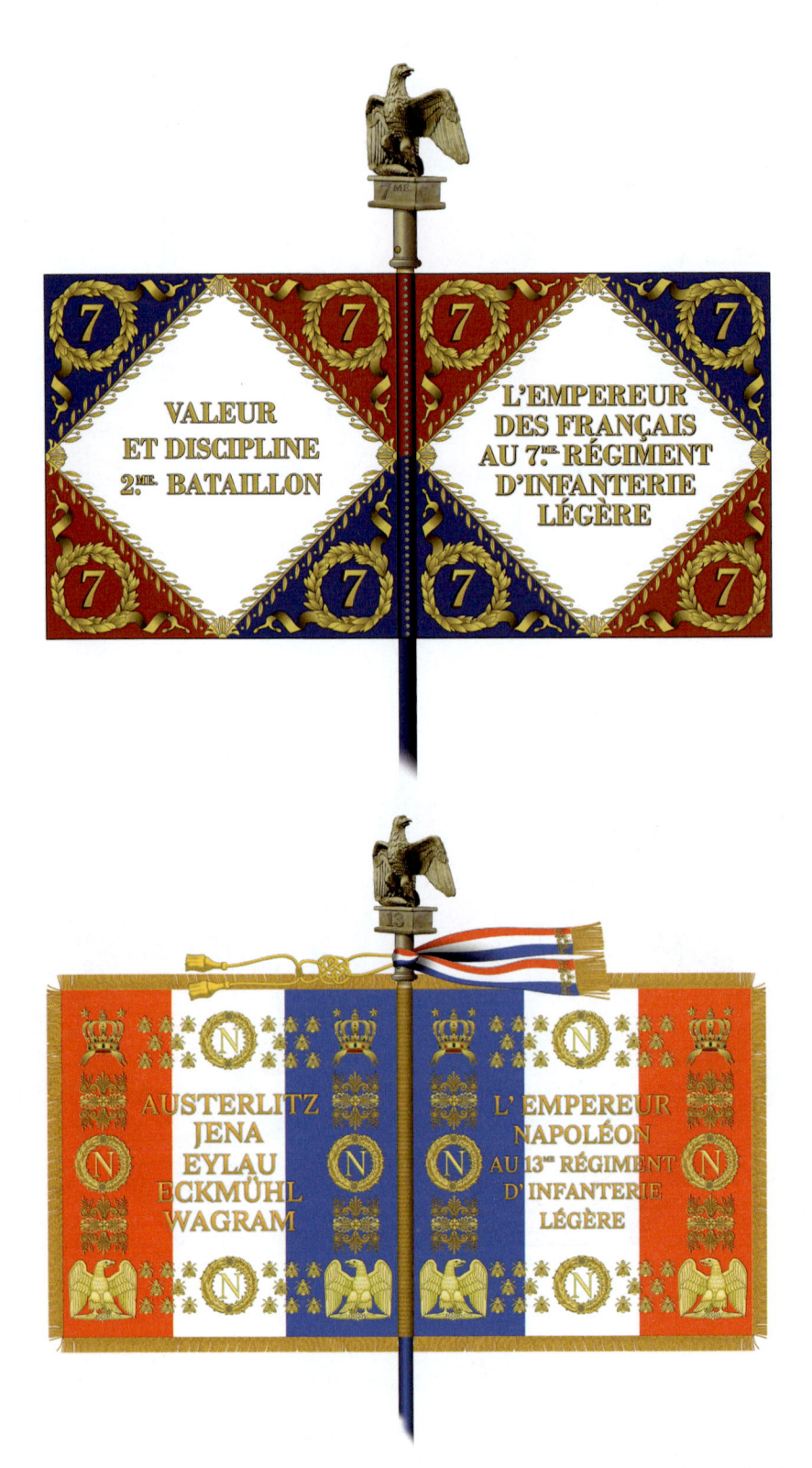

Light infantry flags, 1804 and 1812 models. The 1804 and 1812 pattern flags both carried the same design of eagle. In 1804 one eagle was issued per battalion; in 1812 only one eagle per regiment was issued. The 1812 pattern flag was the most ornate issued by Napoleon. The reverse of the flag carried the regimental battle honours. (Artwork by Anderson Subtil © Helion and Company 2021)

Colonel and flag, 1815. The 1815 eagle and flag was a much simplified design. Here is *Colonel* Despans-Cubières of the 1er Léger having received his new eagle at the Champ de Mai on 1 June 1815. The 1er Légère did not qualify for any battle honours in 1811, but they were present at Lutzen in 1813, and there are examples of this battle honour being displayed on other flags in 1815. The 1815 eagles were due to be presented to the war battalions, but then sent back to the depots; however, it appears the eagle of the 1er Léger was present on the field at Waterloo. Note how the colonel wears riding boots. (Artwork by Patrice Courcelle © Helion and Company 2021)

Chasseur, 1812 'Bardin' uniform. This is the 1812 pattern chasseur uniform designed for the light infantry, but not introduced until after the peace in 1814. The epaulettes of the early empire have been replaced with shoulder straps. The gilet is completely covered by the habit-veste. The greatcoat is rolled and strapped to the top of the haversack behind. The small pin and chain on the right lapel is an *epinglette* (vent pick). This was an essential tool for keeping the musket barrel's touchhole clear during firing. (Artwork by Patrice Courcelle © Helion and Company 2021)

Voltigeur in campaign dress, 1815. This light infantry voltigeur is depicted in typical uniform worn on campaign. His habit-veste is hidden below a beige *capote* (greatcoat). These greatcoats were sometimes white or grey. He is wearing linen *pantalons* and gaiters. His shako is covered by a black canvas cover to protect it from the elements. The yellow aigrette is still visible. He carries a non-regulation canteen (*bidon*). He also carries a sabre-briquet sword. (Artwork by Patrice Courcelle © Helion and Company 2021)

Carabinier officer, 1815. This figure depicts *Capitaine* Jean-Baptiste Joseph Cardron (1784-1845) of the 9e Légère. Much of Cardon's uniform has survived, along with many of his letters. A native of Philippeville in modern Belgium, Cardron volunteered for the army in 1805 at the age of 18. He was one of the tallest men in the 9e Légere at 1.8 metres. Eager for promotion, he reached the rank of *capitaine* and was made a chevalier of the *légion d'honneur* in 1813 after being wounded at Bautzen. His shako has no plate, but instead has a large cockade mounted lower than usual. The Imperial plate may have been removed during the restoration. The surviving coat has an unusual grenade badge on the right side of the collar (not shown). There does not appear to be any precedent for this and was probably a latter addition. (Artwork by Patrice Courcelle © Helion and Company 2021)

Carabinier *Tambour*, 1815. This drummer wears the 1812 pattern uniform with imperial livery. The coat is green and is decorated with embroidered tape depicting imperial eagles and 'N' motifs. The extent to which this uniform was fully introduced is debatable.
(Artwork by Patrice Courcelle © Helion and Company 2021)

Partisan chief, 1814-1815. The French light infantry regiments had their origins in the irregular legions of the eighteenth century. In 1814 and again in 1815, Napoleon raised irregular partisan bands to harry the enemy supply lines and communications. This 'chef de partisans' is a retired officer, fiercely loyal to Napoleon. He carries a *sabre d'honneur* he won during the Consulate. With his native department about to be invade by the allied army, he raises a force of retired servicemen and woodsmen. He wears no uniform, but sports a tricolour cockade and, inside his coat pocket, he keeps a precious passport with the authorising signature of a general, without which he and his men risk being hanged as brigands or spies. (Artwork by Patrice Courcelle © Helion and Company 2021)

Year XII (21 January 1804), formed of volunteers and conscripts at least 5 feet 3 in height, drawn from well-off families who could afford the fees of 200 francs a year. Paying to serve in the army might appear to have little incentive, but a successful vélite could look forward to a commission in the line after four years.

Table 18. Chasseurs à Pied, Garde Imperiale, 1804

Staff	Company
1 *colonel*	1 *capitaine*
1 *major*	1 *lieutenant en premier*
3 *chefs de bataillon*	1 *lieutenant en second*
1 *quartier-maître-trésorier*	1 *sergent-major*
3 *adjudants-major*	4 *sergents*
3 *sous-adjudants-major*	1 *fourrier*
2 *porte-drapeaux* (standard bearers)	8 *caporaux*
3 *officiers de santé* (medical officers)	2 *sapeurs*, rank of *caporal*
1 *élève-chirurgien* (pupil surgeon)	80 *chasseurs*
1 *vaguemestre-sergent-major* (baggagemaster)	2 *tambours*
1 *tambour-major*	
3 *caporaux-tambours* (drum-corporals)	
1 *chef de musique*.	
46 *musiciens*.	
1 *maître tailleur*.	
1 *maître cordonnier*	
2 *armuriers* (1 for the vélites).	
1 *guêtrier*	

In 1806 there was an expansion of the Imperial Guard, with a second regiment of chasseurs à pied added, and then a third, formed mostly from those having served as Vélites (thus creating what became known as the Middle Guard). In 1815 there were four regiments of chasseurs à pied in the Middle Guard and which took part in the ill-fated final attack on Wellington's line.

In 1809 a succession of tirailleur and conscript regiments were formed, half of which were described as chasseurs and came under the command of the colonel of the Chasseurs à Pied of the Guard:

- 1er Régiment des Tirailleurs-Chasseurs de la Garde Impériale
- 2e Régiment des Tirailleurs-Chasseurs de la Garde Impériale
- 1er Régiment des Conscrits-Chasseurs de la Garde Impériale
- 2e Régiment des Conscrits-Chasseurs de la Garde Impériale

These four regiments were reorganised in 1810 to create four regiments of Voltigeurs de la Garde Impériale. It is probably a mistake to think of these as voltigeurs in the sense of the troops in the line and light infantry regiments, but they were composed of the pick of the conscripts and recruits. Two more regiments were added in 1811, seven more in 1813, and three more in 1814, totalling 16 regiments of voltigeurs. With better service conditions, these guard units acted as a magnet, drawing the best conscripts and recruits away from the line. The impact of this must have been significant and ultimately detrimental.

FRENCH LIGHT INFANTRY 1784-1815

Flanquer of the Imperial Guard. The collar, cuffs and piping are yellow, with red turnbacks. The piping and tassels on his gaiters are also yellow. (Collection Yves Martin)

Voltigeur of the Imperial Guard, by Martinet. The plume is green, with a red tip. The shako cords are red as is the border on the epaulettes. In keeping with voltigeurs in line regiments, he has a yellow collar. The turnbacks on his coat are red, with blue hunting horn emblems. Note the pointed, red cuffs piped white. (Collection Yves Martin)

Napoleon's Irregulars 1814-1815

As the First Empire came crashing down following the disaster of Russia in 1812, the cataclysmic defeat at Leipzig in 1813, and the ravages of a typhus epidemic, France faced the prospect of foreign invasion for the first time since 1792. Napoleon responded to this national crisis as France responded in 1792, mobilising the National Guard, declaring a levée en masse in the departments most at risk, and raising corps of irregular light troops. Given the magnitude of the crisis (every major European power had armies massed on the French frontier), Napoleon went a step further, calling for an insurrection and the raising of partisan corps to harry the enemy.

On 1 January 1814, instructions were issued for the defence of France. Four corps d'armée were assembled: The Duke of Raguse (Marmont) at Colmar, the centre at Épinal, under the Prince of the Moskova (Ney); the Duke of Treviso (Mortier) at Langres, and the Duke of Castiglione (Augereau) covering Lyon. Each of these armies would form an 'organisation of insurrection' composed of a general and several superior officers native

A group of exhausted, half-starved chasseurs pause for rest in a contemporary illustration by Beyer (circa.1813). Note the shako covers, and the camping equipment: a *gamelle* (mess pan) and a *grand bidon* (water can) carried on their packs. Note the two different water canteens being carried, and the cup, and piece of bread hanging from the haversack on the central figure, who is using a staff to help support the weight of his equipment. (Collection Martin Lancaster)

to each region. The generals of insurrection would form companies from local villagers and provide orders for the sounding of the tocsin. The generals would also raise corps of partisans, nominating their chiefs and issuing them with patents (thus legalising them as combatants). The insurgents would be armed with hunting weapons and issued with moulds for the manufacture of ball ammunition. The generals organising the emergency levy were instructed to organise free corps from retired soldiers, or those who had lost their corps in the chaos, and deserters. These free corps would serve alongside the regular army in the line.[31]

The partisans were irregulars, protecting their villages, and doing everything possible to cause the enemy harm. In effect this was a declaration guerrilla warfare. On 8 January, Napoleon instructed Minister of War, *Général de Division* Clarke to write to all the generals commanding the insurrection, to gather all the customs men, rural and forestry guards, gendarmes, discharged and pensioner service men, and put them at their disposal.[32] Further instructions were also issued on the subject of partisans. Any citizen was able to raise a corps of partisans, particularly those who had been soldiers, if they could present at least 30 men; 20 on foot and 10 mounted. These partisan chiefs simply had to present themselves to the local general commanding the insurrection to receive a patent.[33] These partisans would put their expert knowledge of the countryside to use to fend off raids

---

31 Napoleon I, *Correspondance*, Vol.XXVII, pp.1-3.
32 Napoleon I, *Correspondance*, Vol.XXVII, p.20.
33 Jean-Marie Thiébaud and Gérard Tissot-Robbe, *Les Corps Francs de 1814 et 1815: la double agonie de l'empire: les Combattants de l'impossible* (Paris: SPM, 2011), p.20.

by the enemy's Cossacks, light horse and jäger. The provisional field service regulations, re-issued in 1809, contained a chapter on raising war parties and this provided a regulatory framework for their operations. According to this regulation, partisan commanders required a passport issued by the commanding general (without which the enemy would be able to hang them as brigands). On returning to the army, these partisans were required to submit all their prisoners and prizes, lest they be labelled as thieves and punished as such.

It is interesting to see that the concept of a mixed corps of cavalry and infantry came back into vogue, albeit at a much smaller scale. Perhaps with some allusion to the old *partis bleues* of the eighteenth century (the illegal 'land pirates'), the resisters of 1814 became known as the 'blouses bleues' (blue shirts). This actually derived from an instruction of 5 March stipulating that these emergency levies would be uniformed in a *habit Gaulois* (gallic coat) or 'blouses bleues' with a shako, cartridge pouch and black cross belt. Worn over their civilian clothes, the blouse (a heavy smock) would serve as their greatcoat.[34] After Napoleon's abdication, the partisan bands were disbanded by a royal order of 6 May 1814. Any partisans who wished to continue military service were incorporated into the regiments of the line, with the remainder sent home.

Their service must have been deemed useful, because soon after Napoleon returned to the throne, he repeated the measure. The decree of 22 April 1815 raised new corps francs in each of the departments along the frontiers of the empire. These corps bore the name of their department, with an identifying number if several were raised. Anyone who believed they could raise a free corps was to address the minister of war or the prefect of the department. The men were to be volunteers from National Guard units which had not been mobilised, retired soldiers, and from forestry guards and other employees. Officers were breveted accordingly. The corps would have no regular uniform, they were to be organised along the same lines as the light infantry and cavalry regiments, with no more than 1,000 infantry or 300 horsemen per corps. The infantry would be armed with muskets and hunting rifles, while the cavalry carried lances. They received no pay and were responsible for supplying their own equipment and weapons. They were also allowed to equip themselves with small calibre artillery (3 or 4-pounders) if they were available, and they were required to hold ammunition for 600 shots per gun.[35]

There were significant incentives for serving within these corps. During wartime they were allowed to draw rations. In the event of invasion, the free corps were to work in the rear of the enemy, bivouacking in the woods, at steep places, or under the protection of a fortification. They were specifically instructed to target convoys and couriers, receiving 30 francs for every prisoner taken. Officers fetched much higher prices, ranging from 100 francs for a lieutenant to 4,000 francs for a lieutenant general. ADCs and couriers fetched 2,000 francs. They were allowed to retain anything of value as a prize, with the state offering to purchase captured military equipment

---

34 Napoleon I, *Correspondance*, Vol.XXVII, p.292.
35 Napoleon I, *Correspondance*, Vol.XXVIII, pp.116-117.

at three-quarters the going price. The decree also allowed departments not on the frontier to raise their own free corps, allowing them to travel to the frontier of their choice after the declaration of war was made. One can see how appealing service with these land privateers might be.

On 1 May 1815 Napoleon again discussed raising free corps and partisans to guard the forests and ravines, and where they might attack enemy convoys and couriers. Every army commander would have an *adjudant-general* staff officer who would correspond with and direct the operations of the partisans. On 9 June, on the eve of the Waterloo campaign, we find the Emperor asking Minister of War, Maréchal Davout to send him a report on the strength of the partisan corps. He wished to order partisans to begin moving to the northern frontier, and to use the Ardennes Forest as a route to push into the heart of Belgium. Others were instructed to follow the mountains into the country around Metz and along the Saar.

The short duration of Napoleon's campaign in Belgium and the disaster of Waterloo on 18 June, meant the free corps soon had armies advancing across their territories. With such significant bounties on offer for the capture of enemy officers and couriers, the partisans certainly caused a nuisance to the allied powers. On 3 July the Austrian *Feldmarschall* Schwarzenberg issued a stern proclamation that partisans and others not serving in regular corps would be shot on the spot. Villages which took up arms would be reduced to ashes, and if an allied soldier was killed the commune responsible would have to pay penalty of ten thousand francs.[36] On 20 July 1815 an ordinance was issued dismissing all corps francs in existence (thereby cancelling any prize money due). The commanders, officers and soldiers of these corps were ordered to return to their homes. Anyone not complying with this ordinance would be arrested, brought before a court martial, and judged against military laws. The partisans were thus delegitimised.

Restoration and 100 Days

Napoleon abdicated on 11 April 1814. On 8 July the Bourbon Louis XVIII formally took the throne, restoring the monarchy the successive governments had sworn would never return. With peace declared the army needed massive reduction and reform. Thousands of soldiers were scattered across Europe in isolated garrisons, and in prisoner of war camps. Desperately organised provisional units needed to be disbanded and unincorporated conscripts needed to be sent home. From an effective strength of 726,000 infantrymen at the end of the First Empire, the ordonnance of 12 May 1814 sought to reduce the infantry to 90 regiments of the line and 15 of light infantry.[37] Each regiment would be composed of three battalions, each of six companies, of which two were elite and four were fusiliers (or chasseurs). The first 15 light infantry regiments would form the core of the new corps, with the others disbanded to complete them to full strength. Included in this reorganisation

---

36   Thiébaud and Tissot-Robbe, *Les Corps Francs*, p.47.
37   Avril, *Essai Avantages d'une bonne discipline*, p.430.

were the 16 regiments of Tirailleurs, 15 of Voltigeurs and two of Flanqueurs of the Young Guard, the majority of which went into the line regiments.

Table 19. Organisation of 12 May 1814

The Staff		Off	Men	Companies	Off	Men
Colonel		1	-	Capitaine	1	-
Major		1	-	Lieutenant	1	-
Chefs de Bataillon		3	-	Sous-lieutenant	1	-
Adjudans-majors		3	-	Sergent-major	-	1
Quartier-maître		1	-	Sergens	-	4
Porte-drapeau (standard bearer)		1	-			
Chirurgiens	Major	1	-	Fourrier	-	1
	Aide-major	1	-	Corporaux	-	8
	Sub-aide	1	-	Grenadiers, Fusiliers, Voltigeurs	-	56
Adjutans-sous-officiers		-	3			
Tambour-major		-	1	Tambours	-	2
Caporal-tambour		-	1	Totals	3	72
Musiciens (inc. a chef)		-	8			
Maîtres	Tailleur-guêtrier	-	1			
	Cordonnier	-	1			
	Armurier	-	1			
Totals		13	16			

The first six regiments took their names from the king, queen and other royal titles. The remaining nine were identified only by a number. On 15 May a separate ordinance stated the Duc de Bourbon would take the title of Colonel General of the Light Infantry.

Table 20. Reduction of Light Infantry Regiments, 1814

1er Régt. Léger du Roi	1er Régt d'Inf Légère
2e Régt. Léger de la Reine	2e Régt. d'Inf. Légère
3e Régt. Léger Dauphin	3e Régt. d'Inf. Légère 1e & 7e Bons, 21e Régt. d'Inf. Légère 31e Régt. d'Inf. Légère
4e Régt. Léger Monsieur	4e Régt. d'Inf. Légère 19e Régt. d'Inf. Légère 1e, 2e & 6e Bons, 23e Régt. d'Inf. Légère
5e Régt. Léger Angoulême	5e Régt. d'Inf. Légère 37e Régt. d'Inf. Légère
6e Régt. Léger Berri	6e Régt. d'Inf. Légère 24e Régt. d'Inf. Légère
7e Régt. Léger	7e Régt. d'Inf. Légère 20e Régt. d'Inf. Légère 26e Régt. d'Inf. Légère 5e & 6e Bons, 21e Régt. d'Inf. Légère
8e Régt. Léger	8e Régt. d'Inf. Légère 34e Régt. d'Inf. Légère 3e & 4e Bons, 18e Régt. d'Inf. Légère
9e Régt. Léger	9e Régt. d'Inf. Légère 1er & 2e Bons, 32e Régt. d'Inf. Légère 1er & 4e Bons, 36e Régt. d'Inf. Légère

10e Régt. Léger	10e Régt. d'Inf. Légère 25e Régt. d'Inf. Légère 30 Régt. d'Inf. Légère 1er, 2e & 3e Bons, 17e Régt. d'Inf. Légère
11e Régt. Léger	11e Régt. d'Inf. Légère 29e Régt. d'Inf. Légère Légion Corse
12e Régt. Léger	12e Régt. d'Inf. Légère 16e Régt. d'Inf. Légère 1er, 3e & 5e Bons, 28e Régt. d'Inf. Légère
13e Régt. Léger	13e Régt. d'Inf. Légère 27 Régt. d'Inf. Légère 2e, 4e & 6e Bons, 28e Régt. d'Inf. Légère
14e Régt. Léger	14e Régt. d'Inf. Légère 5e & 6e Bons, 18e Régt. d'Inf. Légère 3e, 4e & 5e Bons, 32e Régt. d'Inf. Légère 2e & 3e Bons, 36e Régt. d'Inf. Légère
15e Régt. Léger	15e Régt. d'Inf. Légère 3e, 4e & 5e Bons, 23e Régt. d'Inf. Légère 1e & 2e Bons, 1er Voltigeurs

By an additional ordonnance of 10 October 1814 two battalions of light infantry were raised in Corsica. These Chasseurs Corses were formed of nine companies each, one of which was carabiniers, with a force of 549 officers and men.

Upon Napoleon's return from exile, one of his first acts was to attempt to undo the 1814 reorganisation of infantry regiments and restore the imperial army to its original footing. However, because of the rapid turn of events, the 15 regiments of light infantry remained as formed in 1814, but without their royal titles. A decree of 13 April 1815 instructed the increase of the number of battalions in each regiment as follows:

I. Our line and light infantry regiments will be successively increased to five battalions, including four battalions of the line, and one depot battalion. Each line battalion will be made up of six companies, including one of grenadiers or carabiniers, one of voltigeurs, and four of fusiliers. The depot battalion will consist of only two fusilier companies.

II. The staff of each regiment will be composed as follows, namely: *état-major* (staff). 1 *colonel*, 1 *major*, 4 *chefs de bataillon*, 5 *adjudant*s, 1 *quartier-maître-trésorier*, 1 *capitaine d'habillement* (clothing captain), 1 *premier porte-aigle*, 1 *officier payeur* (pay officer), 1 *chirurgien-major*, 4 *aides-chirurgiens*, 5 *sous-aides*; total, 25. *Petit état-major* (Petty staff). 10 *adjudants-sous-officiers*, 2 *second et troisième porte-aigle*, 1 *tambour-major*, 1 *caporal-tambour*, 12 *musiciens*, including a *chef* (leader), 3 *maîtres-ouvriers*; total, 29.

III. The companies will keep the organisation they now have for officers and NCOs: the soldiers will be increased to eighty, which makes six hundred for the battalion, until the 4th and 5th battalions are brought to completion in men: following this, each of them may be increased by twenty-four soldiers.

IV. Our Minister of War will give the necessary orders so that the 4th and 5th Battalions are immediately completed with officers and NCOs. As soon as the

3rd and 4th Battalions are made up to six hundred men, the companies will be increased to 120 men, eight hundred and forty per battalion.
V. There will be provisionally attached a major and a cadre of supernumerary battalion officers to each regiment.[38]

In addition to this, the imperial decrees of 5 May and 9 June 1815 saw the formation of two new battalions of chasseurs under the names of Pyrénées and Alpes respectively.[39]

After Napoleon's second abdication the army which had rallied to his cause was no longer trusted. The regiments of infantry were dissolved by the ordinances of 16 July and 3 August 1815 and the soldiers sent home to their departments of origin. Then 86 infantry departmental legions were formed, each recruiting men from soldiers of that department. Each legion had a staff and two battalions of line infantry, with a battalion of chasseurs à pied, three depot companies, an artillery company and a company of éclaireurs. The line infantry battalions had eight companies, one of which was of grenadiers; the light infantry battalion had eight companies of chasseurs only. The depots of the Napoleonic regiments and the materiel they held in stock were sent to the various departments to form these new legions. While it is true to say the Napoleonic regiments became extinct in September 1815, we know at least where their councils of administrations went. The depots of the 15 light infantry regiments were used in the formation of the following legions:[40]

- 1er Léger became the Légion des Hautes-Pyrénées
- 2e Léger became the Légion d'Eure-et-Loir
- 3e Léger became the Légion des Basses-Pyrénées
- 4e Léger became the Légion de la Gironde
- 5e Léger became the Légion de la Manche
- 6e Léger became the Légion de l'Aube
- 7e Léger became the Légion du Cher
- 8e Léger became the Légion des Pyrénées-Orientales
- 9e Léger became the Légion des Ardennes
- 10e Léger became la Légion du Bas-Rhin
- 11e Léger became la Légion d'Ille-et-Vilaine
- 12e Léger became la Légion du Gers
- 13e Léger became la Légion de la Vienne
- 14e Léger became la Légion de la Drôme
- 15e Léger became la Légion de la Haute-Vienne

In 1820 France moved back to a regimental system. Twenty regiments of light infantry were created, each with two battalions. Although there was no direct administrative or personnel link with the old regiments, the new corps adopted the traditions and battle honours of their predecessors. Subsequently,

---

38 Arthur Chuquet, *Ordres et apostilles de Napoléon, 1799-1815* (Paris: Librarie Ancienne Honoré Champion, 1912), Vol.4, pp.536-537.
39 *Recueil général des lois*, Vol.13, pp.274-277.
40 Susane, *Histoire de l'ancienne infanterie française*, Vol.1, pp.390-393.

in 1840 France created battalions of chasseurs à pied armed with rifled carbines and sword bayonets. The chasseur battalions became seen as the true light infantry and so finally, in 1854, under the reign of Napoleon III, the French army decided there was so little difference between line and light infantry regiments, they ought to be finally merged. Twenty-five regiments of light infantry were converted into line infantry adopting the numbers 76e to 100e. These regiments carried with them the traditions and battle honours of the Napoleonic light infantry regiments right into the Great War of 1914-1918. Thus we see the 84e Régiment de Ligne adopting both the soubriquet of *l'Incomparable*, awarded to the Napoleonic 9e Légère, and the *Un Contre Dix* (one against ten) of the Napoleonic 84e Ligne. If one wishes to read the regimental histories of the Napoleonic light infantry regiments, one must search the regimental histories of the 76e to 100e Line Regiments written before the Great War.

Table 21. Recapitulation of Light Infantry Force 1762-1815

Date	Regts	Bns	Soldiers	Observations
1762 (10 December)	6	/	1,950	Légions
1776 (25 March/31 May)	7	/	2,290	Légions
1784 (12 July)	7	/	2,424	Régts. Chasseurs
1788 (17 March)	/	12	5,430	Battalions à pied
1791 (1 January)	/	14	8,652	Battalions à pied
1794 (12 August)	30	90	96,960	Demi-brigades
1796 (10 Brumaire)	30	90	96,960	Demi-brigades
1799 (23 Fructidor)	26	78	84,006	Demi-brigades
1803 (24 September)	28	86	61,108	Regiments
1808 (18 February)	32	150	107,190	Regiments
1812 (1 September)	37	185	123,070	Regiments
1813 (20 January)	37	185	127,040	Regiments
1814 (12 May)	15	45	20,685	Regiments
1815 (16 July)	/	/	/	Ceases to exist

4

Light Infantry Tactics

One of the most interesting aspects of studying French light infantry is its tactical employment and how it differed to that of the line infantry regiments. With the publication of the first edition of his essay on light infantry in 1806, Duhesme complained how the line and light infantry regiments appeared as the same arm, with the same weapons, organisation, regulations, inspector-generals, equipment and manoeuvres. The only obvious difference between them was in the cut of the uniforms. Duhesme blamed this on the tactical employment of both forms of infantry in the 1790s. Light troops had often manoeuvred as part of the line, while line infantry habitually performed outpost duties. Duhesme even pointed out the somewhat ludicrous observation that even heavy cavalry had been sent off as skirmishers. But there *was* a difference, he said, and people like him who had been at the head of a division on active service, and knew their troops well

> [C]ould not help noticing that, from the very dawn of our present tactics, our free corps and our battalions of chasseurs à pied guarded themselves better at the outposts, were much better at scouting, were more suited to discoveries and parties, fought as skirmishers with more intelligence than our line troops, which, on the other hand, manoeuvred with more order and aplomb on the battlefield, and better resisted the charges of cavalry.[1]

A regiment of line infantry, coolly manoeuvring under enemy artillery fire and 'imperturbable in front of all the most vigorous charges' was, in Duhesme's opinion, less suited to outpost work and skirmishing than even a mediocre regiment of light troops. Duhesme explains why:

> The strength of troops is in their own opinion. The soldier who, in closed ranks, regards himself in his battalion as if in an impregnable fortress, finds himself, if you throw him en tirailleur, very isolated and very compromised, while the trained chasseur à pied, who, in a fight, braves the man on horseback, and who,

---

1   Duhesme, *Précis historique de l'infanterie légère*, pp.2-3.

covering himself with the slightest obstacle, calmly aims his musket shots, often only manoeuvres in the ranks with confusion and uncertainty.[2]

Recruited from the same pool of citizens, armed and equipped more or less the same, the real difference between light infantry and their cousins was therefore one of mindset. They were trained to act independently, to embrace the freedom of operating outside the line, like the *enfants perdus* before them, and were led by officers who encouraged this independence, and, particular the case with young, subaltern officers, embraced the freedoms and opportunities for independent command. On the other hand, if that same recruit had he been sent to a regiment of the line, he would have been trained to act in unison with his comrades, to exhibit immobility and firmness, to find sanctuary in massed ranks. As *Général de Division* Joseph Rogniat wrote in 1816:

> Watch our best line troops, our grenadiers for example, as skirmishers! These soldiers, so brave in the line, are heavy, ponderous, clumsy, shy even in a profession that is foreign to them; they don't know whether to advance, retreat, or pursue the enemy, nor avoid it. If a cavalry platoon fell on them, they did not know how to save themselves or to escape it, nor to congregate to resist it, and they let themselves be cut to pieces without defence.[3]

In this chapter we will explore the tactics employed by light infantry. The techniques of battlefield skirmishing are of obvious interest, and although not exclusive to light infantry, the latter were primarily intended to fight in this manner. It is an interesting subject, with a development from independent skirmishers, acting almost as snipers (a term then unknown, which did not enter the English lexicon until the 1820s), to great masses of skirmishers covering the advance of attack columns, operating as a cordon in extended order, using 'buddy systems'; but first we must introduce the type of warfare which brought the need for light infantry to the fore: the petite guerre operations in which light troops, mounted and on foot, played a leading role.

The *Petit-Guerre*

A great deal of experience in petite guerre was gained in the wars of the mid-eighteenth century. Previous to the war of 1792, a diligent officer of light infantry had at his disposal a number of excellent books on the type of wartime operations he was likely to engage in. The key texts were Frederick the Great's *Instructions Militaires* augmented with *Instructions pour la petit guerre* as published by the Saxon colonel, Georg Faesch in 1777. Before this we have Grandmaison's 1756 work, *La Petite Guerre, ou traite du service des troupes légères en campagne* and de Jeney's excellent *Le Partisan* from 1759. Bardin also lists an anonymous work *Courtes maximes pour la petite guerre*,

---

2   Duhesme, *Précis historique de l'infanterie légère*, pp.4-5
3   Joseph Rogniat, *Considérations sur l'art de la guerre* (Paris: Magimel, 1816), p.95.

FRENCH LIGHT INFANTRY 1784-1815

A study by Carle Vernet showing infantry preparing to ambush a column of troops approaching by road. Mounting ambushes was recognised as an important tactic in petite-guerre. (Anne S.K. Brown Military Collection)

which he attributes to Crevier (1764); along with Laroche's 1770 *Essai sur la petite guerre*, and *L'Officier Partisan* by Ray de Saint-Geniés in 1769.

A provisional instruction for light troops was issued on 1 May 1769 (*Instruction que le Roi a fait expédier pour régler provisoirement l'exercice des troupes-légères*). Bardin believed this regulation was written by Charles François Dumouriez (1739-1823), who was an excellent and respected soldier, at least until he attempted a coup d'état in 1793.[4] Authors rarely mention the document because it was barely implemented at the time and did not survive the disbandment of the legions in 1776.[5] Much of the document describes close order arms drill. It describes an ordinary pace of 60 steps per minute (each pace being two French *pieds*); a double pace, twice the former; and a *pas de course* – a shorter, 18-inch (French) step, which took quarter of a second to complete (in other words it was three times the ordinary pace). There are only several elements which describe the functions of an advanced guard. The chapters are presented here in their entirety:

---

[4] Bardin, *Dictionnaire de l'armée de terre*, Vol.13, p.3881.
[5] Bardin, *Dictionnaire de l'armée de terre*, Vol.10, p.2920.

CHAPTER 17. *Dispositions of an advanced-guard*
The advanced-guards will keep a hundred paces at most from the troop they precede; they will send out in front of them & on the flanks, the dragoons necessary to scout the march.

The commander will also make whatever arrangements he deems necessary with regard to the nature of the terrain he will have to cover.

If he marches against the enemy in an open country, he must have only a few skirmishers ahead of him, the rest of the troop must march in good order.

If it is necessary to pass a stream, a deep ravine, a crossing or covered path, hedges leading to woods, a defile, etc. he must have the ground searched and not go too far before it has been properly checked.

When he marches in thicket country, he will leave a few dragoons between the advanced-guard & the troop, posted from distance to distance & within sight, so that the troop does not take another path.

These advanced-guards will be stronger during the night, they will be followed closely by the troop, & then they will always march sabre in hand, so that if they meet the enemy, they can charge him suddenly & without giving him time to reconnoitre.

These advanced-guards will reunite their troops when ordered by the commander.

CHAPTER 18. *Dispositions of a rear-guard*
The rear-guards will be kept in the same way at most a hundred paces behind the troop; they will be followed at thirty paces by a number of dragoons necessary, to be informed of what is coming behind them; they will get closer to the troop when they march at night, & the dragoons who follow them will stand ten paces behind them.[6]

There are some interesting details elsewhere in the instruction. They describe how a legion should march across open ground, with the infantry in the centre and the cavalry forming two wings either side of it. It also describes methods for training the dragoons at skirmishing, deploying half their number to fire their pistols or carbines independently, while the rest of the troop remained formed in support. Anyone who did not heed the recall signal would be severely punished. During mock battles the dragoons were told to spend a minute clashing their sabres together to accustom their horses to the noise. There was useful advice on conditioning the horses to gunfire and the means of dispersing the soldiers in skirmish formation, which we will return to below.

As for the period between 1792-1815 it is generally believed there was no official instruction or regulation for light troops. This is not strictly true. The 1791 infantry regulations teach soldiers how to load and fire at will. Arguably a skirmisher needs no further instruction. The field service regulations of 5 April 1792 also detail the work of the advanced posts, protecting camps with instructions on the formation of posts, guards, sentries, and the use of

---

6   *Instruction que le Roi a fait expédier pour régler provisoirement l'exercice des troupes-légères* (Paris: Imprimerie Royale), pp.180-181.

passwords. To better understand the principles as they were applied during the opening decade of war, we can introduce the 1803 work of François Jarry de Vrigny de la Villette (1733-1807), a French émigré in British service. When read in conjunction with the regulation of 5 April 1792, Jarry's work illuminates the duties of light infantry during the 1790s.

Prior to the revolution Jarry was a military engineer who served in Prussia and became director of the war academy in in Berlin. He returned to French service in 1790 and became chief of staff to Rochambeau, then had a stint as a diplomat, attempting to keep Prussia out of the war. In 1792 he was promoted to *maréchal de camp* and took command of the advanced guard of the Armée du Nord. During the defence of Courtrai he gained a degree of notoriety, taking the draconian step of burning parts of the suburbs to deny shelter to Tyrolese jäger. After the fall of the monarchy in August 1792, Jarry emigrated, and came to Britain three years later. Recognised as a brilliant military theoretician, the British put Jarry to work schooling young officers, who in truth were probably more interested in boisterous activities than listening to the theoretical ramblings of a French émigré. In 1803 the Duke of York ordered the publication of a translation of his treatise on the *Instruction Concerning the Duties of Light Infantry in the Field*. At the height of the invasion scare, with Napoleon's army massing on the Channel coast, the importance of Jarry's work was clearly seen. Although it was written and translated for a British audience, Jarry explained the French employment of light infantry. In the translator's preface there is a very interesting remark on the importance of learning this system:

> If the French attempt a landing in this country, they will, no doubt, endeavour to disembark a considerable body of troops of this description; and, indeed, all their troops are accustomed to fight en tirailleur. Their army will be constantly covered by sharp-shooters, concealed behind enclosures, hedges, trees, bushes, walls, houses, inequalities of the ground; they must be dislodged by a chain of English sharp-shooters, advancing under the same sort of cover, and driven behind their line.[7]

In his preamble, Jarry reinforces the importance of light infantry in mountainous and broken ground where cavalry is unable to operate. The two arms ought to cooperate as much as possible, and together form a protective chain in front of, or on the flanks of an army's camp. Reading the mass of details in the text it is more than apparent why advanced-guard warfare required special training, particular because it relied so much on junior officers acquainting themselves with the local situation and terrain. It also becomes apparent why light infantry work was so exhausting. For a column of infantry, artillery and its baggage to march through and camp unmolested in enemy territory called for a great deal of energy on the part of those preceding and flanking the column. Using Jarry and the 5 April 1792 regulations we are able to reconstruct the typical process of securing

---

7 Jarry, *Instruction Concerning the Duties of Light Infantry in the Field*, pp.vi-vii.

an army's camp. This system provided security for the camp, preventing surprise attacks and the infiltration of spies. It also deterred desertion from the soldiers in camp, who would also have to break through the chain of *sentinelles* guarding them.

When an army decided to camp, the first duty was to organise a search of the ground in order to confirm the enemy had no concealed parties. Jarry cautioned that a large farm with barns might easily conceal two or three hundred enemy troops, so it was important these places were properly searched. By using local guides and maps, a commander was to familiarise himself with the layout of the ground, noting the roads, villages, woods, heights and rivers between himself and the potential route of enemy attack. The officer was then to determine the extent of his chain of *sentinelles* (sentries) and their location. This in turn would depend on the likely proximity of the enemy and the type of ground to be covered. The system described in fact comprised of multiple chains, providing a robust defence in depth, minimising the chances of an enemy falling on the army's camp by surprise. This succession of chains can be summarised in the following terms, starting from those nearest to the camp or bivouac:

Camp guards: these were formed by the battalions in camp and were composed of 15-18 men, placed one hundred paces in front of the centre of each battalion. Each guard ought to be able to see the next guard in line, and cavalry ought also to provide guards in front of their camping ground.

Grande-gardes (the 'outlying picket'): The *chef de bataillon* would personally supervise the establishment of *grande-gardes*, visiting the posts and ensuring they were sufficiently entrenched. They were located on the principal roads leading to the camp, commanded by an officer and placed in a protected location, such as a churchyard or garden surrounded by a breast-high wall. Where no such protection was available, the *grande-garde* ought to construct field works, cutting down trees, or forming an abatis, or piercing loop-holes through walls. The purpose of these was not to be a point of resistance, but to offer sufficient protection from surprise attack and to buy sufficient time to relay a timely warning back to the camp. The officer commanding the *grande-garde* was also advised to cut pathways through hedges to allow his men to quickly fall back on this post, or to escape from it to a rallying point. The officer commanding the picket would then detach a number of his men forwards to create the chain of *sentinelles* and small posts around 300 paces in front. Jarry recommended retaining between two-third and one half the force in reserve at the *grande-garde*. Ideally there would be a few light cavalry troopers assigned to these pickets in order to relay information swiftly back to the camp. If the enemy appeared to be surrounding the position, the picket was to fall back on the rallying point before it was cut off.

Petits-postes (*small, or detached posts*): Where the *grande-garde* did not have a direct line of sight to the chain of *sentinelles*, or at points where the enemy was most likely to appear, a series of small posts might be placed ahead of the picket. They ordinarily consisted of a *caporal* and four men, concealed in some natural cover, such as behind a hedge or the edge of a woods. Jarry recommended each small post placed one sentry about 15-20 paces in front. Each post must be able to clearly see the *sentinelles* in front of it. The 1792 regulation advised how these posts ought to be withdrawn to the *grande-garde* at nightfall and replaced with *sentinelles volantes* (flying sentries) who would sweep behind the chain in regular patrols.

Sentinelles: These were placed within 300 paces of the *grande-garde*, taking advantage of high ground to have the best view, but taking care to remain hidden, using the banks of ditches, bushes and trees for cover. Each sentinel needed to see the one on his right and left so it was impossible for anyone to pass between them without being challenged. Jarry recommended the *sentinelles* should be doubled, so that one man might go to investigate if they heard or saw something suspicious. If only a single sentinel was posted, the man could do little but shout for help because he was not allowed to leave his post (*sentinelles* were assigned to fixed positions). If there was something to report, the nimblest sentinel would run back to the post and report to the *caporal*; he would then continue back to the *grande-garde* and report to the commanding officer. It was important the same man reported twice, to prevent any confusion or embellishment of the original report. In the event of friendly troops approaching the chain of *sentinelles*, the officer of the *grande-garde* would be called up. There would be a confirmation of passwords, or if the password was unknown because the detachment had been absent for several days, a thorough examination might take place and the detachment brought in with an escort. If there was any uncertainty, the approaching force was to be kept away from the camp until daybreak. Enemy deserters were also to be brought in and escorted under guard to the officer of the piquet. The *sentinelles* and others engaged in the work of the advanced guard were instructed to carry their muskets in the *l'arme au bras* (support arms) position with fixed bayonet. However, Jarry recommended they carried their muskets 'advanced', levelled in their left arm, so the weapon could be faster brought to the shoulder to fire, and so this movement was less likely to be seen. Indeed, sunlight reflecting off a musket barrel and bayonet held aloft could be seen through a spyglass at great distance and betray one's position.

Patrols: Ordinarily formed of two or three men, patrols typically marched two or three hundred paces beyond the chain of *sentinelles* in order to prevent anything coming unawares on the front or flanks. These patrols were usually sent out at daybreak. Larger patrols of four men and a sergeant might be sent out on particular missions, perhaps to approach villages, question the inhabitants about the enemy's patrols and guards. Such a patrol was known as a *découverte*.

The above measures describe the typical system of guarding a camp. These might be modified to allow soldiers to secure fields while foraging.

If a general wished to know where the enemy was, he would order a reconnaissance. Ordinarily, and perhaps increasingly so during the First Empire, reconnoitring was the function of light cavalry, because of their greater mobility and range. Jarry describes a small-scale reconnaissance operation, sending an advanced guard of 100 infantry and 20 dragoons with bread and oats for at least two days. Seven or eight dragoons and a *caporal* would form the van, 700-800 paces in front of the infantry. Two dragoons would maintain line of sight between the van and the main body. At every crossroads the *caporal* of the van would detach a dragoon who would advance 500-600 paces at the fast trop to explore each arm of the crossroads. The infantry would send out a detachment of 12-15 soldiers about 200 paces in front. Seven or eight men and a *caporal* would be detached on both flanks to march parallel to the road about three hundred paces from it. A detachment of dragoons would form the rearguard, ensuring no one came out of hiding once the column had passed. Again, one can imagine the gruelling work performed in these missions, particularly among the flankers covering the wings of the march. These men needed to cover extra distance and perform all their searches without losing any time to the march of the column they were protecting. One imagines many of their manoeuvres were conducted at a light run. Again, the importance of NCOs and subaltern officers directing these searches cannot be stressed too much. Intelligence and energy were required in equal measure.

If the enemy was encountered, the commander of the party would give the order to halt. He was advised to take the nearest piece of high ground or to fall back onto the sides of a road as it passes through a valley or other defile. If there was any chance of the enemy obtaining his flanks, using the cover of a woods, the commander was to detach men on that side to give warning by firing their muskets. Skirmishers would be deployed along the hedgerows and other cover to the front. The commander then had to quickly decide if the force in front of him was a detachment performing a similar mission to his own or was closely followed by the enemy's main force. If the enemy advanced boldly, it likely indicated it was supported in strength. The commander would order the detachment to make a fighting retreat, sending a dragoon back to the main column, if the detachment was believed to be in danger. However, if the opponent also paused and deployed skirmishers, Jarry recommended an attack was made to seize prisoners who might enlighten the commander. Covered by skirmishers who engaged the enemy light troops, a body of infantrymen would rush on the enemy without firing. Jarry pointed out there was an obvious disadvantage of shooting the men one wanted to question.

On the day of battle, Jarry provides some useful advice on the role of light infantry. Their first concern was to cover the deployment of the columns. They achieved this by 'occupying the houses, hedges, hollow ways, and thickets, in front, to the distance of about six or seven hundred paces, according to the proximity of the first artillery batteries of the enemy and the situation of his outposts'.[8] Achieving this might require the light infantry to dislodge the enemy posts, but this should only take place if the general in command ordered it. There was a very real danger of light infantry being committed into a fight without adequate supports being available. If the enemy light troops were entrenched in any way, the commander of the light infantry would look for routes to turn this position; frontal attacks were reserved for

---

8   Jarry, *Instruction Concerning the Duties of Light Infantry in the Field*, p.197.

grenadiers supported by artillery. When the army fought on the defensive, the duty of the light infantry was to identify the ground within musket shot of the main force, and to use cover to mount an obstinate defence, disputing every tree, hedgerow and house. If caught by cavalry in the open, the men were to quickly form a clump, a closed mass, pressed against one another and present bayonets at the horses' nostrils. Faced with such an obstacle, horses would not support nor push each other on. Jarry counselled how the force of a horse could be withstood by seven to eight men standing firmly together. He did not recommend forming squares. There was a great emphasis on maintaining a reserve and Jarry stated the infantry fought 'open and scattered, but without disorder or confusion'.[9] In the aftermath of the battle, the work of light infantry became more fatiguing still. Either a fighting retreat was required to protect the army as it rallied, or a pursuit was required to prevent the enemy from doing the same. The enemy would often be delayed in retreating while in the act of trying to save its artillery. The light infantry ought therefore to attempt to intercept the enemy's guns, setting up ambushes, making as much noise as possible to prevent the enemy attempting to make a stand.

Battlefield Skirmishing – in Search of a Doctrine

The French army of the 1790s and beyond was famous for the use of masses of skirmishers in battle, the so-called 'tirailleurs en grandes bandes'; yet there is surprisingly little written on how their battlefield skirmishers worked. As should now be clear, in order to understand 1792-1815 we must first go back to earlier times and see what went before and how this influenced our period.

One of the most influential military works in the second half of the eighteenth century was by *Maréchal-Général* Maurice, Comte de Saxe, the victor of Fontenoy during the War of the Austrian Succession. His *Mes Rêveries* (My Musings) was originally published posthumously in Amsterdam in 1757. It detailed a system of warfare he believed better suited for the French national character than the rigid, ultra-disciplinarian approach adopted by Prussia. When reading this book we must remember it is an idealised system of warfare, in which de Saxe foretold the use of breach-loading carbines, which did not become available until the following century. However, the book is extremely important in understanding the development of light infantry tactics. It forms something of a foundation stone on which we can build our knowledge.

The following passage is taken from the 1759 English language edition of Saxe's *Reveries*. In the work, Saxe speaks of legions, by which we should read regiments of infantry, formed in 'centuries' and 'half centuries' of light-armed foot and horse, which are actually 70 men strong. The system of skirmishing ahead of a shock action attack appears to be the basis of much of what followed on the subject, so it is worth repeating here in full:

---

9   Jarry, *Instruction Concerning the Duties of Light Infantry in the Field*, p.212.

In the disposition for charging, the light armed foot are to be dispersed along the front, at the distance of an hundred, or from one to two hundred paces, from the legion, and to begin firing when the enemy is about three hundred paces off; which they are to continue, without any word of command, till the enemy approaches within about fifty paces; at which distance, every commanding officer is to order a retreat, taking care to retire gently towards his respective regiment, and in such manner as to be able to fall into the intervals of the battalions by tens; keeping up his fire likewise till he has joined them: by this time the legion must be advancing in charging order, having doubled its ranks, and formed eight deep, while the light-armed foot were skirmishing in front… The whole moving forwards in this order, with a regular and brisk pace, must certainly make a formidable appearance, and greatly intimidate the enemy; for what can they do to oppose the shock? If they would attack the flanks of the centuries, they must necessarily break their battalions before they can be able to do it, which is a very dangerous… How is it to be supposed, that, being only four deep and having been likewise already harassed by the light-armed infantry, they can possibly maintain their ground against troops, which are not only quite fresh, but formed eight deep, with a front at the same time equal to theirs; and which falls impetuously upon them … From hence therefore it appears highly probable, that they must be defeated; and if they trust to flight, they will only expose themselves to more certain destruction: for the moment they turn their backs, the light-armed foot, together with the horse posted in the rear, are to pursue, and will make dreadful havoc amongst them.[10]

Maurice de Saxe was a noted soldier and influential military writer. His descriptions of tirailleur fire protecting the charge of infantry columns reached maturation in the 1790s. (Anne S.K. Brown Military Collection)

Interestingly, Saxe also considered the impact of enemy cavalry on his skirmishers at the beginning of an action:

And although it may be imagined by some, that the enemy's cavalry might disperse my light-armed troops, yet, in the execution, it will be found quite otherwise: for every regiment having but seventy of these irregulars, which will be scattered along its front, and in continual motion, the enemy will have no steady or fixed object to fire at: finding themselves able therefore to do but little, if any execution, and exposed at the same time to a severe fire, they must soon be obliged to retire. But as they will naturally endeavour to remedy this inconvenience, the only effectual method of doing it, will be for them likewise to establish a body of irregulars, trained up to engage mine, and formed upon my principle.[11]

---

10 Saxe, *Reveries*, pp.49-51.
11 Saxe, *Reveries*, p.51.

Here we have the start of something of an arms race. De Saxe concluded that the only realistic way of combatting light troops was for the enemy to have light troops of its own.

There is another interesting passage in de Saxe which helps explain the general French preference for infantry fire by skirmishers. It is on the importance of the rate of fire and improved accuracy which might be achieved by skirmishers:

> Let us suppose them to begin firing at the distance of 300 paces, which is what they must practise at their ordinary exercises, and to continue it, during the space of time necessary for the enemy to march that quantity of ground, which will be from six to seven minutes at least: my irregulars will be able to fire six times in a minute; however, I shall only say five; everyone will therefore have fired thirty times, and consequently the complement belonging to every regiment, at least 2,000 [shots], before the engagement can possibly commence on the side of the enemy. We are, moreover, to consider, that the troops employed on this service, are such as have been incessantly exercised in firing at some very distant mark; which are not drawn up in any close order; and which fire at their own ease and discretion, without being obliged to wait for the word of command, or kept in that constrained attitude, which is customary in the ranks, where the men crowd one another, and prevent their taking a steady aim. I may therefore insist upon it, that a single fire from one of these irregulars perfected in his business, will in general do as much execution, as ten from any other; and if the enemy are drawn up in order of battle, their movement will be so slow, that they must sustain above four or five thousand such fires from every regiment, before they will be able to begin the engagement.[12]

The rate of fire given above does seem too great (Saxe was perhaps speaking of his yet-to-invented breech-loading rifles rather than muzzle-loading muskets). To summarise, we offer the following interpretation. Each infantry battalion ought to have enough skirmishers to cover its frontage. At the time, 700 men was considered sufficient for this. The skirmishers would advance 100-200 paces ahead of the battalion, approximately 60-130 metres (one pace = 2 *pieds* (2 x 32.48 cm = 64.96 cm)). Once dispersed, the skirmishers received no other commands until they were required to retire. Seeking out whatever cover was available, at 300 paces, or at approximately 200 metres from the enemy line, the skirmishers automatically began an independent fire at will (this was known as a '*feu de billebaude*'). Saxe describes the effect of this fire as 'devastating', with a well-trained skirmisher able to deliver ten times the hits of an ordinary soldier, firing from within the ranks. When the enemy reached within 50 paces (approximately 30 metres), the skirmishers were ordered to fall back on the supporting infantry. There were gaps between the battalions which allowed the skirmishers to clear their front. There they would re-form and prepare to give chase to the enemy should it retreat after a shock attack by the line infantry.

---

12 Saxe, *Reveries*, pp.52-53.

LIGHT INFANTRY TACTICS

Other areas of interest raised by de Saxe include the skirmishers' ability to draw enemy fire and attention from the battalion masses manoeuvring behind them. This was particularly the case on an attack against entrenchments, when it was important to reduce enemy fire on the attacking troops. More generally, Saxe believed the light infantry would be 'thoroughly exercised to fire well, and to load briskly'. They would also take advantage of 'hedges, houses, thickets, and all other places' that might be found for them.[13]

As will be seen, Saxe's theories were shared and elaborated on by many other commentators. Jean Colin cites the tactician Bombelles discussing the ordinance of 1754. He believed the French ought to fight with the *arme blanche* without firing. When infantry were required to fire (for instance, when they were behind entrenchments, hedgerows or ditches), he declared the *feu de chasseur* – in other words, independent, aimed fire – was the most murderous, while fire delivered by command only produced a mediocre effect. Independent fire was the type best suited to the French 'genius'.[14]

After the Seven Years War, we see publication of a new ordinance for infantry exercises (20 March 1764). This appears to confirm what Broglie implemented in that conflict and follows the general recommendations of Saxe. Under the chapter concerning firing, we find an early mention of the method of skirmishing:

> [N]othing prevents us, however, every time we march forward or backward, from detaching from the right or the left of each battalion, a half-section to disperse over the entire front, and make a well-aimed *feu de billebaude*, and then retreat at intervals behind the battalion, when we are very close to the enemy.[15]

The same passage then discusses the method of teaching a battalion or a regiment to rally and reform promptly. The method of dispersal is interesting. The troops are sent '*à la paille*' by the beating of the *breloque* drum signal. The literal meaning of this is the troops are sent 'to the straw', but at the time this was also a euphemism for sending a regiment off into a field to perform the necessary functions of nature. In the context of skirmishing, on hearing the breloque the soldiers would be stood at *l'arme au bras* (support arms); they would execute a half turn to the right, then break ranks and disperse. When the commander wished to rally his men, he would have the drummers beat the *rappelle* (recall) at which the men would fall back on their flag bearers and drummers. In order for the companies to reform as speedily as possible, they did not stop too much to look for the correct dressings and position in the line. The commander of the battalion would then dress his line on the flags more correctly.

The provisional instruction for light troops of 1 May 1769 (*Instruction que le Roi a fait expédier pour régler provisoirement l'exercice des troupes-légères*) followed the 1764 regulations. To deploy skirmishers, the drummers would

---

13   Saxe, *Reveries*, pp.320-321.
14   Colin, *L'infanterie au XVIIIe siècle: la tactique*, pp.50-51.
15   *Ordonnance du roi, pour régler l'exercice de l'infanterie, du 20 mars 1764* (Paris: l'Imprimerie Royale, 1764), p.107.

beat *la breloque* and the soldiers would be sent '*à la paille*' – in other words, dispersed as if to gather forage. A few troops would be left behind to mark the alignment of the companies. When the recall was beat on the drums, the infantry and horsemen out skirmishing would 'rally promptly' and maintain absolute silence. No instructions were given for those out skirmishing; there was no advice on forming a chain, or acting in pairs, etc., only the initial instruction to send the men *à la paille* in order to disperse them. What skirmishers did between being dispersed and rallying appears to have been left entirely to their own intelligence and initiative.

In 1770 we find the publication of an influential work by the soldier-tactician Jacques-Antoine-Hippolyte Count de Guibert (1743-1790). An admirer (perhaps even disciple) of Frederick the Great of Prussia, Guibert's *Essai général de tactique* mentions the role of chasseurs and skirmishers. Comparing French light infantry to other contemporary irregular troops (Crimean Tartars, or North African tribesmen), Guibert considered the former identical to line infantry in recruitment, uniform, weaponry and training, and he believed line infantry ought to be trained sufficiently to do the job of both arms. In Guibert's system, column formations were preferred to execute movements with greater speed and security. If the column was threatened by cavalry, tirailleurs ought to be deployed on the flanks and rear where they could shoot at any troopers who came too close. If the enemy cavalry attempted to press home a full charge, the column would close-up with the skirmishers falling back on the front or rear of the column. In an attack by columns, the chasseur companies ought to be scattered in the intervals between them. If the enemy was entrenched, the chasseurs were to draw the enemy fire away from the approaching columns or even penetrate the ramparts if they were poorly defended. The columns marching behind the chasseurs would march at the double until about 200 paces from the enemy (this would be 120 steps per minute), before taking the treble pace (the *pas de course*), then 30 paces from the entrenchment, launching into a full run before seizing it. If the entrenchment was carried, the columns were to deploy into line. The chasseur companies were required to screen this deployment and at the same time quickly seize all advantageous points like ditches, ravines, hedges or houses which might protect them. In the event of the enemy withdrawing, skirmishers ought to maintain a harassing fire and to take prisoners. These tirailleurs had to be supported by battalions in good order who could charge if the enemy attempted to rally. Skirmishers also had an important function against enemy artillery. Guibert wrote: 'The first law of war is not to expose the soldier, when it is unnecessary, then to expose him bluntly, when necessity requires it'.[16] When attacking an enemy position, the columns of infantry ought to take advantage of any natural cover in the ground to remain unseen by enemy artillery. Where this was not possible, the columns ought to move very quickly with scattered companies of chasseurs out front to attract the enemy's attention, to harass the enemy with gunfire, and to direct their fire principally against the gunners of enemy batteries.

---

16   Guibert, *Essai général de tactique*, Vol.1, p.238.

With this in mind let us race ahead to the *Règlement provisoire sur le service de campagne* (provisional field service regulations) of 5 April 1792. This document was published days before the outbreak of the War of the First Coalition and represents the apogee of *ancien régime* military thought. These provisional regulations were reissued in 1808 so were evidently considered to have some validity nearly forty years on since Guibert's essay. How much had the doctrine changed? Not at all. In the chapter titled 'Instruction for the days of combat' we read how to attack a village or entrenched place. There would be a preliminary bombardment; the hedgerows would be cut open to allow the passage of troops; then:

> While the lines are being formed and the batteries are established, the general officers, in order to discover the dispositions and to reduce the effect of the enemy's cannon, will cause the light infantry to march in front of the front of the line; they will have it placed behind the undergrowth, hedges, small ditches or heights, according to the nature of the country, it will be ordered to fire on the enemy batteries, and to endeavour to destroy the gunners. These soldiers will not remain in troops, so as not to draw the cannon on them, but they will separate, taking advantage of anything that can put them under cover, and being attentive to gather together somewhat at the first signal of their officers.[17]

The passage goes on to describe how after the line infantry made its charge, it was to quickly reform and march at the ordinary pace while the pursuit was left to the light infantry and grenadiers who were cautioned not to stray too far from the supporting battalions. We can see how very little this doctrine had changed in the thinking since Guibert's time. Once dispersed the light infantry were left to their own devices to use cover and target enemy gunners during the preliminary phase of an attack. After the shock action was completed, the light infantry then had a follow-up role, helping to exploit advantages, firing on the retreating enemy, seizing prisoners and occupying strong points.

One cannot discuss Guibert without introducing the works of François Jean de Graindorge d'Orgeville, Baron de Mesnil-Durand (1736-1799). Much is written about the merits of the *ordre mince* (the Prussian, thin-line, linear model where firepower was the principle means of fighting) and the *ordre profonde*, as advocated by Mesnil-Durand, which gave preference to shock action breaking the enemy line, because it was believed that trading volleys with an enemy was not the same as driving them away, and prolonged musketry was extremely costly in terms of casualties. Much like Saxe before him, Mesnil-Durand recognised the importance of firepower on the enemy line prior to and following this shock action, and believed trained, specialist light infantrymen were best placed to deliver that fire, working in close support of the advancing infantry battalions.

Mesnil-Durand makes some interesting remarks on light infantry in the opening essay of his 1774 *Fragments de tactique*. Unlike the fusiliers and

---

17   *Règlement provisoire sur le service de campagne du 5 Avril 1792* (Paris: Magimel, 1808), p.129.

grenadiers, who were required to 'march perfectly well in line, to break up & reform the battalions, to form and develop the column, to make large wheels, to execute the various fires with precision, etc.', chasseurs had a different role; therefore it was 'useless for them to waste their time in the battalion on these manoeuvres'.[18] Chasseurs needed to be taught how to be chasseurs. In a colourful description he summarised it thus:

> They must be trained to march together with the greatest lightness; to rally in the blink of an eye; to fight indifferently 2, 3 or 4 in depth, closed up, with open files, or scattered: they must have a better and lighter musket than the others, and that they never regulate their fire with that of the battalion; but make on their own account a regular and continuous fire with the greatest vivacity and without command; and for this fire to be more deadly, they must be continually exercised at target shooting, and if necessary at swallows; in such a way that they succeed in shooting, like those filibusters of yesteryear, who had neither better arms nor better eyes: no troop however able, even entrenched, can withstand their fire; because to shoot from behind a parapet, it is still necessary to show the nose without receiving a bullet in the middle of the forehead.[19]

A number of points are worth exploring here. The importance of target shooting is really emphasised. It makes enormous sense for the chasseur infantrymen to go hunting and to learn marksmanship from shooting at birds in flight (one imagines using *grenaille* – buckshot –rather than ball ammunition) in addition to conventional target shooting. The reference to *filibustiers* is also interesting. These adventurers were the freebooters, pirates or buccaneers of the seventeenth and eighteenth centuries in the West Indies. Mesnil-Durand described the French Canadians as 'heirs to some point' of these filibusters and provided an example of the British blockade of Port-Royal in Acadia (Nova Scotia), where 300 French Canadians fought against 1,800 British soldiers, using skirmishing techniques against a formed battalion.[20] Working onto the flanks and rear of the battalion, the French Canadians were able to deliver very accurate fire causing the British to retreat, while hardly losing a man in the process. This story was told to Mesnil-Durand by an eyewitness, and it clearly made an impression on him.

Elsewhere in this text he states the rather obvious point that chasseurs firing on the enemy line from long range are likely to score hits without losing many men in return. If the enemy retreated from this harassing fire, then it was a victory scored at little cost. If not, then a charge would have to be delivered anyway. He describes this ensuing charge, thus:

> Two battalions charging with a depth of six, or even more, in two columns, will have on their outer flanks the two companies of grenadiers, at the inner flanks the two of chasseurs. These battalions will approach slowly at first, the four small

---

18 François Jean de Graindorge d'Orgeville de Mesnil-Durand, *Fragments de tactique, ou six mémoires précédés d'un discours préliminaire* (Paris: Ant. Jombert, 1774), p.2.
19 Mesnil-Durand, *Fragments de tactique*, p.3.
20 Mesnil-Durand, *Fragments de tactique*, p.3.

troops rushing forward. Immediately they will make a heavy fire, as well as the guns of the regiment which will have followed them and will fire preferably on the enemy cannon. This fire will not fail to cause harm: that of the Grenadiers is very good; that of the Chasseurs, trained as I have asked, much more murderous still. That of the enemy will therefore be much less certain, especially seeing that this is still only a prelude, and that the battalions are marching towards him in good order and with great pace. Moreover the first enemy fire will not be on these still distant battalions, and even when they are closer, it will be badly carried; for the line of Grenadiers, Chasseurs and cannons will mask them, so that he will hardly be able to aim or point at them.[21]

It does not take too much imagination to think ahead to the battles of the French Revolution and see the influence of Mesnil-Durand: the columns of National Guard volunteers and citizen levies massed in attack columns, screened by hordes of skirmishers. It was the perfect system for them. Alas, Mesnil-Durand also detailed how this tactical system could be overcome if the enemy was on higher ground and was therefore able to see over the smoke of the skirmish screen and observe, even fire upon, the columns manoeuvring behind them. Having foretold the tactics of the Revolutionary era, students of Wellington may well wonder if a young Arthur Wellesley had a copy of Mesnil-Durand on his reading list? Troops positioned on higher ground were much less susceptible to these attacks by skirmishers and columns, particularly, as Saxe advised, if they had light troops of their own.

In another striking passage, Mesnil-Durand describes the effect of enemy fire on the skirmish screen. Regardless of how intense the enemy fire was, a screen of 200 men in extended order covering the front of a battalion of 600 men, would only lose a third of a formed line, because the enemy fire was not aimed, but indiscriminately fell on the troops and on the intervals between them. Again, he cited the example of combat in North America, stating: 'good marksmen, low and scattered, not only withstood the fire of a battalion very well, but decimated them in return'.[22] Even if the enemy battalions advanced and fired on the skirmishers, they could maintain a fire while falling back on their oncoming supports. By drawing the enemy fire, they protected the supporting battalions. Now comes the crucial moment. Speaking of the formed enemy troops advancing against a skirmish line falling back on its supports:

> In vain it would give the enemy for a moment the air of victory: it would not surprise our little troops who would be supported very well and closely, nor our battalions who would not have counted on these little troops beating the enemy without them. It would be himself who, if he took this shadow of advantage for something, would be very surprised at the change of decoration that would be presented to him forthwith.[23]

---

21 Mesnil-Durand, *Fragments de tactique*, p.9.
22 Mesnil-Durand, *Fragments de tactique*, p.10.
23 Mesnil-Durand, *Fragments de tactique*, p.11.

Why is this passage so remarkable? Advance from 1774 to 14 June 1800 at about five o'clock in the evening, in the fields to the east of a small hamlet called Marengo in northern Italy. In that battle an action took place which saw a demi-brigade of French light infantry take on an Austrian infantry regiment and a brigade of grenadiers. The battlefield report and campaign journal of *Général de Division* Jean Boudet describes how he and *Général de Division* Desaix bought the French army time to rally for a counterattack, by sending the 9e Légère forwards to 'remind the retreating troops of their courage'.[24] Boudet continues: 'I therefore carried myself forward to within musket range of the enemy's front, which nearing appreciably, obliged me to throw skirmishers forwards, so as to delay their march.' The first Austrian infantry regiment (IR11 Wallis) was thrown back by the 'violent fire' of the skirmishers as it attempted to deploy. The brigade of grenadiers deployed behind and advanced on the 9e's skirmishers, firing as they went. After a time, the supporting battalions of the 9e began to retire back into line with the rest of the French army before commencing a charge. The skirmishers fell back too. Boudet writes: 'I should observe here that this retrograde movement became favourable to us, for in noticing it, the enemy redoubled their hopes, carried forwards with more audacity, and the surprise they felt in seeing themselves then charged, was advantageous to us'. This is exactly what Mesnil-Durand had predicted. The results of this charge are famous. Desaix fell mortally wounded while riding up to the skirmish line to see what was in front of him, and as the advancing battalions charged through the band of skirmishers and crossed bayonets with the Austrian grenadiers, *Général de Brigade* Kellermann executed a charge of heavy cavalry into the Austrian flank to crown the success.

It appears that the crucial element to the success of this attack was exactly the circumstance described by Mesnil-Durand in 1774. The battlefield at Marengo was fairly flat. The Austrian grenadiers could only concentrate their fire on the skirmishers ahead of them. Seeing the skirmishers fall back caused the Austrians to come on more strongly, only then to be surprised to find themselves on the receiving end of a bayonet charge from the formed troops behind the skirmishers. The attack of the 9e Légère at Marengo (which earned them the honorary title *l'Incomparable*) is often cited as a brilliant tactical success. We can now see it really was truly a textbook action.

To conclude this section, at the time of the French Revolution, the employment of skirmishers was widely understood and common in tactical knowledge. Light infantry took the guise of 12 independent battalions of chasseurs à pied and the light companies in each infantry battalion. They were trained in marksmanship and were fleet of foot. On the battlefield their purpose was to screen attacks, seize key points on the battlefield, and target enemy gunners. They generally fought dispersed, using cover where they found it. When attacked they fell back, firing as they went. If the enemy fell back, they pursued. They fired without words of command, as targets

---

24 T.E. Crowdy, 'Marengo and the Journal of General Jean Boudet', *Napoleon Series*, <https://www.napoleon-series.org/military-info/battles/1800/Italy/Marengo/MarengoBoudet.pdf> accessed September 2014.

presented themselves. Once dispersed, the only command ever given to tirailleurs was the instruction to rally. Their basic training taught them how to load and fire their weapons independently, they broke ranks every time they were dismissed. What further instructions did the men need? This very independent approach seems to have begun to change during the wars of the French Revolution, with ever-increasing numbers of soldiers thrown forwards as skirmishers; soldiers with little training in light infantry tactics and unused to fighting independently. These soldiers needed easy systems to help guide them and give them confidence under fire. While a formal regulation was not provided, we do at least find examples of instructions and guides which provide an insight into these skirmishing systems.

The Wars of the Revolution

On 1 January 1791 the chasseur companies in every infantry regiment were abolished. War broke out in April 1792. We can follow the narrative of Duhesme's commentary for the impact of these events:

> At the beginning of this war we had no other light infantry than the twelve battalions of chasseur à pied which were partially drawn (four of these battalions had been formed from the Royal-Italian and Royal-Corsican regiments) from those legions, whose cavalry was, some time before the revolution, organized into regiments of chasseurs à cheval. This number, insufficient for our armies, was not proportionate to the line infantry, considerably increased by the hundreds of battalions of volunteers raised in 1791; for these battalions encamped in line and formed brigades with those of the old regiments. The battalions of these chasseurs à pied who found themselves, in 1792, in the armies of the Rhine, the Centre and the North, united in brigades with the chasseurs à cheval, served in the forward posts. The Austrians initially had more numerous, more skilful and more experienced light troops on foot. Their Tyroleans and their Chasseurs du Loup were known and feared from the first engagements. The panicked terror and the rout of the columns leaving Valenciennes and Lille must be attributed to the skill they had in slipping on the flanks of these columns. Their skirmishers, hidden behind trees, in ditches, ravaged in the first engagements our battalions, which, bravely stood in line, saw themselves decimated without perceiving their enemy. Several good officers were victims of the skill of these good marksmen, who thus had the honour of the first skirmishes. Our pickets were at first opposed to them with little success, because they brought more bravery than intelligence and skill.[25]

It is quite remarkable, saddening in fact, that after all the good reforms, France entered the war woefully unprepared for the inevitable *petite guerre* engagements which followed. Like all good commentators, Duhesme reinforced his point with a human story, one which obviously affected him:

---

25   Duhesme, *Essai sur l'infanterie légère*, pp.108–110.

> A young *caporal* in the Battalion of Saône-et-Loire, my relative, who was placed, being on the picket line, in a clump of trees with about ten men, without any other instruction than that of firing on the enemy, believed he had to die at his post like a Spartan, and, although passed on all sides, he continued to fire in front of him at any chance, until a bullet passed through his chest, and he fell drowning in his blood. Taken prisoner by the Prussians, he was left, as a hopeless case, with some peasants who healed him.[26]

Such was the result of the neglect of training and instruction. The young *caporal* had no understanding of the most basic concept of light infantry warfare, where the object is not to hold fast like a battalion of grenadiers, but to fire and move, forwards or back, and never become cut off by the enemy.

Fortunately for France, at least two its army commanders knew how to do things better. Before they guillotined him on 28 August 1793, *Général de Division* Adam Phillipe, Count de Custine was described by Duhesme as a true advanced-guard general. A veteran of many wars, and sporting a formidable military moustache, Custine bolstered his chasseurs with companies of volunteers drawn from the infantry regiments commanded by handpicked officers chosen for their intelligence. *Général de Division* Charles Dumouriez also trained his soldiers for forward post warfare. Well versed in the combat techniques of the old legions, at Jemappes he threw entire battalions *en tirailleur* supported by light cavalry (a throwback to the tactics of his 1769 instructions for the legions). Duhesme writes how Dumouriez's skirmishers surrounded the Austrian redoubts and threw such a violent hail of lead on the enemy gunners, they were forced to abandon their pieces.

Writing in 1820, *Colonel* Marbot was a supporter of this revolutionary tactic, which he described as 'tirailleurs en grande bande'.[27] Marbot said this type of fighting was largely unknown before the Revolution but had proved itself effective in twenty-five years of fighting. When an enemy was well dug into a formidable position, protected with artillery, a conventional attack would see a quarter of the attacking force knocked out before it could even begin to engage the enemy. Therefore, a whole regiment, or even a brigade would be sent on each flank of the enemy, while another formed in front, out of cannon range threatening the front of the enemy position. At a given signal, the troops on the flanks would advance through the woods and over rocks, working their way into the rear of the enemy position. When in canister range, the advanced would become a fast bayonet attack, at which point the troops formed in front of the position would form column and attack at speed. At this point the defending troops had to decide whether to be cut down at their guns from troops on all sides or flee. Marbot credited the development of this type of attack to the great generals of the early part of the war, Dumouriez, Custine and Dugommier, and wrote the system was later perfected by Massena and Augereau, both of whom became marshals in the First Empire.

---

26 Duhesme, *Essai sur l'infanterie légère*, pp.147-148.
27 Marcellin Marbot, *Remarques critiques sur l'ouvrage de M. le lieutenant-général Rogniat*, pp.60-64

As the National Assembly decreed the formation of new legions, and the compagnies franches were formed into light infantry battalions at the front, the situation stabilised. In fact, by the end of 1793, fighting *en tirailleur* became the prevalent form of combat. This led Duhesme to make perhaps his most memorable statement: 'It can be said with truth that at the end of 1793 the French armies had only light infantry'.[28] This is a bold statement, but unlike the vast majority of commentators on this subject, Duhesme was at least an eyewitness to events (Marbot was a 10-year-old boy when Duhesme went to war). We have seen him in the National Assembly in September 1792, taking his oath before leading his free company to the front. Why should we doubt him? Let us allow him to expand on and qualify this statement fully:

> We never manoeuvred in line; there were then no or few battalions 'embrigaded'; even those of the old regiments hardly knew the School of the Battalion, and it would have been difficult to manoeuvre under the same command four battalions together. The armies were divided into divisions of very unequal strength: they were five thousand or twenty thousand men. The brigades were also more or less strong, composed of one or two regiments of cavalry, or of six or fifteen battalions of infantry; and as there were hardly any colonels, except in the cavalry, the battalion chiefs were the chiefs of their corps, and received orders and instructions directly from the brigadier generals. Each corps thus manoeuvred in isolation; some battalions of volunteers were even formed in two ranks, following the instruction of M. de Noailles [note: following National Guard instructions]. Should they go to the enemy, attacking a post, part was detached en tirailleur, the rest marched in line, then set off in the run without keeping their ranks, leaving the flag behind, which often found itself isolated after the affair, not having ten men for an escort. The first successes had sharpened the courage and intelligence of the soldiers; their officers, brave as themselves, were always with the most advanced, and directed them; one even saw generals at the head of these masses of skirmishers, showing them the points of attack. The Austrians, stunned by this new type of combat, in vain reinforced their light troops by detachments of their heavy infantry; but their skirmishers could not resist the number and the impetuosity of ours, and soon their line, surrounded by a hail of bullets, was forced to fall back. There began the *furia francese*. The clamours and the gunshots redoubled, and the baffled corps, no longer hearing any commands, laid down their arms or fled down the road.[29]

There is much to reflect on in this passage. The key point is perhaps the importance of leadership. All the military writings before 1792 assumed sufficient time would be available to train chasseurs, turning them into expert marksmen and to have them rehearse the techniques of dispersing and rallying. To what extent were the light infantry volunteers in the free companies and legions of 1792 adept at these skills? To what extent were the line troops thrown forwards as skirmishers prepared for this type of combat? Even in the *ancien régime* model, one imagines that skirmishers

---

28 Duhesme, *Essai sur l'infanterie légère*, p.114.
29 Duhesme, *Essai sur l'infanterie légère*, pp.114-116.

were directed to a certain extent by their NCOs and officers. We can see from Duhesme's description the impact of leadership became all the more important as the tactical ability of the troops declined, where even generals found themselves leading the attack from the skirmish screen (one can argue the merits and faults of this). We certainly see what an impetuous force was beginning to emerge from the chaos.

Although a somewhat chaotic and even perhaps a tactic of desperation, the importance of skirmishers on the battlefield in 1792 should never be underestimated. Read the following commentary in Schneider's 1823 work on light infantry:

> [T]his army, improvised in 1792, could not fight by manoeuvres against what was called the first infantry and the best cavalry in the world, against those Prussians trained by the immortal Frederick, or the Austrians who learned from fighting him. Intelligence and courage made up for the defect of science; these imposing masses fought as skirmishers, and each infantryman, gifted with courage and intelligence, thus became a skilful skirmisher, helped to defeat the enemy by attacking him as and where he had to be defeated.[30]

This is an extremely valid point and worth re-emphasizing. Volunteer French skirmishers defeated what was arguably the most sophisticated military machine of the eighteenth century.

After the victory of Fleurus (26 June 1794), Duhesme indicates the situation stabilised for the French. Writing about the Armée de Sambre-et-Meuse, Duhesme states the instruction of the line and light infantry was finally perfected. Daily skirmishes in the advanced guard helped hone their techniques. Duhesme reflected that the army began to learn the science of warfare in a way previously unknown to it. They formed something of a camp of instruction on the heights of Tongre opposite the Meuse and Maestricht. In the mornings, the troops worked on entrenchments and in the evening were exercised in line by their general officers. Even the method of camping became more regular, although tents had been lost by then. The men learned how to build huts from straw. These huts were aligned in a uniform fashion, and muskets were arranged neatly in faggots of arms. This was in sharp contrast to the disorder and confusion previously encountered, where the army's 'camp' resembled something of a 'Tartar's halt'. The advanced guard was placed three or four leagues ahead of the army covering all the points where the enemy might arrive from. Theirs was a defence in depth, with two or three chains of outposts which protected the army and would give two- or three-hours' notice of an enemy attack. The light troops, placed in the defiles and learned to fortify their advanced posts, to better use the advantages of the terrain, to place their advanced guards, to make patrols and reconnoitre.

Duhesme gives several examples where experienced officers left several pelotons in reserve on which the skirmishers might fall back, particularly

---

30   *Colonel* Virgile Schneider, *Résumé des attributions et devoirs de l'infanterie légères en campagne* (Paris: Dondey-Dupré, 1823), pp.8-9.

A pair of line infantry tirailleurs in action, circa 1794. Despite losing their chasseur companies in 1791, line infantry continued to form ad hoc light companies to skirmish and scout for the battalion. (New York Public Library)

when threatened by cavalry. A good example was at the Battle of Schliengen (24 October 1796):

> Throughout the day our light troops were continually at grips with the enemy advanced-guard; they kept watch for the army, and their march was a continual skirmish in which our tirailleurs lost nothing of their superiority. I will only speak of the battle we won there to describe the manner in which our light infantry supported themselves in front of our positions. The division I commanded was spread out on a plateau from Schliengen to Liel, two outlets which the enemy had to try and occupy. The heights opposite us were lined with vines; in particular they dominated the path leading to Schliengen. I had only the 21e Légère in the forward-posts in the vineyards and the defiles. The enemy threw perhaps three times the number of skirmishers to force it to quit its position, without being able to succeed. The *chef de brigade* who commanded it had been careful to form three small reserve corps so well placed that all his tirailleurs, when they were repelled, came back, and that he could support them appropriately to make them resume the offensive. Besides that, he was careful, when he saw them tired or their cartridges were spent, to send a relief to them. This reinforcement made a joint effort with them to retake the line. So the officers were careful to bring back to the battalion the former skirmishers who were resting and stocking themselves with ammunition to return again.[31]

---

31   Duhesme, *Essai sur l'infanterie légère*, pp.139-140.

Writing in 1816, Rogniat also saw the absolute necessity of supporting *grandes bandes* of tirailleurs with formed troops, even in woodland. Rogniat cited an example from the battle of Hohenlinden in 1800 where *Général de Division* Moreau needed to eject Austrian skirmishers from a strategically important wood. Rather than attempting to march whole battalions through the woods in support of his counterattack, Moreau sent infantry in isolated companies, each of which formed a small column, better able to penetrate the woods and help drive away enemy skirmishers. These formed supports bolstered the line of skirmishers and deterred enemy counterattacks.[32]

From the above examples, we can conclude the light infantry demi-brigades which were formed in 1794 were made up of soldiers who had endured an incredible baptism of fire and had improvised then consolidated their tactics over the first two years of the war. The tactics of desperation which saw hordes of skirmishers thrown into battle actually proved very successful. France's opponents could not match the volume of light troops thrown at them. Every skirmish was a lesson learned – and they learned fast. While patriotism and revolutionary fervour no doubt had some importance, the key to the success in light infantry warfare appears to have been good and dynamic leadership by young, aspirational officers, hungry for promotion. Service in the advanced-guard offered opportunities for independent command, even for a junior officer, and even modest successes paved the way for unprecedented levels of promotion in those early years.

Schèrer's Instructions of 1793

Much of our focus has been on the main theatre of operations, in the campaigns against the Austrians and Prussians along France's north and eastern frontiers and in the Low Countries. We should also remember French troops were engaged in a brutal insurgency conflict in the Vendée in western France, also along the Pyrenees against Spain and the Alps against the army of the King of Sardinia. This last conflict is particularly interesting, but is not so well known, as there is little focus on the theatre until the arrival of a certain Napoleon Bonaparte in 1796. Having annexed Savoy, Monaco and the County of Nice in 1792, the French found themselves engaged in a difficult war for control of the Alps. As one can imagine, this type of mountain warfare was particularly suited to light infantry.

In Colin's study *Tactique et Discipline* we find an instruction composed by *Général de Division* Schèrer towards the end of 1793. Schèrer would eventually be replaced by Bonaparte and his stewardship of the army and campaigns have been somewhat eclipsed by the illustrious successor. However, Schèrer laid some groundwork for his success, and he is particularly interesting for students of irregular warfare, not only for the following instruction, but for founding an excellent intelligence service in the Armée d'Italie, one which

---

32 Rogniat, *Considérations sur l'art de la guerre*, p.101.

LIGHT INFANTRY TACTICS

Bonaparte reaped many rewards from.[33] Schèrer recognised that when the French broke through the barrier of the Alps, warfare in the Italian plains would require a completely different approach to that taken in the mountains. The infantry would have to learn to withstand cavalry attacks in the plain. He described how the line infantry would need to fight in three ranks, unless it was fighting in entrenchments, when the third rank could be used as a reserve. Of the light infantry he wrote the following:

> The light infantry will usually be formed in two ranks, because this arm is mainly intended to fight by fire, to move with agility, sometimes even without order and scattered, to trouble the enemy on its flanks and its rear, it is natural that its usual order of battle is less deep than that of the line infantry, intended to act mainly by impulse, and to fight the enemy with the bayonet … I will assume that a division made up of four demi-brigades of the line and a light one is tasked with attacking part of the enemy line head-on. Here is the order of attack that I would prescribe: the three battalions of light infantry would move forward, formed in two ranks, the files distant from each other at two or three paces apart, so as to that these three battalions cover the front of the twelve battalions of the division and mask its movements …

Schèrer then describes how the 12 battalions would each form in column of divisions (i.e. two company frontage) with three paces gap between each division, before continuing:[34]

> When the signal of the attack is given, the light infantry battalions, 150 paces from the front of the columns, will march briskly forward making a sustained fire. The twelve columns will follow them at the manoeuvring pace, and when the light infantry has reached 50 paces from the enemy's front, they will stop; if the enemy stands firm, it will redouble its fire; the closed columns *en masse* by divisions, the first charging the bayonet, the other three with arms held aloft, will double the pace while maintaining their order of depth, will pass through the light infantry, which will place itself into pelotons in the intervals, and will rush with the bayonet on the enemy line.[35]

This instruction is particularly interesting in the way it describes the light infantry demi-brigade fighting in open order, rather than dispersed. There is a significant difference between these two formations. In this system, the skirmishers are standing in two ranks, but with two or three paces (approximately one metre) between each file. The officers and NCOs would presumably have taken their normal positions in the rank of the file closers behind their respective companies, and all three battalions would have stepped off at the same time. This is a much more regulated screen – a chain of

---

33 See Alain Montarras, *Le General Bonaparte et le Renseignement: la periode Revolutionnaire et la Première Campagne d'Italie* (Paris: SPM, 2014), pp.62-65.
34 Jean Colin, *La tactique et la discipline dans les armées de la Révolution* (Paris: Chapelot et Cie, 1902), p.LXXIV.
35 Colin, *La tactique et la discipline*, p.LXXIV.

skirmishers rather than dispersed individuals taking pot shots at the enemy. To have executed such a formation would have required commands, to open the files, to fire while advancing. One would also expect higher casualties from this type of attack than if the men were freely dispersed and able to use cover. So why the change? It is perhaps the scale of the battles. In his essay on chasseurs, Mesnil-Durand speaks of two battalions with their grenadier and chasseur companies attached. In using a full demi-brigade, Schèrer is committing 24 companies of chasseurs to the skirmish screen (assuming the three companies of carabiniers were detached or in reserve). Perhaps it was too difficult to coordinate so many skirmishers without them retaining something of a formation? By using open order, and only in two ranks, the casualties would be far fewer than a unit in close order. Here every two files occupied the same space as five files in closed order.

We should also remark on the infantry columns formed behind the skirmish screen. The official French tactical doctrine followed the model of manoeuvring in column, then deploying to fight in line. The above description shows a different reality. With so many skirmishers deployed and firing on the enemy, there was no need for the columns to deploy. Schèrer's columns had a two-company frontage, and were four companies deep, with an interval of just three paces between each company. These columns were a dense mass of men, 12 ranks deep, moving very quickly, enough to plough through an enemy line through sheer weight of numbers, much like an ancient phalanx.

There is a great deal of sense in Schèrer's instruction. There were real risks in attempting to deploy a column under fire, or even engaging in a toe-to-toe fusillade with the enemy (*Général de Brigade* Rivaud had such a firefight at Marengo and lost half his line in 15 minutes). Duhesme cautioned against attempting to deploy a closed column under enemy fire, giving an example of the 20e Ligne being broken by enemy fire while attempting this at the Battle of Caldiero in 1805. Perhaps predicting what his

Adam-Philip de Custine (1740-1793) had an excellent knowledge of *petite-guerre* operations. Here he studies his maps, watched over by a *representant du people* – a type of political commissar sent to enforce the bidding of revolutionary politicians. A former noble, Custine was guillotined on 28 August 1793. (New York Public Library)

colleagues might attempt at Waterloo, with columns formed of battalions in line, he also cautioned against attempting to advance in line over too great a distance, as natural obstacles would cause the wings to turn and the centre to break. For Duhesme the only way to break a determined enemy line, was, like Schèrer, Mesnil-Durand and Saxe, through the combination of skirmish fire and the impulse of a charge of battalions in closed column. Duhesme admitted that a skirmish screen presented less muskets than a battalion drawn up in line, but the fire of trained skirmishers was 'surer and more deadly'. Duhesme then provided some metrics to support his argument:

> Thus, having 800 skirmishers over the extent of my line, I would have 2,400 musket shots per minute; for, although the soldier can fire 5 or 6 rounds per minute, mine will fire only three in order to be able to march and better aim. The lines will always take ten minutes to approach; multiplying 2,400 rounds by ten, it will happen that before approaching the enemy, we will have fired 24,000 musket shots, and even if only a tenth have struck, it is already 2,400 men killed or wounded on a line of 8 to 10,000 men, and, for sure, the collective fire of enemy battalions could not wreak so much havoc on the narrow fronts of our masses and on the scattered men.[36]

Of course, the above tactics are negated if the skirmishers are unable to get close enough to the enemy line because it had sufficient skirmishers to protect it. Indeed, Marbot observed that two opposing lines of '*tirailleurs de bataille*' (as he called them), often 'mutually neutralised one another and decided nothing',[37] Success in those situations would have to be bought at a very high cost.

Guyard's Éclaireur Instructions, Year XIII

During the 1790s we have seen a change in the employment of skirmishers, from small numbers of independent chasseurs using cover, to great, open-order chains screening the front of a division. Trained to load and fire at will, these skirmishers needed no other formal instructions than 'disperse' and 'rally'. Everything else was left to their own intelligence and that of the NCOs and subaltern officers accompanying them. At the other end of the scale, we have Schèrer's great chain of skirmishers, which in effect worked on the same lines as a battalion, albeit in two ranks, with open intervals between each file. What about in the circumstances where just a few skirmishers were needed to go forwards ahead of each company? How did commanders release their men?

In 1804/1805 (Year XIII) an *Instruction pour le service et les manouvres de l'infanterie légère en campagne* was published. The author was a *Colonel* Guyard (latterly of the 1er Régiment de Hussards à Pied) who complained there was not the least instruction for the service and manoeuvres of light

---

36   Duhesme, *Essai sur l'infanterie légère*, pp.449-450.
37   Marbot, *Remarques critiques sur l'ouvrage de M. le lieutenant-général Rogniat*, p.59.

Excellent study by Godfrey Engelmann (1788-1839) showing voltigeurs firing from behind a wall. Note how the officer with cape is retrieving cartridges stored in a sash around his waist. (Anne S.K. Brown Military Collection)

troops on campaign.[38] Why, he asked, did light infantry commanders waste their time teaching their soldiers the complex evolutions of the line, but not the manner of dispersing as skirmishers, and rallying? As an officer serving on the advanced posts in 1792, he maintained a journal and these notes formed the basis of his work.

In Guyard's system, the peloton appears to be formed only in two ranks. This is not to say pelotons habitually formed in two ranks, but in Guyard's opinion, if light infantry were fighting behind a hedge, or in woods, or ditches, behind a house, the third rank was useless. If a chief wanted to disperse one or two files of each peloton to fire in front or to scout his flanks, he would command: *Éclaireurs, en avant! – Marche!* At the command to march, the file leads would continue forwards in a straight direction. The men in the second rank would fan out, arriving level with the file leads. They would occupy a front equal to the platoon behind them. They ought never to be more than 100 toises (fathoms – 200 yards) in front of their battalion, but at least 50 or 60 toises (100-120 yards) away. These éclaireurs needed a command structure to support them. According to Guyard the number of NCOs and officers detached ought to depend on the number of men deployed. If two files per peloton were sent forwards (four men, or 32 per battalion), the first

---

38   Guyard, *Instruction pour le service et les manoeuvres de l'infanterie légère, en campagne*, p.52.

sergent and *caporal* of the first peloton and the last *sergent* and *caporal* of the eighth peloton would go forwards with the éclaireurs. The *lieutenant* of the first peloton would march forwards and take command of this detachment. If four files were sent out from each peloton, the first captain and *sous-lieutenant* would also go forwards. The advantage of Guyard's system is a battalion could cover its front, without losing a whole company, and the deployment of skirmishers would be more quickly achieved.

There are some other interesting remarks in Guyard's essay. Light infantry, Guyard observed, almost always fought as skirmishers, and only maintained a battalion mass in order to protect the retreat of these skirmishers. Every time a troop marched on the enemy it ought to be preceded and followed by an advanced-guard and a rearguard. When the troop marched in line, it required éclaireurs in front, or flanqueurs when in column. The 'carpenters' of the corps should always march at the head of the column, with their axes in their holsters and carbines slung over their right shoulder (pioneer troops existed but were not officially recognised until 1808). These pioneer troops were required at the front in order to remove obstacles and cut through hedges. He remarked that men sent out to scout the march of the column sometimes took their freedom from the ranks as an opportunity to pillage. This resulted in the column blundering into an enemy. He also recommended light infantrymen adopt short hair, in the *à la Titus* fashion, and that they should have their heads shaved every month to avoid not being able to see for having hair in their eyes. This might appear a bizarre suggestion, but it was common to cut the soldier's fringe along the line of the brow and tie back the remainder of the hair in a queue behind. On campaign it is easy to imagine hair continued to grow and may well have fallen into a soldier's eye while firing.

'French tirailleurs' (1800) by Jan Anthonie Langendijk (1780-1818). The black leather cross belt is interesting, as are the blue culottes which are too short for his light infantry gaiters. (Anne S.K. Brown Military Collection)

It was essential light infantry received training, particularly in firing at targets. From this training the soldier would learn how to adjust his shot and not to use too much powder. Without these basic skills experience had shown that for every 100,000 shots fired by skirmishers, barely 100 struck their target. The result of this was to embolden the enemy. Guyard provides advice on aiming, either at units (aim for the cross belts) or when aiming at individuals (use a tree or hedge to steady the musket), and even against moving horsemen (fire five or six lignes in front of the target). He goes so far as to recommend sentinels make themselves a rest or fork for their musket from branches of a tree. Guyard states that carabiniers ought never to provide éclaireurs but remain formed up and ready to march on any point indicated. In other words, they acted as grenadiers rather than the marksmen they were originally intended to be. During a retreat the colours were to be conducted by the carabiniers.

We ought to consider the importance of Guyard for a moment. Was his publication a vanity project, or was it widely consulted? Remarkably we find Guyard's work reappearing in an 1816 work called *Examen de la legislation sur le service en campagne et dans les place assiégés*. The foreword of this book explains how on 17 August 1811 the Duc de Feltre (Clarke) charged two general officers and a superior officer to review the field service regulations which had been re-issued to the Armée d'Allemagne in 1809. The superior officer turned out to be none other than Bardin. He did not publish his findings until 1816, but he must have considered Guyard's work relevant, because he inserted the document in its entirety.[39]

Duhesme's Voltigeur Instructions, 1805

In his 1814 essay on the light infantry, Duhesme explained the key instructions he provided to the voltigeur companies of his division in the Italian campaign of 1805. These instructions are particularly valuable because they were actually issued to troops at the outset of a campaign. Duhesme suggested there were two main tactical situations to consider. The first is where voltigeurs are protecting the regiment, throwing a protective screen across its front and flanks. The second is when the regiment was on the offensive. In the first case, notice how few voltigeurs are actually deployed as skirmishers at any one time:

> When a regiment of three battalions is in line, the first battalion has its company of voltigeurs to the right, a hundred or a hundred and fifty paces away, the third to its left, at the same distance, and the second behind or in front of him, at, about the same distance. This first arrangement announces to the two companies of the wings, that they must guard the flanks of the corps, and to that of the centre, that they must scout the front and furnish the advanced sentinels on the march; they usually manoeuvre in two ranks. If the regiment forms a column to the enemy, the column will be preceded and flanked throughout the march by these three companies, which will march, that of the centre in line and that of the wings by file, always taking the heights, and detaching a third of their men as skirmishers. If the column passes into order of line, the company of the left puts itself into a run,

---

39 Étienne-Alexandre Bardin, *Examen de la législation sur le service en campagne et dans les place assiégés* (Paris: Magimel, 1816).

LIGHT INFANTRY TACTICS

to take up, in the direction of the new line, a position suitable for guaranteeing the left, and thus covering the movement; that on the right is similarly carried at the most favourable point for guarding the right; that of the centre is put in line in front of the front: all detach some skirmishers in the avenues by which one can approach the line. One makes, for the closed column, the same arrangements as for the other. If the column is deployed, and it is to fire, which in war the approach of the enemy would indicate, the company of the centre and its skirmishers will run out to the flank where one most fears being turned, in order to protect it more effectively, either by redoubling the number of skirmishers, or by placing itself en potence (if necessary), always taking up the advantages of the terrain.

If we form attack columns by battalions, which announces that we want to march on the enemy, it is then that the captains of the voltigeurs will launch almost everyone en tirailleur to join the terrible effect of the masses and at the pas de charge, the deadliest effect of a hail of well-directed musket shots. However, they will do well to keep with them a third or a quarter of their men to serve as a rallying point in case one is pushed back, especially by cavalry charges. We will sometimes assume this case; then, at a whistle or other signal from the captain, the skirmishers must return to him and form themselves first in a somewhat convex line, and then retreat behind the battalions through their intervals. If the battalions retreat in a checkerboard, the companies of voltigeurs will move and extend so as to cover them, the skirmishers also support each other by their fire in their retreat; that the one who withdraws while loading his weapon is supported by another who faces forwards, his weapon made ready, and does not fire until the other has stopped in his turn, In the column against the cavalry, the voltigeurs facing almost everywhere, will protect the preliminary manoeuvres with their fire, and then will retreat at the run by the angles or other intervals, into the centre, where they will reform to make sorties.[40]

From the single stripe on the forearm, this appears to be a voltigeur sergeant. The plume is yellow with a green base. The epaulettes are also green. (New York Public Library)

There many discussion points in the above passage. Did voltigeur *capitaines* have whistles? They do not appear to have been widely used, do not appear in contemporary iconography, and they are hardly mentioned in Bardin's dictionary, although he does state whistles were used at the beginning of the war of the Revolution by Belgian corps in French service.[41] Perhaps Duhesme saw this and thought

---

40 Duhesme, *Essai sur l'infanterie légère*, pp.214-218.
41 Bardin, *Dictionnaire de l'armée de terre*, Vol.3, p.1632.

FRENCH LIGHT INFANTRY 1784-1815

it an idea worth adopting; but this does not mean it was adopted. Another interesting aside is the idea of two soldiers covering one another: one loaded and ready to fire while the other loads. Elsewhere in his book, Duhesme confirms this 'buddy system'. Giving advice on managing a skirmish line he writes:

> In dispersing them along the front of the line, their officers will ensure that they are all at about the same level, that some are not too far ahead, others not too far back; that they always stay, as long as possible, vis-à-vis the gaps of which they have left, to regain them more easily: they will be united two by two, and these two companions, who should always be two friends, must not leave each other, in order to help each other when they are pressed; one should always keep his fire and only release his shot when the other has reloaded. As the lines approach each other, the skirmishers will unmask the front of the closed columns of the first line and will close up vis-à-vis the gaps, which they will then enter, placing themselves in one rank with their reserve, which, being in two ranks, will commence a well sustained fire by file, but in which the soldier will be recommended to shoot more accurately than with speed. It is understood that the skirmishers should never cease fire, but on the contrary redouble it.[42]

'Embuscade de Voltigeurs' by Félicie Fournier (1828). Voltigeurs sheltering behind a wall fire on the flank of enemy cavalry charging at infantry. (Anne S.K. Brown Military Collection)

---

42 Duhesme, *Essai sur l'infanterie légère*, p.306.

LIGHT INFANTRY TACTICS

It might well have been the case that a type of buddy system had always been in place. However, none of the previous writers mention this, and instead emphasise how skirmishers were dispersed and unformed. However, returning to Schèrer's instructions, in which light infantry fought in two ranks, in extended order (that is, three paces between each file), the men of the first and second rank in effect formed a pair. Duhesme also recommends the voltigeurs were formed in two ranks only, and therefore a similar pairing is naturally created. In the latter quotation the idea the two companions ought always to be friends, is intriguing, perhaps invoking the spirit of the Theban band of antiquity, or more prosaically, an instruction for the two men to form a strong bond between one another. What is different about Duhesme's instruction and the one issued by Schèrer in the decade before, is the importance of a formed reserve, even when closely supported by attack columns. Duhesme had learned the importance of this in his early campaigns and reinforces that message throughout his work. The reserve acted as both a rallying point and also allowed the commander to send men to reinforce a particular part of the screen, or to replace soldiers who had expended their ammunition.

A chasseur takes aim. Firing with the feet apart was a natural stance for a marksman, but this was impossible when formed in ranks. (New York Public Library)

Morand's Instructions, 1811

Perhaps the best surviving example of an instruction for skirmishers was penned in 1811 by *Général de Division* Charles Antoine Morand (1771-1835). Entitled *Manoeuvres pour une compagnie de Tirailleurs ou de Flanquers*, this instruction was discovered by the Russians in *Maréchal* Davout's captured correspondence in 1812 and published in 1903. Before looking at the instructions in detail, we must understand why they came into being. In a letter dated Hamburg, 16 October 1811, Davout wrote to Morand confirming he had received a copy of the instruction and was so impressed by it, he had sent it to all his generals commanding infantry divisions (Friant, Gudin, Dessaix, Compans and Barbanègre) with an instruction for them to spend the rest of the autumn exercising their troops in this manner. Davout recommended at first mixing the men of the centre companies with the voltigeurs, because the latter already knew the manoeuvres and could pass

121

on their knowledge. Writing to the other generals listed, Davout confirmed it was recognised as harmful to take a certain number of men from each company to act as skirmishers and flankers and that it was preferable to take whole companies instead. As elite companies, voltigeurs could not be expected to do this service so it was important the centre companies knew what to do in their absence, and that there was a uniform system for performing this service. The training was to be given to all regiments, light and line alike.

This is a very interesting development. Firstly, Davout indicates voltigeurs were not always able to perform these services. The letter says it was because they were an elite company, but this probably meant the elite companies were often detached, rather than this type of service was 'beneath' an elite company. Davout also clearly thought light infantry centre companies also needed training in these arts, which suggests they were deficient in this regard. Moreover, it confirms that in 1811 there was no formal system of skirmishing which had been adopted by the Grande Armée, which is in itself extraordinary after 19 years of warfare. The remark about a preference for whole companies to be used rather than taking men from each company is also interesting. This indicates battalions had previously detached a number of files or called for volunteers to quit the ranks and skirmish. This practice (described by Guyard above) presumably created gaps in the line, which had a detrimental effect on alignment.

The system of covering the front of a line and scouting for the head of a column worked as follows. We must first assume the voltigeurs and grenadiers are already detached (hence the need for a centre company to skirmish) and that only the four centre companies remain. At full strength, each company would be composed of forty-three files in three ranks. The deployed company would march 200 paces from the battalion, and take up a position at the centre of the space which had to be covered, for example, in front of the centre of a battalion in line. On arrival at this point, the *capitaine* would divide his company into three sections (ordinarily a company formed two sections). The *capitaine* would command the centre section

A group of voltigeurs wearing the 1812-pattern uniform, but with the earlier style plumes. These were replaced with short aigrettes in the 1812 regulations. (New York Public Library)

(with the *sergent-major*, two *sergents*, two *caporaux* and two *tambours/cornets*), with the *lieutenant* taking the right section and the *sous-lieutenant* taking the left. The centre section would act as the reserve while the flank sections marched 100 paces to the right and left respectively. The *lieutenant* would then order the first two ranks of the right section to face left, with the *sous-lieutenant* ordering his two first ranks to face right. At the command: *à 15 pas par file, prenez vos distances – marche* (at 15 paces per file, take up your distances – march) the deployed men would march, leaving a 15-pace gap between each file until they met in the middle. Once deployed the skirmishers would advance forwards by 100 paces. The third rank of the left and right sections remained in reserve with a *sergent*, the *caporaux* and (if available) a *tambour* or *cornet*.

The instructions on deployment were followed by some qualifying remarks:

> These reserves must provide replacements for the line, reinforcements at the points strongly attacked, and for the officers some escorts who must never leave them: these escorts, intended to serve as points of rallying and retreating, must be at least 6 men. If a non-commissioned officer is detached to carry orders to the skirmishers, he must always be accompanied by a fusilier drawn from the reserves…
>
> Skirmishers must always march two together in order to help each other. They should only fire one after the other, so that one of them always remains loaded. As far as possible, the line of skirmishers covering the head of a column should describe a portion of a circle of which the head of the column would be the centre. … During the retreat of a line, the cordon of skirmishers must remain parallel to the line. The captain of the company of skirmishers must never lose sight of the column or the lineage: in the event that the ground prevents him from seeing it, he will place non-commissioned officers or soldiers, so as to keep him informed of all his movements. The pace of the skirmishers is adjusted to that of the column or the line.[43]

We can therefore see the cordon of skirmishers is 300 paces from the line, (approximately 200 metres) with the supports 200 paces (approximately 130 metres) from the line. The remark on protecting a column is also interesting. In order to prevent the skirmish cordon from becoming too extended, it would form something of an arc, pivoted at the centre of the front of the column. If the company had to cover the flank of a column, the same dispositions would be made, with the reserves marching in file. However, if both flanks of a column had to be protected, the *capitaine* would send the flanking sections off to cover each wing at a distance of 100 paces and move with his reserve to the flank he felt was most exposed. The *capitaine* would maintain contact with the other section by sending a *sergent* with a verbal message, or through use of signals (drums/cornet).

---

43   Kharkevich, *Outgoing correspondence of Marshal Davout*, pp.7-8.

Group of light infantry from 1797 after Alfred de Marbot. The central figure is portrayed as a voltigeur with a green, yellow-tipped plume, and a yellow collar. The carabinier would have been better portrayed in a mirliton cap. (New York Public Library)

All of the above is quite formulaic, but one must remember this system is a training tool to teach centre companies a different manner of fighting. Experienced skirmishers may have had greater flexibility in how they acted. Indeed, a greater level of dynamism is indicated in several ensuing paragraphs of remarks which are repeated here in full:

Not only will the skirmishers have to be trained at the ordinary and accelerated pace; but also at the *pas de course*, because it is at the run that they will have to make the changes of direction, of front, and in a charge to take a wood, a village, and all the positions where they have no fear of being charged by cavalry. It is also at the run that they will have to fall back on the reserve pelotons, when the cavalry presents themselves to charge them, unless they can hide in a hole, a ditch, a hedge from which they can shoot on them safely. In the plains, the tirailleurs will have to march in the greatest order with calm, coolness and silence; spare their firing and be ready to carry out any movements that will be ordered. When one places tirailleurs on the flanks at the head or tail of a column marching in an open plain, one must remember not only to be informed of the movements of the enemy; but also to keep the infantry and cavalry skirmishers far enough away so that their bases do not reach the column. If the plain is furrowed with ravines and presents small hills or clumps of wood, the skirmishers will have to enter the ravines to search them, climb the summits of hills, turn and search the clumps of trees. As they advance, the officers of tirailleurs must pay their attention not only to the movements of the enemy and their troops, but also to observe carefully the form of the ground which they can use in the event of a combat of firm footing or retreat, and notice the resources available, either to build little bridges or to retreat in haste, if necessary.[44]

The instruction also provided detailed advice on attacking villages or entrenchments and formations against cavalry. With villages, the main tactic was to cause the enemy to stretch this line and to weaken his centre. This was achieved by sending skirmishers out onto the enemy's flank. Once the centre was weakened, the reserve was to attack the centre and overwhelm the defenders. Key to success was the soldiers being used to running from the centre to the flanks and rear of the enemy, and back to the centre again. When faced with cavalry the reserves of skirmishers ought to be prepared to form a circle the moment they were threatened. If the reserve was in a column, it would close up and the files face outwards.

One of the most interesting aspects of the instruction is it details the various horn and drum calls which were used by skirmishers. These were existing signals but given a new meaning in the context of skirmishing. In a nice piece of continuity back to the 1760s, the signal to deploy remained '*la Breloque*', the call to send out working parties, or as we might put it in modern parlance: 'go to work'. The signals are shown in Table 22. Relatively few signals were required, and there is no signal for 'open fire' or 'cease fire'. This means skirmishers were still entrusted with using their intelligence to open fire as targets became available. The original instruction concluded with a caution relating to these signals. There was a risk of drum signals for the columns and the skirmishers being confused. To that end, the drum majors were cautioned not to use '*la Grenadière*' or '*les trois coups de charge*' when the column was flanked by skirmishers.

Table 22. Tirailleur Signals, 1811

Movement	*Sonneries* (calls)	*Batteries* (Drum rolls)
Déployement (Deploy)	*Déployement*	*La Breloque*
Ralliement (Rally)	*Ralliement*	*Aux Drapeaux*
Retraite (Retreat)	*Retraite*	*Retraite*
Marcher à droite (right)	*Marche à droite*	*La Grenadière*
Marche à gauche (left)	*Marche à gauche*	*Les trois coups de charge**
La charge (charge)	*La charge*	*La charge*
Marche lente (slow)	*Pas ordinaire*	*Pas ordinaire*
Marche précipitée (fast)	*Marche précipitée*	*La Charge avec roulement***
S'arrêter (stop)	*La Messe*	*La Messe*

Notes:
* Three beats of 'the charge'.
** 'The charge' with a drum roll.

---

44   Kharkevich, *Outgoing correspondence of Marshal Davout*, pp.9-10.

While Morand's instructions are the most complete available today, the system of deploying the cordon of skirmishers appears somewhat over-engineered, with the need to divide the peloton into three sections, rather than two, and with the formulaic method of deploying the cordon, which may not have been practical as the unit began to suffer from wartime attrition. We can compare it to another system which was only documented after the Napoleonic Wars, but which has some similarities. *Colonel* Virgile Schneider (1779-1847) published his *Résumé des attributions et devoirs de l'infanterie légères en campagne* in 1823. As colonel of the 1820s-vintage 20e Légère, the work contains one of the most practical methods of deploying a company *en tirailleur*, and although the work was published after the wars, we know Schneider was a Napoleonic veteran, graduating from the École Polytechnique in 1799 and ending the wars as an aide to *Général de Division* Rapp. In the preface of his work Schneider explains his project to develop a set of instructions for light infantry. After submitting his findings to the Minister of War and the Inspector Generals of Infantry, Schneider was told: 'We have not yet decided on the specialty of our instruction'.[45] This at least confirms that no one system of skirmishing survived the Napoleonic Wars.

In Schneider's system the company charged with skirmishing ahead of a battalion advances out at the accelerated pace in the required direction for 100 paces and then halts (Schneider was less fixated with deployment distances and writes that the officer in charge ought to decide where to deploy his troops, taking advantage of the best cover). With the third rank remaining in reserve, the first two ranks advance 15 paces. Two files are withdrawn from the left flank to form the *lieutenant*'s escort, and two from the right to form the *sous-lieutenant*'s escort. A *caporal* joined each of these escorts. The *capitaine* remained with the reserve, which formed itself into two ranks. The *capitaine* then ordered the first section of the front two ranks to face right, and the second section to face left. The files marched at the accelerated pace, opening a 15-pace distance between one another. The *capitaine* then ordered the skirmishers to advance by 100 paces, the soldiers in the second rank remaining three paces behind the first rank, and three paces to the left of their file leader (this presumably allowed each soldier a clear space in which to load and aim). Each pair of skirmishers worked as a team, with the front-rank firing first, and the second rank holding fire until his file leader had reloaded.

Published the year before Schneider's book, another interesting work is the *Instruction pour les voltigeurs de l'infanterie légère et de ligne*. This is another important document, because the author based it on instructions issued in 1815 by *Général de Division* Reille to the voltigeurs of his II Corps at the beginning of the Waterloo campaign. The author of this work is Eugène-Alexandre Husson (1786-1868), a graduate of the Fontainebleau École Militaire and light infantry officer, who saw service in the 25e Légère and then was a *capitaine adjudant-major* in the 1er Légère in 1815, serving in

---

45   Schneider, *Résumé des attributions et devoirs de l'infanterie légères en campagne*, p.10.

Reille's corps. Husson was wounded at Waterloo, then finally quit the army in 1822, publishing several useful guides.

Husson's instruction cautioned troop commanders never to deploy more than two thirds of their force and to always retain one third in reserve. After marching a few paces in the direction which needed to be covered by skirmishers, the *capitaine* would send forwards one section from the peloton (first or second) and instruct the *lieutenant* to form it rapidly into two ranks. At the command, '*Formez la ligne des tirailleurs*' the section would face left and right of the central file and then march, '*Prenez vos distances*' at 10 or 15 paces. Meanwhile the *capitaine* would send ten men from the section which had not deployed as a reserve to the right of the cordon, and ten more to the left. These reserves would be command by the *lieutenants* and stand 30-40 paces behind the centre of each wing of the cordon. The *capitaine* would detach more men if he felt the cordon was menaced at any particular point. While this instruction reflects at least what Reille's troops did in 1815, Husson found it might take too long to perform in certain situations. A simpler version was for the deployed section to advance, form into two ranks and to gradually fan out as they advanced until the 15-pace distance was achieved. An interesting detail in this instruction was that during a retreat, the second rank would run back 50 paces, then halt, covering the withdrawal of the front rank. Soldiers were encouraged to learn how to load their weapons while marching. Tirailleurs were to practice firing and loading while knelt and laying down. Husson states (somewhat controversially) that tirailleurs ought not to fire with their bayonets attached, because it made aiming the weapon fatiguing and caused the firer to aim low. It took just five seconds to fix the bayonet to the musket if the need arose. One of the most interesting aspects of the instruction is it tells the tirailleur to choose a target, to ensure it is in range and to fire by preference against officers directing the movements, on groups (in other words, there was a better chance of hitting them than firing at individuals) and principally on persons on horseback who appeared to be 'behind the curtain of the enemy skirmishers' observing the course of events.[46] The deliberate targeting of enemy officers by French skirmishers is confirmed elsewhere and is important to stress. In 1820, *Colonel* Marcellin Marbot wrote:

> In the campaigns of 1806 and 1807, our skirmishers did so much harm to the enemy, by killing their officers whom they distinguished by their uniforms, that the two great northern powers then at war with us, ordered all their army officers to wear the uniform of a simple soldier without any kind of apparent distinction, hoping that by this disguise they would escape the eye and the muskets of our skirmishers, who, before this change, in spite of the enemy skirmishers, chose the officers in the midst of their troop and shot them one after the other.[47]

---

46   Eugène-Alexandre Husson, *Instruction pour les voltigeurs de l'infanterie légère et de ligne* (Paris: Cordier, 1822), p.21.
47   Marbot, *Remarques critiques sur l'ouvrage de M. le lieutenant-général Rogniat*, pp.53-54.

The effect of targeted fire was also noted by Charles Stevens, who was on the receiving end of it during the British expedition to Holland in 1799:

> I was Lieutenant of grenadiers at the time I was wounded, but had command of a battalion company; and Ensign Favell and myself, who were the only officers of that company, were both wounded before a single man of the company were hit, which was a proof that we were picked off by the French riflemen, numbers of which they had in front of their Army; we, unfortunately, had but few in front ours ... The riflemen the enemy had gave them a great advantage over us, and in consequence of their having so many light troops many of our officers were picked off by them, and the proportion of killed and wounded officers was very great.[48]

Returning to Husson's voltigeur instructions, he again repeated the maxim that skirmishers in the same file ought never to fire at the same time, but for one of them to remain loaded. When fighting in covered ground, the skirmish line should only advance eight to 10 paces between each shot, or 15 to 20 paces while in open ground.

There are obvious similarities between Morand's 1811 instruction and the two published after the wars. The advantage of Reille's instruction and the one described by Schneider is the way the skirmish cordon flows out from the centre, rather than having to march off to a point and then deploy inwards. If Husson considered Reille's instruction too slow, others must have felt the same about Morand's instruction. Despite this, there are enough similarities for us to draw some conclusions about skirmishing in the latter part of the First Empire. Voltigeur and chasseur companies still formed themselves in three ranks. If skirmishers were required, one company was detached to provide these skirmishers. One third of the men were to remain in reserve, but close enough to the skirmishers to support them. The cordon or chain of skirmishers can be described as an open order line, in two ranks, often with a 15-pace interval between files. The *lieutenants* commanded each wing of the chain, and each had a small, formed escort with them acting as a close reserve and a rallying point. The *capitaine* and the signallers remained with the main reserve. Lastly the soldiers in the cordon acted in pairs, one of them always ready to fire while the other loaded.

Voltigeurs Réunis

There are numerous references to voltigeurs being detached from their battalions to form ad-hoc advanced-guard units or elite battalions known as voltigeurs réunis (reunited or assembled voltigeurs). Title 1 of the infantry regulations of 1 August 1791 states that when both battalions of a regiment exercised together, the grenadier companies would unite to form two pelotons. The grenadiers of the second battalion stood on the left of the grenadiers of the first battalion. Title 3, Article 7 of the field service regulations of 1792,

---

48   Stevens, *Reminiscences of my military life*, pp.10-11.

Detail of a dynamic illustration by Charlet depicting light infantry in an assault. Note the cape worn by the officer bottom right. (Collection Yves Martin)

states that when a brigade of infantry is formed, the companies of grenadiers of each brigade will be united into a battalion, which will be commanded by a superior officer chosen by the général de brigade. When the voltigeurs were created, this same principal sometimes appears to have been applied to them, with them being brigaded together and serving outside of the battalion.

Writing on St Helena, Napoleon mused on various aspects of military science. Discussing the ideal composition of a battalion, he expressed preference for regiments being formed of two battalions, each of six companies, including one of grenadiers and one of voltigeurs (as per the 1808 formation). When such a regiment was assembled it would in fact form three battalions, each four companies strong, with the grenadiers and voltigeurs uniting to form an elite battalion.[49] While this was a theoretical paper, it is perhaps based on some evidence, and sure enough we find examples of these special units being formed, and even 'grenadier divisions' formed of elite companies from various regiments.

Perhaps the most famous of these united units were the Grenadiers of Oudinot. In order to create more active battalions, the grenadier/carabinier and voltigeur companies of the third, depot, battalions of light and line infantry regiments serving in the Grande Armée were gathered together and formed into battalions of 'grenadiers'. The term grenadier was applied, even though the battalions were 50 percent composed of voltigeurs. By January 1807 the

---

49 Napoleon I, *Correspondance*, Vol. XXXI, p.505.

grenadier division was composed of four brigades, each of two regiments, each formed of two battalions of six companies. The only exception was the fourth brigade which was composed of one small battalion of two carabinier and one voltigeur companies, plus an artillery and engineer component.

There was some interesting analysis made on the role of light infantry during the First Empire by Waldor de Heusch in his *Étude sur l'infanterie légères*. Heusch provides numerous examples of voltigeurs and grenadiers réunis, some of which are highlighted here an examples.[50] During the Jena campaign, Ney formed elite battalions to reinforce an advanced guard composed of a brigade of light cavalry and a regiment of light infantry. At Eylau, Friant's division (part of Davout's III Corps) used some companies of light infantry to occupy a village, while all the voltigeur companies in his division were united to form 'a cloud of skirmishers'. In 1809 Friant used a combination of light infantry and united voltigeur companies to counter Austrian light troops. At Wagram on 4 July 1809 Massena united 1,500 voltigeurs to either swim or be boated across the Danube to drive away Austrian skirmishers. In Spain, *Maréchal* Lannes instructed *Général de Brigade* Wathier to form a detachment of 600 horse and 1,200 voltigeurs to put down Spanish insurgents disrupting the siege of Saragossa in January 1808. Later that month Lannes formed a detachment of all the voltigeurs from the 14e and 44e de Ligne from Grandjean's division. These were preceded by a detachment of sapeurs. Suchet did similar at the assault of Tarragona in 1811, reuniting grenadiers and voltigeurs under the command of an engineer officer.[51]

Speaking of the war in Spain, Girod de l'Ain's excellent memoirs provide several first-hand examples of his time as a subaltern voltigeur officer. In his early operations in Spain around Balmaseda in October 1808, Girod describes in detail how his voltigeur company worked with others as they approached the main Spanish army:

> We soon encountered the enemy. My company, which formed the vanguard, was reinforced by the other companies of voltigeurs of the regiment and of the 24e de Ligne. We formed a strong line of skirmishers with them, and we fought all day without the order to advance.[52]

The next passage is from the Battle of Somosierra on 30 November 1808. It is remarkable for describing in detail the work of an advanced-guard. To protect the road to Madrid the Spanish had taken up a formidable position in the mountains, cutting the main road and establishing artillery batteries. Girod describes the approach of the French army:

> Battalions of voltigeurs were formed, and I found myself right up in the vanguard. On the 30th, in the morning, a thick fog completely hid us from the view of the

---

50 Heusch, *Étude sur l'infanterie légères*, pp.25-34.
51 Heusch, *Étude sur l'infanterie légères*, p.35.
52 Girod de l'Ain, *Dix ans de mes souvenirs militaires de 1805 à 1815* (Paris: J. Dumaine, 1873), p.96.

enemy's positions. We set out, however, marching up the main road, and the emperor came, in person, to stand for some time between the two sections of my company which formed the head of the vanguard. We had already entered into the mountain defile when, suddenly, we received on our left flank a discharge of musketry which warned us of the presence of the enemy. A few skirmishers were immediately detached on this side, who, through the fog, climbed the mountain, and found an abandoned bivouac at a short distance. The column continued its march forward on the main road, and soon we reached a large ditch, which the enemy had dug across the defile. We immediately started to fill it, and, at once, I was sent forward at the head of 50 voltigeurs with orders to dispose them en tirailleur on the left of the high road and to push everything that I could find before me. I soon met the enemy's skirmishers, and for some time I chased them from rock to rock, when suddenly the fog rose like an opera curtain and let me see at short distance the Spanish lines crowning a fine position from which I was separated only by a shallow ravine. My little troop, as soon as it was sighted, was judged worthy of a general discharge of the enemy's first line, and I instantly lost nine men, killed and wounded; I myself had two balls through my coat.[53]

After Somosierra, the army marched on Madrid. On 3 December, Napoleon announced an assault of the city would begin at 10 o'clock. Girod again found himself at the front:

Battalions of voltigeurs were again formed and charged with the attack. Each of these battalions provided a vanguard of 100 men, commanded by three officers chosen by rank of seniority... I was designated as the sous-lieutenant to be part of the vanguard. At the appointed hour, we approached the city under the protection of some cannons; some other corps attacked at the same time on different points. The fire of the enemy was most lively; in order to suffer less, we dispersed ourselves en tirailleur and, at the run and in the midst of canister fire, we gained a small, isolated house within pistol range of the city walls; our intention was to lodge ourselves there, from thence to shoot the enemy gunners at their pieces.[54]

This is the classic function of light infantry. Having used open order to lessen the impact of artillery fire on them – notice also how the voltigeur battalion itself forms a vanguard, selecting the three most senior officers to command it – the voltigeurs ran to the shelter of a house to open fire on these gunners to reduce the fire on the columns which advanced behind them. Girod tells us, they dug through the rear wall of the house with their bayonets and entered the building, using furniture to create a fire-step along the outer wall. Their fusillade began to have an effect on the gunners, who turned their guns on the house 'which made a horrible ravage there: the demolitions, the splinters of stone and wood, as well as the cannon balls and the canister shot, caused us telling losses.' When the French guns succeeded in demolishing part of the city walls, Girod noticed the Spanish artillery fire 'suddenly slowed'. With a cry of *vive l'empereur*, the voltigeurs rushed in a crowd to the foot of the

---

53 Girod de l'Ain, *Dix ans de mes souvenirs militaires*, pp.101-102.
54 Girod de l'Ain, *Dix ans de mes souvenirs militaires*, pp.104-106.

walls. Girod climbed up on the shoulders of one of his men to climb into the breach. A bitter combat ensued, with the voltigeurs fighting as skirmishers. On one occasion *Général de Brigade* Labruyère arrived on the scene and admonished the *capitaine* of voltigeurs for fighting *en tirailleur*. Much to everyone's surprise, Labruyère ordered the *capitaine* to form his men into line:

> Nothing could have been worse imagined than this disposition: it was, indeed, obvious that the enemy's fire converging in the same direction, would be more deadly, while our soldiers, being unable, in ranks, to load and to aim at will, would do much less harm to their adversaries. Our captain had the firmness to resist the orders of his general. The latter, seized by a fit of anger, took a non-commissioned officer by the arm and planted him in the middle of the street, commanding that they should line up; but the voltigeurs, feeling how much their captain was in the right, continued to fight as skirmishers. The general, rebuffed, withdrew and sought elsewhere officers and soldiers more docile.[55]

Girod claims the general had a death wish after been rebuked by the emperor earlier in the campaign. He eventually led a charge on a barricade only to fall dead pierced by several balls. What is most interesting about the above remark is the voltigeurs' reluctance to fight in line and to lose the ability to load and fire at will. We also see intelligence from the voltigeur *capitaine* who is equally reluctant to expose his men needlessly to enemy fire. One last reflection on the above passages: notice how the battalions of voltigeurs are only formed on the day of battle, or as otherwise required. They are not permanently formed.

When one thinks about the subject, the practice of habitually creating elite battalions of voltigeurs makes no sense at all. All the way through this narrative we have seen how infantry battalions required their own complement of light troops for various functions. By removing the voltigeurs from their parent battalions, the latter still required close support and would have needed to draw off éclaireurs, flankers and tirailleurs from the four remaining fusilier companies. The practice appears more nonsensical still when each division habitually had at least one regiment of light infantry quite capable of any task set for the voltigeurs. It demonstrates how in the First Empire the tactical distinction between line and light infantry regiments was increasingly forgotten. Indeed, it is often said voltigeurs were the only true light infantry in this period. Duhesme bemoaned the practise. Writing about the employment of voltigeurs as shock troops in sieges he hit upon the crux of the problem with combined battalions:

> It is a great mistake to unite companies of voltigeurs to form elite battalions; in no case, should these short men, whose first merit is to be skilful and nimble in skirmishing outside the ranks, like the Velites outside the Roman Maniples, be united to fight *en masse* and often hand to hand; above all, they should not be

---

55   Girod de l'Ain, *Dix ans de mes souvenirs militaires*, pp.107.

employed in sieges in the same service as grenadiers, who need strength and size to drive in a line with the bayonet, escalade walls and climb a breach.[56]

There is some truth in Duhesme's statement: voltigeurs, the shortest men in the army, with shortened muskets, acting as close combat shock troops. This type of fighting was previously anathema to light infantry.

On Rifles

One interesting discussion point in this subject is why the French did not widely adopt the use of the rifled carbine during the Napoleonic wars? We saw experiments with the chasseur-carabiniers in 1788, but this type of infantry did not survive beyond the reforms of 1791. They were resurrected in 1793, but these 'riflemen' were no more equipped with rifles than the grenadiers carried grenades. Two useful commentators on the subject are Duhesme and Bardin, both of whom commanded light infantry during the early years of the war. We also have some interesting data from an 1814 trial subsequently published by Gassendi in 1819. These sources combined clearly explain why France never seriously pursued the use of rifles in this period.

When the French first encountered the Austrian rifle-armed Jägers in 1792, they were so surprised by the losses inflicted, their natural response was to equip their own free corps in imitation of the enemy light infantry. Duhesme complained not enough rifles were produced and so only the elite carabinier companies received them. In the Parliamentary Archives we see an extract of a letter from the National Assembly's *comité militaire* to Robert Paté, Premier Controller of the arms manufacturer at Charleville, dated 12 June 1792. It speaks of some rifled carbines at Charmont which were provided by the entrepreneurs of Liege, which had been paid for but not delivered to the armies. At the same time these carbines were ordered from Liege, the Minister of War placed a separate order for an additional 10,000 rifles at Charleville. This order was then downgraded to a provisional one for 5,000 rifles, even though the arms workers were practically unemployed at the time. It is unclear how many rifles, if any, were actually produced. A month later the *Archives Parliamentaires* record an instruction from 23 July 1792 authorising the generals of the Armée du Rhin to requisition part of store of rifles which had been manufactured in Liege under the direction of a Mr. Gorden in 1790. These were presumably the same ones at Charmont mentioned previously. Of these it is worth mentioning M. Bezançon of the *comité militaire* wrote: 'I will say only a word about the carbines which are in Charlemont and which were supplied by the entrepreneurs of Liege: it is that I cannot be convinced we will ever make use of these weapons for any troops for any reason'.[57] Alas he did not state what his reservations were, but perhaps Duhesme can enlighten us.

---

56 Girod de l'Ain, *Dix ans de mes souvenirs militaires*, p.462.
57 Mavidal and Laurent, *Archives Parlementaires*, Vol.L, pp.619-620.

FRENCH LIGHT INFANTRY 1784-1815

Despite his self-professed lack of experience in warfare, at the end of 1792 Duhesme reveals he was already uncomfortable with the use of rifles: 'I could not help feeling,' he wrote, 'that the soldier, armed with only a projectile weapon, would only be good at fighting from afar, and that he would never approach his enemy with as much courage and assurance as if, with the same weapon, he found, with the means of striking him from afar, the advantage of fighting him closely'.[58] Duhesme complained about the lack of a bayonet for the weapons. He had the rifles equipped with a straight, double-bladed sword. This was attached to the side of the barrel by means of a spring. Although the weapon looked threatening enough, Duhesme concluded it was next to useless. Some of his carabiniers had the long blades snapped by their adversary's musket. Bardin concurred, complaining about the difficulty of fixing a bayonet, which in any case was absolutely useless, except for the soldiers in the front rank.[59] These complaints demonstrate the French clearly misunderstood the advantages of a rifle – in other words, fighting at distance. We must remember, at the same time rifles were being experimented with in 1792, people were seriously discussing reintroducing the pike as an infantry weapon. The French were seemingly obsessed with shock action combat.

The lack of an effective bayonet was only the tip of the problem. The rifling effect was created by scoring the inside of the weapon's barrel with seven, equidistant and pronounced, spiral grooves. This caused an inequality of calibre, which meant the soldiers could not use standard musket balls. According to Bardin, there were as many bullet moulds as there were weapons. Duhesme confirms this. He complained that after a hard day's fighting, his exhausted carabiniers had to sit about all night melting lead to make their own ammunition for the following day.

The loading of the weapon was complicated and potentially dangerous. It required specialist equipment, powder horns and even a mallet. Rifle shooters used a *calpin* (patch) to separate the ball from the gunpowder charge and to fill the rifled grooves to ensure the pressurized hot gases did not pass around the ball. If this occurred, the charge would lose its force and range. The *calpin* was usually a piece of ticking, leather, or round cut fabric impregnated with a fatty substance, 20-22 millimetres in diameter. It was placed over the muzzle of the rifle barrel before the ball was inserted. The ball was then rammed home and became wrapped in the *calpin* as it was forced down the barrel. Hammering with a mallet was usually required to ensure the patch and ball was pushed all the way down the barrel, sealing

Chasseurs de Byron (1792) showing some of the specialist equipment required to load a rifled carbine, including mallet. The utensil in his right hand is described as a steel *fourchine*, a type of forked rest and bayonet. The *chapeau* is a variation of the cocked hat. (New York Public Library)

---

58 Duhesme, *Essai sur l'infanterie légère*, pp.221-222.
59 Bardin, Étienne-Alexandre, *Dictionnaire de l'armée de terre*, Vol.2, pp.1021-1025.

the grooves, but also deforming the ball in the process. If there was a gap between the charge and the patch, serious accidents could occur. When fired, the hot gases would rapidly expand in the gap between the powder and the patch and ball. This expansion of gases could be sufficient to cause the barrel to burst. Given the slowness of this operation, Duhesme wrote that his carabiniers often omitted to use the patch and rammed the ball without it. While this was a much faster means of loading, it resulted in a dramatic loss of range and accuracy, and so the standard infantry musket, with its longer barrel (and bayonet), was much preferred.

Other complications included the need to block the priming touchhole with a pin or feather tube during loading, and the requirement for fine powder for the priming charge (this powder was held in the powder horn). If the weapon was fouled, it was difficult to clean, and if the rifle would not fire because the powder had become damp, one could not remove the ball and gunpowder charge with a worm attached to the ramrod, as one could with the infantry musket. With all these factors combined, it is no wonder Duhesme wrote: 'After a few months, the carabiniers requested the standard issue musket with its bayonet and were much better off in the fighting'.[60] Bardin concurs: 'Some excellent carabinier companies were found, so to speak, sometimes disarmed, for the very reason that they had rifles'.[61]

Compare the above descriptions of rifles to the performance of the infantry musket, as written by Napoleon himself:

> The infantry musket with its bayonet is the most perfect weapon invented by man. Its point-blank range is 60 *toises* (116 metres). It is very murderous at 120 *toises* (233 m) and strikes at 300 (584 m). Its cartridge only weighs only 1 ounce and a fifth (36.7 grams). It can shoot sixty in a row without interruption in the space of thirty minutes, or even in twenty minutes, without needing to be washed.[62]

In spite of all the disadvantages outlined above, rifles made something of a comeback under Napoleon. During the Consulate the French arms factories

Study of a light infantry carabinier 'instructor' by Charlet. The baggy *pantalons* with a stripe down the outer seam are a common feature in Charlet's work. (Collection Yves Martin)

---

60 Duhesme, *Essai sur l'infanterie légère*, p.222.
61 Bardin, Étienne-Alexandre, *Dictionnaire de l'armée de terre*, Vol.2, pp.1022.
62 Napoleon I, *Correspondance*, Vol. XXXI, p.430.

FRENCH LIGHT INFANTRY 1784-1815

and especially that of Versailles, made some rifles. These weapons were given to the voltigeur officers and NCOs when these companies were formed. The thinking behind this is explained by Napoleon himself, writing while in exile on Saint-Helena:

The Tyroleans have rifles of this kind; the light troops of the king of Württemberg were armed with more or less similar carbines with bayonets; but this weapon is difficult to load, it clogs easily, it is badly balanced. We cannot arm whole companies with them, because these companies could not perform two rank firing, would not have bayonets; they would be destroyed. But it is possible without any inconvenience to distribute a few rifles to each company of voltigeurs, provided they are of the calibre of twenty bullets to the pound: it is good to battle the enemy from as far away as he battles you. We could also advantageously arm with these rifles some bourgeois companies, in a fortress, to shoot from behind the walls.[63]

This is an interesting rationale. Each company of voltigeurs might have three officers, four *sergents*, a *sergent-major* and a *fourrier* (*caporaux* would not have been armed with carbines because they fought in the ranks): in other words, nine rifles per company. Just because the officers and NCOs were required to carry them, they could easily have passed the weapons to marksmen to shoot on a particular target if the need arose, particularly, as Napoleon alludes, if someone was firing on the company from long range with rifles of their own. During the First Empire carbines were also carried by subaltern officers in the light infantry regiments. A letter by Jean-Baptiste Cardron from 1810 declared he was armed to the teeth in Spain: 'That is to say, a large sabre, two pistols and a carbine. These are the arms of all the officers that make war with these brigands'.[64] Part of the reason for so many weapons is because they fought dispersed and officers therefore needed an array of close protection weapons.

Of these 'voltigeur rifles' we even have some data on their performance. In terms of accuracy, a study made in Magdeburg in March 1814 by two artillery officers firing carbines and muskets at a horizontal trajectory at 70 *toises* from the target produced the following results (as published by Gassendi). Twenty shots from a marksman armed with an infantry musket would hit the target five times. In that same time, 16 carbine shots would hit the target 13 times. The rifle sounds very favourable in these terms. However,

Sergent of voltigeurs of the 31e Ligne by Zimmermann. As per regulations, the sergeant is armed with a short, rifled carbine. (Anne S.K. Brown Military Collection)

---

63 Napoleon I, *Correspondance*, Vol. XXXI, p.432.
64 T.E. Crowdy, *Incomparable: Napoleon's 9th Light Infantry Regiment* (Oxford: Osprey Publishing, 2012), p.300.

both Gassendi and Bardin discounted the improved accuracy. Bardin stated in battlefield conditions, the rate of fire of a rifle was more like twelve to fifteen shots an hour. Gassendi admitted the weapon was difficult to use and considered the weapon one of 'patient and phlegmatic assassins' better suited for use in fortresses.[65]

To conclude then, while other nations did adopt the rifled carbine, the weapon appears not to have suited France's needs and national temperament. It is somewhat telling to read Duhesme's main complaint about the weapon (the advantages of which were to enable aimed shots at greater range) was its lack of a functional bayonet. This clearly demonstrates a misunderstanding of the purpose of weapon. All the way through this study we have seen the two most important characteristics of the French tirailleurs were speed of movement and rate of fire. A rifle enabled neither of these.

A voltigeur officer carrying a rifled carbine. His cartridges are stuffed into a sash around his waist. By Nicolas-Toussaint Charlet (1792-1845). (Collection Yves Martin)

---

65 Gassendi, *Aide-mémoire à l'usage des officiers d'artillerie de France*, Vol.2, p.566.

5

Uniforms and Equipment

It is often said light infantry differed only from the line by the cut of the uniform. Why then, with repeated opportunities to standardise the design of uniforms, did the French supply light infantry a different uniform to their cousins in the line? Even the famous Bardin uniform introduced in 1812 coloured the uniforms differently. Was it a recognition that the different services provided by light infantry required a different type of uniform, or was it merely a fashion statement on the part of light infantrymen? With the short *habit-veste* introduced in the 1790s, the light infantry uniform was perhaps more functional, but it was also more cutting-edge, introducing elements of light cavalry fashion, and introducing items such as the shako and trousers long before they reached the line. Most of all, any study of the uniforms of the French Revolution and Napoleonic Era, before the advent of photography, is usually a voyage into the unknown. On one side there are regulations and on the other, reality. Did regulations copy what already existed, or did they drive innovation? Did finances and time permit the manufacture, or were the men often dressed in what they found. It is a frustrating subject, where it is difficult to be certain of anything without supporting evidence from regimental inspection reports. Our mental image of these soldiers is often corrupted by inexact iconography and anachronisms introduced by later artists, who often drew and painted an idealised image of soldiery to inspire and please their own audiences.

Light Infantry Uniforms 1784-1791

At the creation of the chasseur regiments in 1784, the French army wore a uniform described by the regulation of 21 February 1779. This regulation replaced the one of 31 May 1776, which was described in the opening preamble of the 1779 document as inconvenient and too expensive. The infantry uniform consisted of a *habit à la Françoise* (French coat – a dig at the Prussian style coat of 1776) in *drap* (woollen broadcloth), a *veste* (jacket or smallcoat) in the same material with collar and cuffs in the distinctive colour, a sleeveless *gilet* of woollen stuff and *culottes* (breeches) made of *tricot* (a soft, flexible woollen fabric), lined with *toile* (linen cloth). On 10 August 1784 a provisional regulation detailed the uniform to be worn by the chasseurs. This described the chasseurs as wearing a dark green habit with a *chamois* (buff) *veste* and *culottes*, very much in the design of the standard infantry uniform, although the regulation did not specify a *gilet*.

Each regiment had a distinctive colour worn on the *habit's* lapels and cuffs. The coat had white metal buttons stamped with a *cors de chasse* (hunting horn) insignia with the regimental number in the centre. The distinctive colours were listed:

- Chasseurs des Alpes, lapels and cuffs in scarlet, with white buttons
- Chasseurs des Pyrénées, lapels and cuffs in crimson, with white buttons
- Chasseurs des Vôsges, lapels and cuffs in lemon-yellow, with white buttons
- Chasseurs des Cévennes, lapels and cuffs in buff, with white buttons
- Chasseurs des Gévaudan, lapels and cuffs in 'aurore', with white buttons
- Chasseurs des Ardennes, lapels and cuffs in white, with white buttons

Note, eighteenth century '*aurore*' (literally, dawn) is variously described as yellow with a light red tone or golden yellow.

A member of the Troupes Provinciaux and a chasseur à pied in 1785. The lemon-coloured lapels and cuffs suggest the chasseur belongs to the Chasseurs des Vôsges. However, the casque helmet was not adopted until 1791. (New York Public Library)

On the left shoulder of the *habit*, the soldiers wore an epaulette with a white fringe and background, with a lozenge design in the regimental colour. On the right shoulder was a contre-epaulette of the same dark green cloth as the habit. The drummers wore a *habit* of blue *drap* decorated with the King's Livery. Their cuffs and lapels were in the regiment's distinctive colour. The men wore a white neck collar and a pair of long, over-the-knee gaiters, which were worn with garters and buckles. There was one pair of white gaiters for parade and two black pairs for general service. They wore a felt bicorn hat, with a tuft of green wool and a white cockade. Their equipment consisted of a cartridge pouch on a shoulder belt, and a belt for carrying a short, grenadier sabre, a calfskin haversack and a cloth distributions sack. The uniform of the officers was the same, except made from better quality cloth and silvered buttons.

On 1 October 1786 a more detailed regulation appeared. This regulation began to move the chasseur uniform away from the design worn by line infantry. The coat was dark green, lined in the distinctive colour of the regiment. The turnbacks were decorated with a green *cors de chasse* (hunting horn) badge made from the same material as the coat. Other than the removal of the pockets marked on the coattails, the habit remained similar to the

FRENCH LIGHT INFANTRY 1784-1815

Chasseur à Pied from the Chasseurs des Alpes in 1786. Watercolour by Charles Lyall (1899). (Anne S.K. Brown Military Collection.)

line regiments. The *veste* was also green, with no distinctive markings on the collar or cuffs. *Bas-officiers* (an archaic term for *sergents*) and chasseurs à cheval were allowed a surtout and gilet in the style of heavy cavalry and dragoons. The text is ambiguous if this included all *bas-officiers* or just those belonging to the cavalry arm.

The *culottes* were made into *pantalons*, a style of trouser cut just four inches above the ankle. These were dark green. The external seam of the *pantalon* was open up to the level where the garter strap was previously worn (that is, just below the knee), from where it was closed by six small buttons. The gaiters were black and cut to resemble Hungarian hussar boots. They were closed by 10 small buttons with a double buttonhole at the top, which fastened the gaiters to one of the buttons on the trouser leg. The neck collar was changed from white to black. The chasseurs wore a felt bicorn hat trimmed with a border of black wool. In wartime, an iron skull piece was to be fitted on the outside of the hat for protection against sword cuts. A flat, round, woollen disk or 'lentil' was worn above the cockade, with company distinguishing colours: 1st - scarlet, 2nd - sky-blue, 3rd - pink, 4th - marigold. The men were also be issued with a forage cap or *bonnet de police* cut in the dragoon style and made from the material recycled from old coats.

The officers' uniform again differed only in the quality of cloth and by the buttons which were silvered. The officers' hats were bordered with a black silk tape, without plumes or feathers, absolutely identical to the design to those of the chasseurs, trimmed above the cockade, by a lentil in goat hair, of the company identifying colour, and with staff officers wearing white. Chasseur officers were allowed green cloth cloaks with a silver lace-edged collar, faced in serge with the regiment's distinctive colour. Instead of gaiters, the officers wore boots in the Hungarian style. Officers were also equipped with a musket and a cartridge pouch in addition to a sabre as well as a *giberne* (cartridge box). The sabre was decorated by a knot or cord mixed with threads of gold & fire coloured silk. Lastly, all chasseur à pied officers, including those of the état-major, were to wear a gilded copper *hausse-col* (gorget) ornamented with a silver medallion in the middle bearing the King's Arms.

At this point, a few words of summary are required. The 1786 introduced the concept that chasseurs à pied could wear a uniform in the style of light cavalry. Although there was no doubt an element of fashion in the design of the gaiters, short gaiters were far more practical for men required to move with flexibility, to run, to kneel behind cover and other perform other

UNIFORMS AND EQUIPMENT

movements which tight, long infantry gaiters restricted (these were designed to keep soldiers upright and rigid). The adoption of the dark green trousers and jacket was evidently a move towards a rudimentary camouflage, and there was a certain poetry in the adoption of silver and white metal: silver representing moonlight (the moon goddess was the ancient deity of hunting), rather than the golden colour of sunlight. These distinctions served as a template for the classic uniform to come.

The ordinance of 17 March 1788 creating the Chasseurs du Roussillon mentions they will be armed, equipped and uniformed like the other light infantry battalions, but with several differences 'relative to the national costume of the inhabitants of the mountains and valleys of Roussillon'. Likewise the Chasseurs-Cantabres would wear national costume of the Cantabrians and other inhabitants of the Pyrenees. Alas, the precise nature of these regional variations is not recorded. Subsequent to this, on 27 May 1790, the chasseur battalions adopted the tricolour cockade in favour of the Bourbon white cockade the army had previously worn.

By the spring of 1791 the chasseur uniform had changed again. The army replaced the elegant, but militarily-useless, felt *chapeau* with the *casque*. This was a boiled leather helmet which was blackened, varnished, and topped by a horsehair (bearskin for officers) crest running from the peak to the back of the helmet. There was a band or turban running around the base of the helmet, approximately six centimetres high and made of fake leopard or panther skin (probably painted goatskin). A leather visor covered the eyes and a brass band crossed over the leather from ear-to-ear, protecting the skull from sabre cuts. Unlike the *chapeau*, which sometimes fell off while conducting arms drill, this elaborate piece of headgear did at least offer the wearer protection from the elements and while in battle. The *casque* had a tricolour cockade affixed to the left side, with a small leather loop for holding a white plume tipped in the distinctive colour. A provisional instruction of 1 April 1791 permitted infantrymen to wear the plume on parade days, otherwise replacing it with a woollen, egg-shaped *houpe*.

This same instruction recorded chasseurs wore a white woollen cloth gilet and it modified the habit slightly, with three buttonholes beneath the left lapel removed. The lapels were dark green, piped in the distinctive colour. The cuff received a cuff-flap with three buttonholes, fastened by three small

An officer of the Régiment de Chasseurs des Pyrénées in 1786, after Alfred de Marbot (1830). (New York Public Library)

FRENCH LIGHT INFANTRY 1784-1815

uniform buttons. The distinctive colours for each light infantry battalion were as follows:

- 1er Bataillon - scarlet collar, cuffs and cuff flaps
- 2e Bataillon - scarlet cuffs only
- 3e Bataillon - scarlet collar and cuff flaps only
- 4e Bataillon - daffodil collar, cuffs and cuff flaps
- 5e Bataillon - daffodil cuffs only
- 6e Bataillon - daffodil collar and cuff flaps only
- 7e Bataillon - pink collar, cuffs and cuff flaps
- 8e Bataillon - pink cuffs only
- 9e Bataillon - pink collar and cuff flaps only
- 10e Bataillon - crimson collar, cuffs and cuff flaps
- 11e Bataillon - crimson cuffs only
- 12e Bataillon - crimson collar and cuff flaps only
- 13e Bataillon - white collar, cuffs and cuff flaps
- 14e Bataillon - white cuffs only

One inclusion in the provisional instruction is the mention of epaulettes and the *bonnet à poil* bearskin caps for infantry grenadiers and the carabiniers. This is somewhat confusing, because a separate instruction of the same day supressed the carabiniers in the chasseur battalions. The carabinier bearskin was similar to the grenadier bearskin but was two inches shorter (at 11 inches French), with no brass plate at the front. In addition, the provisional instruction allowed grenadiers and carabiniers to have an ordinary *chapeau* as well as the *bonnet à poil*. How are we to explain this provision? Firstly, we must ask if carabiniers wore a bearskin cap before 1791? When the 1786 regulations were issued, chasseur-carabiniers did not exist, and there is no mention of bearskin caps even for grenadiers. This does not mean they did not exist (Bardin says an instruction of 1782 allowed them). Although the chasseur-carabiniers did not form a distinct company of their own, it is entirely possible some were issued the cap, but they were more likely to have dressed identically to the chasseurs (the 1788 inspection report of the Chasseurs des Cévennes records the presence of the chasseur-carabiniers but does not list bearskins – nor for that matter does it mention anything about them being issued with rifled carbines). The instruction of 1 April 1791 is something of a hotchpotch instruction, intended to clarify elements of, but not replace, the regulation of 1786. Although we see the instructions for carabiniers grouped with those for infantry grenadiers, the likelihood is these clauses were intended for the mounted carabinier regiments, not the light infantry. When light infantry carabiniers were eventually reformed into an elite company, they may have adopted the carabinier bearskin as described in this provisional regulation – after all, the regulation did not specify which type of carabiniers could wear it.

Excellent study of the chasseur uniform at the beginning of the war in 1792 with the leather *casque* helmet and longer tailed habit, by Duplessis-Bertaux. (Collection Yves Martin)

UNIFORMS AND EQUIPMENT

To conclude, the uniform worn by the chasseur battalions at the start of the war was a combination of the 1786 regulation and the 1791 provisional instruction. It included the leather *casque*, a black neck stock, a green *habit* piped in the distinctive colour, a white woollen, sleeved *gilet*, green *pantalons*, and Hungarian-cut gaiters. It was highly functional for the type of service the chasseurs were likely to encounter.

Uniforms of the Volunteers

In this section we consider the vast subject of the uniforms worn by the various units of National Guard chasseurs, free corps and legions. A word of warning at the outset: only by searching through every dossier in the French army's archives relating to these units, could anything approach the full truth be found.

Commencing with the National Guard of Paris, the basic uniform (eventually adopted by the line infantry) was a representation of the new French national colours – blue coat, red collar, white trim. Contemporary iconography shows chasseurs initially wearing a uniform very similar to the regular chasseur battalions, with green breeches and coat. There are small flourishes, including embroidery, or Hungarian knots over the upper thigh. There are depictions of chasseurs wearing a sash around their midriff holding a brace of pistols. In 1790 there in a picture of a chasseur from the city barriers, which depicts a uniform in the national colours, with a blue coat with white lapels and a red collar. However, the figure wears blue *pantalons* and short gaiters, and is therefore an early precursor of the uniform the light infantry would adopt in 1793. This figure also has Hungarian knots on his breeches, with a red stripe down their outer seam.

The decree of 28 May 1792 which instructed the creation of 54 *compagnies franches* included an article on the uniform and armament of these companies. It would 'in substance' be the same as the light infantry, however the commanders-in-chief of the armies could request changes depending on 'the circumstances and the country where these corps will be employed'. On 7 July the National Assembly issued a new instruction stating the 54 *compagnies franches* would wear a grey *habit* rather than the green of the light infantry. This was an unwise decision, as grey uniforms were worn by enemy jäger. On 19 July the National Assembly changed this instruction again, this time decreeing that the uniforms intended for the free companies 'will be of white woollen cloth', in other words, copying the uniforms of the regular line infantry. This impractical decision was quickly realised to be a mistake. Note the following minute from the meeting of Friday 24 August 1792:

> M. Fouquet, in the name of M. Georges Goliche, commander of a free company, arriving at that moment from the Army of the North, asks that the troop that he is responsible for forming, be dressed in cloth of any other colour than the white decreed by the National Assembly. He observes that this colour is too bright for the kind of service for which free companies are intended. The Assembly accepts

FRENCH LIGHT INFANTRY 1784-1815

the proposal and refers to the Executive Power, which it authorizes to provide for the clothing of the free companies in the colour which will be considered most suitable.¹

A separate decision, one month before, on 23 July 1792 appears to confirm the National Assembly knew it had made a mistake. A decree allowed the chasseurs of the Armée du Rhin to dress 'in the manner and in the colour which they consider the most suitable and economical'.² On 8 August the commanders of the Compagnie Franche Allobroge helpfully presented a model uniform to the National Assembly. The uniform was green, with a 'French style' casque, bonnets, boots and breeches in the Hungarian style, with the belts in black leather.³ On the other hand, the free company of Chasseurs Bons Tireurs were instructed to go out and purchase their own uniforms on 10 September.⁴

Such a haphazard approach was unsustainable. The companies and battalions of chasseurs lacked the support of formal depots; they lacked the expertise in maintaining and repairing uniforms. A company might be fitted out at great expense in the spring and summer, but then what could it do to sustain these uniforms after six months of living in the field, through the extremities of winter and through constant combat in the advanced posts? One imagines that the uniform over the winter months in 1792-1793 was 'the national cockade' and whatever else might be found. A national uniform would be required, in the same way a new organisation for the infantry was required. We come therefore to the reforms of 1793 and the creation of the demi-brigades.

Légion du Midi (1792) by Marbot. The uniform is described as a deep sky blue, with red lapels, green epaulettes and piping on the gaiters. (New York Public Library)

The Uniform of the Light Infantry Demi-Brigades

Thus far the uniform regulation of 1786 remained in force, with the modifications described in the provisional instruction of 1 April 1791. The uniform worn by the light demi-brigades was described in the decree of 7 September 1793 *Décret qui determine l'uniforme des bataillons d'infanterie légère*). This decree is so short it can be reproduced below:

> All light infantry battalions will wear the uniform as follows:
> *Habit-veste* (coatee), gilet (jacket) and breeches, in national blue woollen cloth.

---

1   Mavidal and Laurent, *Archives Parlementaires*, Vol.XLVIII, pp.686.
2   Mavidal and Laurent, *Archives Parlementaires*, Vol.XLVII, p.74.
3   Mavidal and Laurent, *Archives Parlementaires*, Vol.XLVII, pp.558-559.
4   Mavidal and Laurent, *Archives Parlementaires*, Vol.XLIX, p.515.

UNIFORMS AND EQUIPMENT

The piping of the coatee, in white cloth.
Cuff-flaps, scarlet.
Small upright collar, scarlet.
Blue lining for the coatee.
Big and small yellow buttons of the republic, with the number of the battalion.
The headgear will be a varnished leather helmet, green in colour.

There are numerous reflections one can make on this rather concise document. Why did the French abandon green, the natural colour of light infantry? There was little economy in the change from green to blue and any arguments about natural green dye fading into yellow are poorly made, because the chasseurs à cheval and dragoons retained that colour. If we return to the *Archives Parliamentaires*, there is a short commentary preceding the adoption of the decree. It was made by Étienne-Nicolas de Calon, Deputy of the Oise Department:[5]

Wonderfully flamboyant interpretation of a French light infantryman with woman from 1803, by Jan Anthonie Langendijk. Note the double-breasted gilet and oversized cravat. (Anne S.K. Brown Military Collection.)

I come on behalf of your War Committee to propose that you decree the uniform of the light infantry battalions. In fixing your attention on the form of the coat, it thought that it would appear to you more advantageous for the good of the service and more in the spirit of the subsequent organization of the troops of the Republic to bring it as near as possible to the national uniform and to make it common to all the battalions of the light infantry by designating them each by the number on their buttons.

As stated above, the adoption of blue is perhaps best described as a political one, that they wanted all the infantry, be they white coats, blue coats, or green coats, to merge into one great national army, and rather than different facing colours, the only difference in the uniforms between each corps would be the number on the buttons.

---

5   Mavidal and Laurent, *Archives Parlementaires*, Vol.XXIII, p.495.

The report also admits that the light infantry coat is not the same as the one worn by line infantry and alludes to the fact that that it was not possible for the light infantry cut to be same as the former. The coat described here is not a *habit*, but a *habit-veste* (known as a coatee in contemporary English). This coat had shortened tails, which did not extend below the buttocks. There were several inspirations for this. Firstly was one of practicality. The last thing a light infantryman needed while pushing through the thicket was a pair of useless coattails snagging on a bush. The coats worn by Austrian light infantry were cut without long tails, and the Brabant light infantry in French service had also adopted short-tailed jackets in imitation of the Austrian style. More widely, the short-tailed jacket was becoming more prevalent in society. The Carmagnole jacket was a French adoption of a tail-less working jacket adopted by Jacobins. Rather than the aping the long tails of the *ancien régime*, a short working-man's jacket was much more politically correct. That said, the tails on officers' coats remained more amply cut and were a reminder of a more elegant era.

The addition of white piping and the scarlet cuff-flaps and short collar represented the new national colours, and therefore each coat became something like wearing the national flag (this visual patriotic display persisted into the twentieth century, and even when being butchered by machine guns on the western front in the Great War of 1914-1918, the French only adopted a 'camouflage' grey after finding a clever way of achieving this colour from weaving together blue, white and red threads). Another important distinction between line infantry *habit* and the light infantry coatee was the pointed blue lapels and cuffs, which served to give the coat a darker appearance than the coat worn by the line.

A small item to note: Traditionally the light infantry had white metal buttons, not brass. Surviving examples of the brass button indicate the new pattern had the number in a *cors de chasse*, surrounded by a clasp, with the words République Française written around the outer edge. The *cors de chasse* emblem would also have been displayed on the turnbacks of the *habit-veste*. There is no description of the type of gaiter worn with this uniform, but there is nothing to suggest the Hungarian cut model no longer applied, although iconography shows a simpler, short, straight-topped gaiter being worn.

The 1793 decree remained the basis of the uniform until the adoption of a new uniform pattern in 1812. However, the thing which must be remembered is uniforms were made by the corps, and this allowed numerous economies and embellishments depending on the whim of the commander, and the state of the finances. At formal inspection reviews a model uniform would be presented for comment. While contemporary iconography is an important source on actual uniforms worn, the surest information is contained within the surviving inspection reports within the regimental dossiers in the French army's archives. Here for example, one might find a comment from the likes of *Général de Division* Mortier confirming '*pantalons à l'infanterie légère*' were tolerated but ought to have a closed seam down the outer leg, not fastened with buttons like hussar stable dress. This particular example is from an inspection report of the 9e Légère in 1802, which is further corroborated by a depiction of the regiment in Lejeune's painting of the Battle of Marengo, in which the soldiers of the 9e are shown with blue breeches, but with a thick red stripe down each leg. Thus here we have artist and inspector confirming a variation of the standard pattern.

The most significant development of light infantry uniform came with successive changes in headgear. The 1793 decree stated light infantry should wear the leather *casque*. However, by 1794 most soldiers wore the felt *chapeau* in the style of the National Guard. Unlike the leather *casque*, which provided the wearer with a peak to protect the eyes and offered some protection from sword cuts, the *chapeau* had no functional benefits at all, except perhaps it was lighter and more comfortable. When worn correctly, the brim of the hat got in the way of the movements of the musket, so soldiers began wearing the hat, *en colonne,* giving it a quarter turn to the left. This took the hat away from the shoulders and also provided shade to the eyes and neck.

There was always an affinity, or perhaps an affectation, by light infantry troops for wearing a uniform in the style of the light cavalry. Hussars wore the mirliton cap, which was a tall, conical hat wrapped with a decorative triangular piece of cloth called a flame. The hat did not have a brim, but careful folding of the flame could create one. This hat was adopted by the chasseurs à cheval and the horse artillery, and then adopted by some light infantry carabiniers. This hat was 11 inches high and tapered inwards slightly towards the top. In turn, this flamboyant style of headgear gave way to the shako which began to be adopted by light infantry around 1798. This cylindrical leather hat had a detachable leather visor, a cockade in the national colours, a plume on the left side with a brass plaque (normally in the shape of a lozenge) at the front. Although the shako was widely adopted by the Consulate, the shako was only officially recognised as the headgear of light infantry by the law of 4 Brumaire X (26 October 1801). Line infantry regiments, and therefore their voltigeur companies, would not adopt the shako until 25 February 1806.

What of bearskin caps for carabiniers? Given the extreme state of the public finances in the 1790s, did the carabiniers wear these caps or not? Carabiniers were the first to wear the mirliton and then the shako, so perhaps the bearskins became a feature of the late Consulate/early Empire? For example, we see in Napoleon's correspondence a decision

Study of a mid-Empire French carabinier with white trousers rather than the usual tight, blue *pantalons*. Where funds allowed, regiments were allowed to provide linen trousers to their men. (Anne S.K. Brown Military Collection)

FRENCH LIGHT INFANTRY 1784-1815

to grant the colonel of the 27e Légère bearskin caps on 24 December 1804.[6] Clearly this regiment did not have that headgear before this date.

The 1793 decree explains nothing about the petty equipment carried by men. For this, one has to return to the 1786 regulations. Here we find confirmation each soldier should have three good shirts, two collars, two pairs of *culottes* (this would have applied for *pantalons*), two pairs of shoes, a pair of white linen gaiters, a pair of black linen gaiters, a pair of woollen gaiters lined in linen, two handkerchiefs, two pairs of hose, a buckle for the collar (line infantry required buckles for their culottes and gaiter garters), a bag containing power and puff, a button stick, a comb, a brush for the hat and coat, two shoe brushes, a leather brush, a brush for whitening the belts, a needle and thread, a button-pull, a ball extractor, a vent pick, a turnscrew, some patches of old cloth for repairs, and old linen for cleaning the weapon. All of these items were still required by soldiers. Then we read nothing in the laws about the issuing of greatcoats to the republican era infantry, but iconography suggests these garments existed. There is little doubt of this, for without them, the men would have frozen to death in their bivouacs. They must therefore have been supplied, or requisitioned locally, or perhaps procured by the men themselves, as and when they were able to afford or 'find' them. There would have been little uniformity in these garments, as the iconography suggests.

tambour-major and child musicians from 1800 by JOB. True enough, the regimental children were able to supplement the musicians with fifes, but drummers had to be aged at least 14 before going on campaign. (New York Public Library)

On 17 Frimaire Year XI (8 December 1802) there was a significant change in the way regimental accounts were managed. The new law (*Arrêté sur les Masses*) provided a comprehensive list of the uniform and equipment then provided for light infantrymen.[7] This law saw the merging of the uniform and maintenance *masses* (funds) to produce a new *masse générale*. It set out the responsibility for providing and administering articles of uniform and equipment and set the duration of each item. The law details all the various effects worn by the various arms, (which for light infantry included the habit, *veste, pantalons en tricot,* canvas *caleçon* (drawers), shako or bearskin bonnet, white buff cross belts and musket sling, cartridge pouch, drum, belts and

---

6   Napoleon, *Correspondence*, Vol.X, p.105.
7   *Journal militaire*, 14th Year, Part 1, pp.202-217.

UNIFORMS AND EQUIPMENT

drumsticks. The *masse* also provided for epaulettes for the *adjudant*s and carabiniers, but there is no mention of those for chasseurs, which we know existed from the iconography; *galons* (braid) for the NCOs and the long service stripes of veterans, those of the musicians; the plumes for shakos, aprons for the sapeurs (interesting – because this type of soldier did not officially exist until 1808, but obviously did). Use of the funds of the *masse générale* for any other purpose, than that determined above, was expressly prohibited.

There then follows some qualifying remarks on some of the more interesting items. The *tambour-major* was not allowed to wear any other stripes or braid than those assigned to the distinction of his rank. The musicians were to have no other distinction than a simple piece of gold braid, ten lines wide, on the facing of the coat. The non-commissioned officers and soldiers were provided with a *bonnet de police* (cloth fatigue cap), which was made from the economies of the cut of new clothing, and the best pieces of the debris of the old clothing. The *pantalons* were replaced every year, and at the end of each year, the old ones were said to belong to the soldier; but so that he always had two pairs available (as stipulated in the 1786 regulation), he could only dispose of the old pair after two years. This is an interesting detail. In probability it meant the soldier had a 'best' pair, and then the pair he used on manoeuvres, which were by then probably quite heavily patched. If regimental funds allowed it, officers and soldiers were allowed to provide themselves with white linen breeches for the summer months. The funds for this would come from the *masse* of linen and shoes (this in turn came from deductions to the men's wages). In addition, each ordinary (mess group) or barrack room would be provided with a sufficient number of *sarreaux* (smocks) and linen trousers for the men to carrying out their chores.

Material was provided to renew the coats and jackets every two years. The old ones remained the property for the corps, with the best ones retained for dressing the new soldiers, for the guardhouse, the prison and the *salle de discipline* (guard room); the others were used for repairs. Soldiers who were discharged were allowed to take a coat, a jacket, breeches and a hat, taken from among the best of those in their last year of service. The clothing effects of men who died in external hospitals was returned to the corps, if the transport costs did not exceed the value of the effects. Otherwise, the councils of administration of the military hospitals and the administrators of

Rear view of the light infantryman in greatcoat by Duplessis-Bertaux. (Collection Yves Martin)

civilian hospices would notify the regiment, which decided whether to sell them or send them on.

From these various clues, we can see how the light infantry uniform developed in the 1790s into the classic uniform of the First Empire, when initially at least, the light infantry regiments were sufficiently well-funded and organised to dress in a manner approaching something close to uniformity. Even then, small details were left to the whim of the *colonel*, such as the design of plumes, epaulettes, the 'dragon' or decorative knot on the hilt of the sabre.

The Uniform of the First Empire 1804-1812

The classic uniform of the light infantry was a dark 'Imperial blue' *habit-veste*, with blue lapels, short turnbacks, red cuff-flaps and collar and white piping. Beneath the coat was a *veste* or *gilet* made of blue woollen cloth, or linen in the summer. The chasseurs wore tight blue *pantalons*, with short gaiters, cut in the Hungarian style for parade, or square-cut for ordinary service. The shako was universally adopted, with bearskins worn by some carabinier companies. Each man was armed with a musket and bayonet, with a *sabre-briquet* (short sword) and equipped with a hide backpack. Officers wore a blue, tailed-coat, or *surtout* coat for undress. They wore tight blue *pantalons*, with boots either cut in the Hungarian style of light cavalry, or in the style known as *à l'anglais*, with a turned-down upper section. The majority were armed with an *épée*, but some carried a sabre with a broader, curved blade. Officers were required to wear a metal *hausse-col* or gorget. Instead of backpacks, officers were allowed a leather portmanteau which was carried with the regimental baggage. Senior officers were mounted and all manner of extravagances occurred on campaign (*colonels* 'finding' carriages, subaltern officers and even *caporaux-fourriers* purchasing captured horses). The sutler-women accompanying the regiment wore civilian costume, not a paramilitary garb as became fashionable in the mid-nineteenth century.[8]

Detailed sketch of a light infantryman in greatcoat and *chapeau* by Duplessis-Bertaux. Note the wide, open lapels of the greatcoat. (Collection Yves Martin)

Several important modifications occurred to the uniform. The first came with the creation of the voltigeurs. Initially the only distinction between the uniforms worn by chasseurs and voltigeurs was the latter had a habit with a *chamois* (buff) coloured collar. The epaulettes and plume would therefore be green, like the centre companies. In some regiments the voltigeurs wore

---

8   For more information on the sutler-women attached to the French army see Terry Crowdy, *Napoleon's Women Camp Followers* (Oxford: Osprey Publishing, 2021).

UNIFORMS AND EQUIPMENT

the same green plume tipped in red as the chasseurs, while some wore green tipped *chamois*. Although the regulation only called for the collar to change colour, before long cuff flaps became made from the same *chamois* cloth, while epaulettes retained a green fringe, but were otherwise pipped in *chamois*.

On 25 February 1806 the infantry adopted a new pattern of shako which was to be implemented with the replacement headgear in 1807. This version was made partly of felt and was eight to twelve inches in height. Unlike the earlier pattern, cylindrical shako, the new pattern was semi-conical, with the top wider than the brim. The plume moved to the front of the hat, positioned over the cockade. Initially the shako was decorated with ornate cords and tassels (*raquettes*) which were suspended from the sides of the shako. These decorative cords were used to tie the plume to the *sabre-briquet* scabbard when not in full parade dress. Metal chin scales were later added, which led to the removal all *raquettes* in a circular of 9 November 1810, which called for greater economy and uniformity. In this circular, shako cords were supressed for all grades. Officers were allowed to replace these with one or two *galons* (braid) of gold or silver (depending on arm and rank). This *galon* would be 34 mm for the *colonel*, with a second *galon* of 14mm placed above at 20mm distance from the first. Other grades would only have a single *galon* measuring 34mm for *majors*, 27mm for *chefs de bataillon*, 20 mm for *capitaines*, 18 mm for *lieutenants*, 14 mm for *sous-lieutenants*. Plumes were suppressed, except for *colonels*, *majors* and *chefs de bataillon*. Those of the *colonel* were white, those of the *majors* half red and white, red being the top half, *chefs de bataillon* entirely red. Everyone else would be issued with a woollen *houpette* coloured white for staff, red for grenadiers and carabiniers, yellow for voltigeurs, and diverse colours for the other companies, later confirmed in a circular of 21 February 1811 as dark green (*vert foncé*) for the 1st company; sky blue (*bleu céleste*) for the 2nd; 'sunrise' (*aurore*) for the 3rd; and violet for the 4th. There were no longer to be leather chevrons on the lateral part of the shako. The body would be made from felt, with a cow leather top. The interior would not be lined in paper or cardboard, only an adjustable, canvas *coiffe*. The plaque and chinstraps, or *jugulaires*, would be white metal for all corps. The plaque was be formed of a lozenge with an eagle emblem stamped on it and the

Officers of voltigeurs and chasseurs by JOB. The addition of a light cavalry colpack and sabre may be an embellishment too far. The packs of the infantry greatcoats have a connecting strap across their chests – this would have been more usual in the Prussian or Russian armies. (New York Public Library)

regimental number within a *cors de chasse*. The loop supporting the cockade was removed, and a maximum price for each shako established at 9 francs 40 centimes.

There then followed the specific measurements of the shako. It was 19 centimetres high. The diameter at the top was 24.4 centimetres. The specific details of the light infantry shako were:

BODY OF THE SHAKO.
Inside and out, like the shakos of the line infantry.
ACCESSORIES
Plaque. A diamond-shaped plate, made of tin, weighing seventeen grams, the same height and width as that of the line infantry, having in the centre a hunting horn of four centimetres high, in the middle of which is the regiment number.
Cockade and gusset for the *houpette*. Same dimension as for line infantry.
Chinstrap. Same details as for the line infantry, with the exception of the scales, which must be in tin rather than yellow copper, and of the button, in the middle of which must be a hunting horn instead of a star.[9]

It should perhaps be noted that light infantry had reverted to the white metal or silver buttons and decorations during the Consulate and early Empire, thus ending the brass buttons of the republican period.

On 7 October 1807 the sabre-briquets were withdrawn from the voltigeurs of the line and light infantry, the soldiers of the light infantry centre companies and from the foreign regiments. Each regiment was instructed to return their sabres in good condition to the artillery stores. On 15 October 1807 a regulation appeared, putting the decree into action. This offered some clarifications. *Sous-officiers*, *caporaux*, grenadiers, carabiniers and drummers were allowed to retain their sabres. Further to this, a letter was sent from the Minister of War to the councils of administration in each infantry regiment (this is reproduced in the *Journal Militaire* for 1807). The reason for withdrawing the swords was because Napoleon thought they were useless in war and 'only served to overburden them with an embarrassing weight'.[10] One can imagine the removal of these sabres was a cause of sorrow for many, for while the sword may well have had limited use, it did confer a certain prestige to the soldier carrying it. Of course, in Napoleon's mind there was no real difference between fusiliers and chasseurs, something which is reinforced by an interesting piece of terminology used in this decree, which had a ring of the *ancien régime* about it. The companies of chasseurs were referred to as the '*basses compagnies*', literally the 'low companies' rather than centre companies. The regulation also distinguished between '*sous-officiers*' (sub-officers, that is *sergents*) and *caporaux*, again, a pre-revolutionary distinction previously supressed in 1791.

---

9   Étienne-Alexandre Bardin, *Mémorial de l'officier d'infanterie* (Paris: Magimel, 1813) pp.717-718.
10 *Journal militaire*, Year 1807, Part 2, p.115.

UNIFORMS AND EQUIPMENT

A chasseur sergent *with two long service stripes searches for English contraband. A brilliant study by Geissler. Notice the cut of the collars on the men's coats, revealing the black neck stock. Their epaulettes are green with red edging. Note the side-mounting of the plume and the powdered hair worn in a queue (the white powder has covered the back of his coat). The cane gives the* sergent *a degree of respectability. (Anne S.K. Brown Military Collection)*

When the army went to war in 1805, greatcoats (*capotes*) were still not formally issued as a standard uniform item, except for soldiers performing garrison guard duty or in exceptional circumstances, such as winter campaigns. This is not to say the demi-brigades did not have them. When first planning the invasion of England and forming the camps along the Channel coast, on 25 Prairial Year XI (14 June 1803), Bonaparte instructed Général de Division Dejean to manufacture and gather 80,000 capotes and 120,000 pairs of shoes by mid-September.[11] We know the 6e Légère already had greatcoats in 1803, because of a letter from Bonaparte to Berthier dated Saint-Cloud 11 Vendemiaire Year XII (4 October 1803). This instructed two battalions of the demi-brigade to march to Montreuil-sur-Mer to form camp with the 69e Demi-Brigade de Ligne. The First Consul instructed Berthier to have the two demi-brigades bring their *capotes* with them.[12]

Despite *capotes* being manufactured, not all troops had them when they departed the Channel coast and marched against Austria. For example, the 9e Légère was forced to confiscate the greatcoats of Austrian prisoners after

---

11   Napoleon, *Correspondance*. Vol.VIII, pp.448-449.
12   Napoleon, *Correspondance*, Vol.IX, pp.24-25.

FRENCH LIGHT INFANTRY 1784-1815

Officer and voltigeur from the 21e Ligne (1808). The officer is wearing a surtout and the blue pantalons are an interesting variation, giving him the appearance of a light infantry officer. (Anne S.K. Brown Military Collection)

the capitulation of Ulm. The following spring, a decree was issued on 25 April 1806 confirming the uniform requirements of the army. This included the instruction for certain line infantry regiments to introduce a white *habit* commencing from 1807, completing the project by 1809. All line infantry regiments were to be issued with a '*capotte*' (sic) or '*redingote*' in beige woollen cloth. Light infantry regiments were not required to change the colour of their uniforms, but they were to introduce a *redingote* in beige woollen cloth. The word *redingote* was a corruption of the English 'riding coat'. Its form was described in the 1786 regulations as having a *rotonde* (rotunda) across the shoulders, in other words a short cape. However, it may simply have been a double-breasted coat with a turndown collar.

The army found itself facing a second winter campaign in 1806 which stretched well into 1807. Despite the regulation, many regiments in the Grande Armée embarked on this campaign with no greatcoats, because we see a flurry of orders instructing their manufacture and requisitions of them. The orders begin from Saint-Cloud on 22 September 1806, with Napoleon instructing the *majors* at the regimental depots to begin manufacturing capotes for their regiments. Then from Berlin on 28 October 1806, Napoleon orders collecting cloth sufficient for 100,000 *capotes* and *pantalons*, and to procure 100,000 *chapeaux* and shoes.[13] On 2 December *Maréchal* Murat is ordered to have 8-10,000 capotes made in Warsaw if Davout's III Corps needed them. The same letter recorded *Maréchal* Lannes was given greatcoats at Stettin.[14] In a note to *Intendant Général* Daru dated Posen, 12 December, Napoleon let rip calling the commissariat in charge 'a rascal' with no idea of his profession and concluded there was no administration of uniforms.[15] Despite having ordered 50,000 greatcoats from Hamburg, 6,000 from Frankfurt, and 4,000 from Stettin, Napoleon had no idea if these had been delivered or not. The letter recorded there were 9,200 Prussian greatcoats seized when they entered Berlin, Bernadotte's troops took 5,000 more when they entered Lubeck. Leipzig

---

13 Napoleon I, *Correspondance*, Vol.XIII, pp.431-432.
14 Napoleon I, *Correspondance*, Vol.XIV, pp.15-16.
15 Napoleon I, *Correspondance*, Vol.XIV, p.88.

provided 80,000 bolts of cloth, which ought to have been enough to make 25,000 capotes. Evidently this continued to be a problem. On 2 February Napoleon complained that the shoes and capotes ordered from Berlin had not arrived and that the capotes from Leipzig were 'ridiculously small' and hardly even reached the knee.[16]

All this said, the *capote* became a vital part of the uniform from this point in the war. In an earlier letter to *Général de Division* Dejean, dated Berlin, 11 November 1806, Napoleon describes how the arrival of fresh troops ought to be accelerated:

> To speed up the training and the departure of these battalions it will not be necessary for the conscripts to be trained, it will suffice that they have eight or ten days of training, that they be armed, that they have a veste, breeches, gaiters, a uniform chapeau and a greatcoat. We must not wait until they have a habit.[17]

From the snippets of many such letters we can conclude that the Grande Armée which fought at Jena, Eylau and probably even Friedland, was uniformed in an extremely haphazard manner, and that soldiers were as likely to be dressed in a Prussian army greatcoat, or one manufactured in Germany, than anything issued in France. We see also that conscripts arrived at the army without a uniform habit. The ragtag appearance of Napoleon's soldiers often depicted in contemporary artwork by the likes of Geissler is therefore no exaggeration – and this was the First Empire at the height of its military success.

Before introducing the 1812 uniform, a short note ought to be made here about the regiments of the Grande Armée which went from Germany to Spain in 1808 and remained in the Iberian Peninsula, the Pyrenees and southwestern France until peace was declared in 1814. In many respects these regiments form something of a forgotten army, because once Napoleon left the theatre after the British were driven from Spain in the early part of 1809, the ensuing Peninsular War was one which the emperor delegated to his brother Joseph and the generals who served him. For the most part these regiments were so far from their regimental depots in France, they had to form petty depots

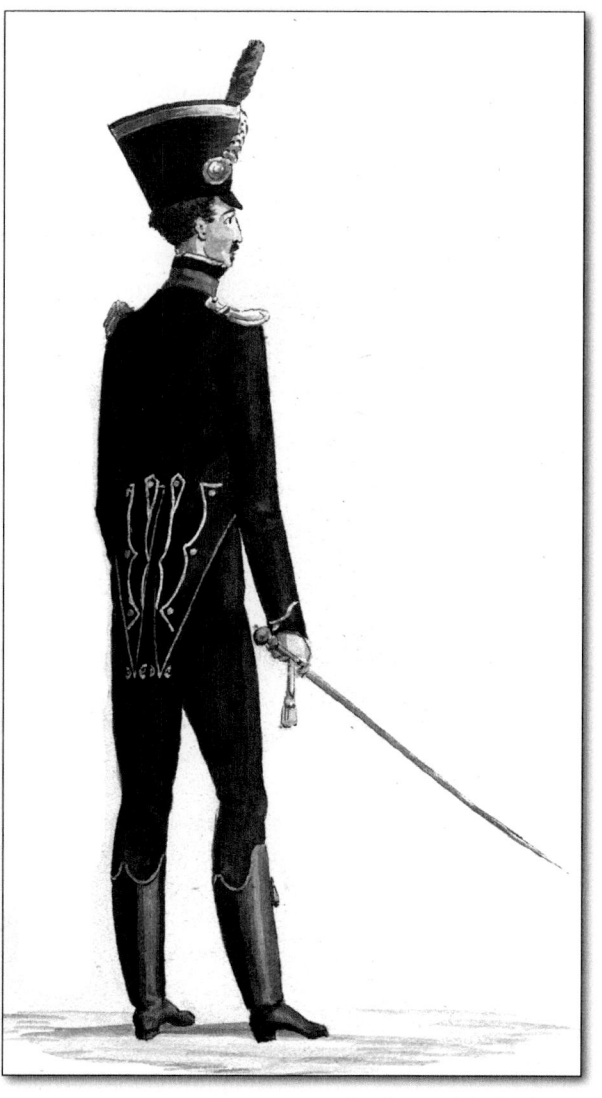

Excellent study by Freyberg showing the detail on the reverse of an officer's habit. Note the pointed cuffs piped white. (Collection Yves Martin)

---

16 Napoleon I, *Correspondance*, Vol.XIV, pp.345-346.
17 Picard & Tuetey, *Correspondance inédite de Napoleon 1er*, Vol.1, p.393.

around Bayonne, near the Spanish border. The convoys bringing replacement uniforms were often attacked once they crossed the border into Spain, and even once they reached Madrid, they then had to be sent on to whichever part of the Peninsula the regiment was posted to. One can imagine the impact on uniforms which were well past their replacement date, and that trousers in particular became made of local cloth, or even from captured enemy stores. Regional variations must have developed. The memoirs of Girod de l'Ain speak of the officers wearing '*pantalons à la Mameluck*', which would have been very loose, baggy trousers in the Ottoman style; but he also had *culottes*, stockings and shoes for his evening wear.[18] The soldiers may well have attempted to conserve their precious blue uniforms in their packs, making more daily use of linen trousers, jacket, and the greatcoat.

The 1812 Pattern Uniform

In Napoleon's correspondence we find a letter from the emperor to *Général de Division* Berthier, dated Ostend, 26 Thermidor Year XI (14 August 1804):

> My cousin, it appears the army is asking for a change in clothing. We would like to do away with chapeau, adopt the pantalon, boots and short coat, giving the soldier a greatcoat for winter. These changes were often attempted in the French army, but it did not take long to go back to the costume which is still in use.[19]

Piecemeal changes did occur, including the shako and greatcoat, but these ambitions did not begin to be realised until the introduction of the so-called Bardin regulations of 19 January 1812.

Colonel Bardin was part of a commission set up in 1811 to standardise the French army's uniforms. Bardin was nothing but meticulous, describing every element of the uniform and equipment. Sections of the text form part of Bardin's 1813 *Mémorial de l'officier d'infanterie* and also the first part of the *Journal Militaire* of 1812. Before summarising the new uniform, a word of caution. Uniforms were manufactured to last a set period of time; for example a pair of *pantalons* ought to last a year, a *habit-veste* or *gilet* for two years and the *redingote* for three. Replacement articles were issued in a staggered fashion so the regimental tailors were not overwhelmed with work. Therefore, when one speaks of a new uniform regulation being introduced on 19 January 1812, we should consider how long it took for the patterns to be distributed to each corps; how long the regimental tailors sat pawing over the patterns and producing specimens of their own for the *capitaine d'habillement* and the *major* to consider. Then the process of manufacture would begin at the next cycle. Even in a time of peace, the rollout of a new uniform would have taken several years to complete. To introduce an entirely new uniform at a time of great national crisis, with battalions scattered across the continent, with thousands of conscripts spending a matter of just

---

18   Girod de l'Ain, *Dix ans de mes souvenirs militaires*, p.166.
19   Napoleon I, *Correspondance*, Vol.IX, pp.592-593.

UNIFORMS AND EQUIPMENT

a few days at the depot before marching off to theatre, is an entirely different matter. This 1812 uniform is therefore better described as the uniform intended for Waterloo rather than the uniform of the Russian campaign.

The light infantry uniform would compose of a new style *habit-veste*, which was cut square across the waist, with blue lapels pipped white. The light infantry coat had blue cuffs with white pipping in a pointed style. The coattails were short. When a man was kneeling, the '*basque*' on the coat would be 300 millimetres from the ground. The rest of the uniform consisted of a sleeved *gilet*, *pantalons* of tricot, gaiters (square cut), a pair of linen drawers, a pair of linen *pantalons*, a beige *capote* (greatcoat), a shako, and a new style of *bonnet de police*, commonly called a 'pokalem'. Soldiers were issued with a pair of white, '*toile*' (canvas) *pantalons* which we amply cut and were worn over the gaiters, cut 110 millimetres from the ground. Bearskin caps were no longer worn by carabiniers, but their shakos were 15 millimetres taller than the ones worn by the chasseurs (referred to as fusiliers in the regulation), and decorated with a red 'aigrette' (a short, feathered plume). The voltigeur shako had the same dimensions as the chasseurs but with a yellow aigrette. The *habit-veste* worn by voltigeurs had a *chamois* collar and epaulettes, with a chamois hunting horn symbol on the turnbacks.

The most distinctive element of the Bardin regulations was the uniform of the drummers. In a return to the style of the *ancien regime*, the drummers would wear a liveried coat. This was described as green, embellished with a dark green tape embroidered with imperial eagles and the letter 'N'. This tape was applied to the collar, the cuffs, pockets and with four double ranks up the front of the coat, and seven on each sleeve. From the illustrations of this uniform by Carle Vernet, we see the drummers in tight green *pantalons* with black gaiters, or the white *pantalons* worn over the gaiters. Of course, this new design was an aspiration rather than actual reality.

After the fall of the imperial government, on 13 April 1814 the provisional government adopted the white cockade and instructed the army to wear this in place of their tricolour cockades. As the remnants of the regiments and prisoners of war returned to their depots, the 1812 uniform could at last begin to be implemented. Table 23 provides the official tariffs for the manufacture and supply of this uniform for the 15 regiments of light infantry in 1815 and, except for the cockade and royalist symbols on cartridge pouches, this would have formed the basis for the uniform worn at Waterloo. Of course, regulations are one thing, their implementation was entirely another.

Drum-major of light infantry and grenadier. The colpack is probably fanciful and influenced by later styles. The grenadier's capote would be better coloured beige and his shako cover would more likely have been black. (New York Public Library)

157

FRENCH LIGHT INFANTRY 1784-1815

Nicolas-Toussaint Charlet's 1823 study of a voltigeur *sergent*. Notice how the single stripe rank insignia is worn on the sleeve of the greatcoat. (Anne S.K. Brown Military Collection)

UNIFORMS AND EQUIPMENT

Table 23. Tariff for General Effects, 8 February 1815

Designation of objects			Price
Habillement (uniform)	Toile for lining		1f 40c
	Toile for *pantalons* and *caleçon* (drawers)		1 65
	Buttons	Medium (per dozen)	0 26
		Small (per dozen)	0 18
	Tailoring	*Habit veste*	2 45
		Habit de tambour	8 50
		Gilet with sleeves	1 15
		Pantalon	1 00
		Capote	1 50
		Bonnet de police	0 60
		Linen *caleçon*	0 40
	Galons (stripes)	Silver for *sergents* and *fourriers*	5 60
		White for *caporaux*	0 60
		Red wool for chevrons	0 55
		Silver for *tambour-majors* and musicians	5 60
		Livery for *tambours*	0 90
	Epaulettes	Red wool for carabiniers (the pair)	3 40
		Adjutant sous-officier (the pair)	22 00
	Aigrettes	Carabinier (red)	3 50
		Voltigeur (yellow)	2 50
	Houppettes for centre companies in diverse colours		0 60
	Agrafes (hooks and eyes) for the *habit* and *gilet*		0 10
	Braces for the *culotte*		0 60
Coiffure (headgear)	Carabinier shako, without neck-cover, garnished in scarlet stripe,10-18 *lignes* wide, with a plaque with the new French coat of arms, chin straps and number hollowed out		10 20
	Shako without neck-cover for chasseur and voltigeur, with new plaque and chin straps.		8 40
	Coiffe exterior shako cover		1 60
	Shako plate in white metal, new model (separately)		0 40
	Chin straps in white metal (separately)		0 65
	Chin strap buttons (separately)		0 20
Grand équipement	Cartridge pouch for sub-officer with ornaments on the outer flap.		4 40
	Cartridge pouch à LL and crown in white copper cast and burnished, or in metal, for chasseurs		4 85
	Cartridge pouch with grenade in white copper cast and burnished, or in metal, for carabinier		4 85
	LL and crown in white copper or in metal, together, without the cartridge pouch		0 45
	Grenade or *cors de chasse*, each, separate to the cartridge pouch.		0 45
	Cartridge pouch belt for *sous-officier*, without bayonet holder, 31 *lignes* wide		4 15
	Cartridge pouch belt for grenadier, voltigeur and soldier, with bayonet holder, 31 *lignes* wide.		4 15
	Musket sling		1 01
	Baudrier 31 *lignes* wide		4 65
	Drum case		36 00

FRENCH LIGHT INFANTRY 1784-1815

Grand équipement	*Collier* of drummer	4 50
	Cuissière (thigh cover) of drummer, in buffed sheepskin	2 60
	Cuissière of drummer, in buff or calfskin	4 60
	Axe of a *sapeur*	36 00
	Porte-hache (axe carrier)	12 50
	Sapeur's apron in sheepskin	72 60
	Cornet with cords and *houpette*	5 78
	Sapeur's gauntlets and cuffs	4 05

Petit équipement	Shoes (a pair)	5 00
	Shirt	4 75
	Half-gaiters black (a pair)	2 90
	Half gaiters grey (a pair)	1 85
	Half stockings in yarn (the pair)	0 90
	Pantalon de toile	3 10
	Black collar	0 40
	Distributions sack	3 70
	Haversack in veal skin, with buff trimming	8 30
	Cockade	0 15
	Turn-screw	0 30
	Vent pick	0 10

6

Lilies and Eagles – Light Infantry Colours

Other than providing them with battalion guns, there was nothing worse one could do for light infantry than to issue them with ceremonial colours. These emblems were absolutely necessary to enable line infantry to keep their direction of march straight and true; or to serve as a rallying point in a desperate hand-to-hand melee, something which they might surround like a living fortress of flesh and blood to withstand an enemy charge; but for true light infantry, designated to fight in the advanced guard and as skirmishers, nothing could embarrass them more than a heavy piece of cloth on a pole, which honour dictated they must protect at all costs. What possible use was a standard while racing through woods, or attempting to mount an ambush? The soldiers of the *ancien régime* knew this and issued no flags; but when national emblems became the vogue, when soldiers dressed themselves in the national colours, it was inevitable that light infantry would follow suit. Not to have had standards would have implied a lack of prestige, even a lack of patriotism and political allegiance.

The 1791 Colours

The decree of 30 June 1791 granted a flag in the national colours to all battalions of light infantry. At the time, only the original twelve chasseur battalions had been formed, but it appears subsequent chasseur battalions also adopted the standard. For example, the 17e Bataillon d'Infanterie Légère declared to the National Convention that they had attached the *acte constitutionnel* to its flag and were going off to force the enemy to read it.[1] The pattern of these flags is believed to have followed the model of the first battalion of each line regiment, but with the incorporation of a hunting horn emblem.

---

1 Hollander, *Les Drapeaux des demi-brigades d'infanterie de 1794-1804*, p.108.

From surviving examples, the flag measured approximately 1.54 metres high and 1.62 metres wide. The cloth was white taffeta, with a broad white cross, which created four quadrants of equal size. The top left quadrant had three horizontal bands in the national colours (from the top: blue, white, red), and the outer edge of the other quadrants was bordered alternately in red and blue. There was originally a fleur de lys symbol at each of the four extremities of the cross, but these were replaced by lozenge-shaped patches in the national colours. The flag bore the legend DISCIPLINE OBÉISSANCE À LA LOI, with a central laurel wreath, inside of which was a golden *cors de chasse*. At the top of the wreath was the letter 'B' (indicating 'battalion'), with the battalion number at the bottom of the wreath. The staff was 2.8 metres in length, painted in a spiral effect in the national colours. The pike head was originally cast with a hollow centre in the shape of a fleur-de-lys symbol. After the abolition of monarchy, this dangerous royalist symbol would have been filed into a lozenge (rhombus) or the replaced with a completely new pike head.

It is unclear what happened to the flags, particularly after the amalgamation of 1794. While the colours of the demi-brigades de bataille were discussed in a report of 12 Ventôse Year II (2 March 1794), there was no mention of those belonging to the light infantry. There are occasional, sometimes contradictory, clues that some of the newly created light infantry demi-brigades had them, but the likelihood is the majority did not. Those demi-brigades serving in the Armée d'Italie in 1797 were issued flags by Bonaparte in a ceremony of 12 August 1797. These colours were emblazoned with battle honours and legends. Any demi-brigades which had older colours handed these over in return for the new colours. While no doubt popular with his soldiers, the issuing of flags by an army commander rather than the state did not sit well with the government. With Bonaparte safely shipped off to Egypt, the government issued a law on 3 Thermidor Year 3 (21 July 1798) stating that any flags with legends were to be handed over to their councils of administration as a keepsake, and new flags would be issued.

The light infantry demi-brigades from the Armée d'Italie which went on the expedition to Egypt in 1798 would have had flags. There is documentary evidence that the 21e and 22e Légère had flags issued to them before departure, and the colour of 3e Bataillon 21e Demi-Brigade Légère was captured in 1801 at the Battle of Alexandria, fragments of which were recorded by Hollander.[2] Incidentally, the colour was captured while the battalion was skirmishing, with a guard of just 30 men to protect it. According to an account in the *Moniteur Universel*, all perished in its defence.[3]

The Consular Colours 1802

After Marengo, the First Consul decided to award flags to the light infantry demi-brigades. A special set of colours was first issued to the 9e Légère in recognition of its valour at Marengo. Designed by Challiot de Prusse, the

---

2   Hollander, *Les Drapeaux des demi-brigades d'infanterie de 1794-1804*, p.112.
3   Hollander, *Les Drapeaux des demi-brigades d'infanterie de 1794-1804*, p.113.

flag was square, with a white lozenge in the centre. In each corner of the lozenge was a blue triangle containing a flaming grenade with lightning bolts. The lozenge was surrounded by a green border, filled with golden hunting horns. The corners were red triangles with the number 9 painted in gold with black shadowing. At the centre of the lozenge was a sunburst effect at the centre of which was a laurel wreath containing the motto L'INCOMPARABLE. Above the laurel crown was a scroll in silver with the words RÉPUBLIQUE FRANÇAISE, with a second one below it with the battalion number. As Hollander points out, the inclusion of the colour green with the national colours was an interesting variation which is only found replicated in the colours of the Chasseurs à Pied of the Consular Guard.[4] This flag was given to the demi-brigade at a parade in the courtyard of the Tuileries on 4 June 1802. No mention is made of older flags being handed over in return, so we must conclude the 9e Légère fought at Marengo without colours.

The special flag awarded to the 9e Demi-Brigade Légère on 4 June 1802. This flag bore the motto 'L'INCOMPARABLE' in recognition of their bravery at the Battle of Marengo on 14 June 1800. (New York Public Library)

Following this special ceremony, a law of 21 Prairial Year X (10 June 1802) stated that flags were going to be issued to all the light infantry demi-brigades. This included every light infantry demi-brigade except the 9e (which had already received its flags) and the 5e and 11e which were part of an expedition to Saint-Domingue (modern Haiti). A deputation from each demi-brigade including the *chef de brigade*, the first *capitaine*, a lieutenant and a *sous-lieutenant*, a *sergent-major*, a *sergent*, four *caporaux* and one soldier per company, and the standard bearer (a *sergent-major*) went to Paris for a parade at the Carrousel on 14 July. There is a surviving example of this flag, belonging to the 2e Bataillon of the 6e Légère. It is described as square taffeta, measuring 1.63 metres on each side. In the centre is a white lozenge. In each point of the lozenge was a blue triangle containing a golden hunting horn. The four corners of the flag were red and contained the number of the demi-brigade, displayed in gold, with a black shadowing effect. At the centre of the flag were rays of sunlight, with a green laurel and oak crown surrounding an inscription painted in golden letters: LE PREMIER CONSUL A LA 6ME DEMI-BRIGADE *LÉGÈRE* LE 25 MESSIDOR AN 10. Above the laurel crown and was a silver scroll lined in blue with the inscription RÉPUBLIQUE FRANÇAISE and one below with the inscription VALEUR ET DISCIPLINE. On the reverse, the central inscription was replaced with a trophy, formed of an epee with a golden hilt, two crossed sabres and two crossed muskets, tied with a tricolour ribbon. The inscription read RÉPUBLIQUE FRANÇAISE with 2ME BATAILLON (or the battalion number) on the lower scroll. The staff was topped with a gilded copper pike head.

---

4   Hollander, *Les Drapeaux des demi-brigades d'infanterie de 1794-1804*, p.116.

The 1804 Model Eagle

Nothing symbolises the First Empire more than the iconic 'eagle' emblems Napoleon awarded to his army at a ceremony in Paris on 5 December 1804. The new imperial emblem was a gilded bronze eagle, with wings outstretched and with its right talon resting on a spindle of Jupiter. The regimental number was displayed on the front and back of the plinth, which was 40mm high and 120mm wide. The eagle measured 310mm high and 255mm across the wing tips. Of secondary importance, the accompanying flag measured 810mm square. It was made of a single sheet of oiled silk. The application of oil strengthened the flag and allowed it to be painted on both sides. The design was a central white lozenge, framed by four triangles, alternating in red and blue. A laurel wreath in each corner carried the regimental number. In the centre of the white lozenge were the letters: L'EMPEREUR DES FRANÇAIS AU [number]ME RÉGIMENT D'INFANTERIE *LÉGÈRE* on one side and VALEUR ET DISCIPLINE with the number of the battalion on the other.

Initially one eagle was awarded to every battalion. These emblems were taken on campaign by light infantry regiments, carried by a *sergent-major*. This remained the case until an order dated Osterode, 26 March 1807, when all light infantry regiments were instructed to return their eagles to the depots. 'This arm will not have an eagle before the enemy', the order read.[5] The reason for this instruction was probably two incidents which had occurred earlier that year. In the first case, a battalion of the 9e Légère lost their colours in an engagement at Mohrungen on 25 January. The battalion was dispersed as skirmishers when it came under heavy attack. When the initial eagle bearer was killed (it appears this was in fact a certain *Lieutenant* Donot, not a *sergent-major* as the regulations stipulated), there was an unsuccessful scramble by some nearby carabiniers to get the flag to safety. The 9e Légère did not report the loss because of a technicality. The gilded eagle had broken off its plinth before the battle in an accident, so they mounted this on a hop pole and hastily paraded it round when rumour of the loss started to spread. However, the Russians took the flag and the plinth with the regimental number and Napoleon eventually found out the truth. A few weeks later, at the brutal battle of Eylau (8 February), it is said the 10e Légère lost an eagle to the Russians, although this claim was not made official. This time the battalion in question was not deployed but formed in column supporting the left wing of Saint-Hilaire's division. Reports appear to vary, but during a snowstorm the regiment was ridden over by Russian dragoons before it could form a square.[6] No one on the Russian side claimed the capture, and the French remained quiet on their side, but an eagle belonging to the 10e was later found in a church in Potsdam. Regardless of the reason, after March 1807 the eagles of light infantry regiments returned to the regimental depots.

After the decree of 18 February 1808, the number of eagles was reduced to one per regiment. The other battalions received fanions. These were described on 8 April 1809 in a letter from the emperor to Marshal Berthier

---

5 Napoleon I, *Correspondance*, Vol. XIV, p.682.
6 Andolenko, *Aigles de Napoléon contre Drapeaux du Tsar*, p.150.

LILIES AND EAGLES – LIGHT INFANTRY COLOURS

as being quite simple, without any motto, bearing only the number of the regiment and the battalion number. Those battalions serving in the Corps of Oudinot were each to have a small tricolour flag, with the number of the demi-brigade on one side, with their parent regiment and battalion number on the reverse, for example: 1er DEMI-BRIGADE LÉGÈRE and then 4e BATAILLON DU 6e D'INFANTERIE LÉGÈRE. Napoleon concluded the letter with a promise to issue some much nicer flags as soon as possible.[7]

On 28 June 1809, Napoleon issued an instruction regarding the *deuxième* and *troisième porte-aigle*. Although light infantry regiments were officially required to keep their eagles at the depot, an instruction of 18 September 1809 to the Inspecteurs aux revues confirmed it applied to infantry regiments both de ligne and légère.[8] Also note the text of the order below erroneously refers to the *1er* and *2e porte-aigles*. In fact the premier porte-aigle was the bearer of the eagle. The text should read *2e* and *3e porte aigles*, something again confirmed in the instruction of 18 September:

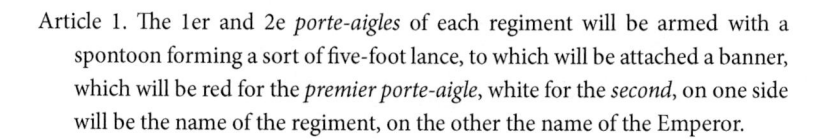

Officer of the 14e Légère in *tenue de ville* (walking out dress) in 1805 by Jacques Hilpert (1905). (New York Public Library)

> Article 1. The 1er and 2e *porte-aigles* of each regiment will be armed with a spontoon forming a sort of five-foot lance, to which will be attached a banner, which will be red for the *premier porte-aigle*, white for the *second*, on one side will be the name of the regiment, on the other the name of the Emperor.
>
> Art. 2. These spontoons will be supplied by the Minister of War, but in the meantime the regiments will be authorized to obtain them. This spontoon will be a kind of lance which will be used as a bayonet. The white and red banners will be used to mark the location of the eagle.
>
> Art. 3. The *premier* and *second porte-aigles* will carry, independently of the spontoon, a pair of pistols, which will be in a case, on the chest, on the left, in the manner of the Orientals.[9]

---

7   Napoleon I, *Correspondance*, Vol.XVIII, pp.524-526.
8   Gournay, *Journal militaire*, Year 1809, First Part, pp-188-189.
9   Picard & Tuetey, *Correspondance inédite de Napoléon Ier*, Vol.3, pp.106-107.

FRENCH LIGHT INFANTRY 1784-1815

The 1811 Model Eagle

In 1811 Napoleon asked for a new design which would incorporate the regimental battle honours since the time of the Camp of Boulogne. The project manifested itself in the decree of 25 December 1811. Henceforth a single eagle would be given to each regiment of infantry with a complement of over 1,200 men, and to cavalry regiments numbering more than over 600 horses. The eagle would be assigned to the first battalion. The other battalions would receive *fanions* without inscriptions to which no importance would be attached, and no honours rendered. The flags were coloured white for 2e bataillon, red for the 3e, blue for the 4e, green for the 5e, and yellow for the 6e.

The flag attached to the eagle, or ensign as it was now officially designated, was formulated in the first months of 1812. The standard for foot troops would be 0.83 metres on each side, not including the fringe. Three cravats would hang from the top of the flag would measure 1.06 metres by 0.18 metres and be coloured blue, white and red. The flag consisted of three vertical bands in blue, white, and red, with elaborate gold embroidery depicting bees and crowns, and Napoleon's initial 'N'. The centre of the flag carried the inscription l'EMPEREUR NAPOLÉON AU [number] RÉGIMENT D'INFANTERIE

Voltigeur and carabineer from 1809. The yellow stripe down the voltigeur's trouser leg is an interesting detail, but may have been influenced by later periods. (New York Public Library)

LÉGÈRE. On the reverse of the flag were the battle honours of the regiment. The battles allowed were Ulm, Austerlitz, Jena, Eylau, Friedland, Eckmühl, Essling and Wagram. This flag would be replaced every two years by the Ministry of War. In terms of the battle honours awarded to light infantry, Hollander reconstructed the allocations (see Table 24). Hollander noted the 1er, 14e, 19e, 22e, 31e, 32e regiments did not received any inscriptions. The other missing numbers were vacant. He also noted some regiments did not receive the new standard until 1813.

Table 24. Battle Honours, 1811 Standards

Battle/ Regt	2e	3e	4e	5e	6e	7e	8e	9e	10e	12e	13e
Ulm			X		X	X		X	X		
Austerlitz								X			X
Jena					X	X		X			X
Eylau					X	X		X			X
Friedland	X		X		X	X		X		X	
Eckmühl		X				X			X		X
Essling		X			X			X	X		
Wagram		X		X	X		X	X	X		X
Battle/ Regt	15e	16e	17e	18e	21e	23e	24e	25e	26e	27e	28e
Ulm			X	X			X	X	X	X	
Austerlitz	X		X				X		X		
Jena		X					X	X	X	X	
Eylau		X					X	X	X		
Friedland		X						X		X	
Eckmühl	X						X	X			
Essling		X	X		X		X	X	X	X	X
Wagram	X	X	X	X	X	X	X	X	X	X	X

In terms of the ban on light infantry taking their colours into the field, Hollander cites a letter from Berthier to Napoleon dated 22 March 1812. Berthier had been asked by the *colonel* of the 7e Légère is they could retrieve their eagle from the depot. Berthier added he thought light infantry ought to carry their eagles like other regiments.[10] Napoleon's response was to reiterate that all regiments with their eagles in the depots ought to keep them there. This raises an interesting question. Did light infantry regiments adopt the plain battalion colours, and if so, what colour did the first battalion use?

First Restoration and the 100 Days

After Napoleon's abdication the remaining eagles and flags were either stolen as trophies by the victorious allies, melted down and burned, or hidden from the authorities and put into safe keeping. A more conciliatory course of action might have been to retain the French tricolour as the national emblem, but for the Bourbons in 1814, national colours of the revolution were too deeply

---

10   Hollander, *Nos drapeaux et étendards de 1812-1815*, p.32.

FRENCH LIGHT INFANTRY 1784-1815

Porte-guidon 1807-1812 by JOB. Notice the chasseurs have lost their sabre-briquets by this time. (New York Public Library

tainted by the memory of the act of regicide and judicial murder of so much of the old nobility.

The new infantry flag was carried by an officer of the first battalion. They were white, 1.5 metres square, embroidered with golden fleur-de-lys and rosettes, and fringed in gold. In the centre of the flag was the inscription: LE ROI AU RÉGIMENT DE [title then number] D'INFANTERIE LÉGÈRE. On the reverse of the flag was the French coat of arms and other royalist symbology. The first distribution of the new royal flags to light infantry regiments took place on 24 September 1814, the Régiment du Roi, the Régiment de la Reine, Régiment de Monsieur, 12e and 15e Légère. As part of the ceremony the flags were blessed and the soldiers took an oath to the new regime, all to the repeated cries of *Vive le Roi!*

On 9 March 1815, the tricolour cockade and flag were resurrected at Grenoble. Napoleon had returned, and in so doing appealed to his former army to take up their eagles. With Louis XVIII and his court again in exile, on 9 April 1815 Napoleon announced there would be a new distribution of eagles. The new standards had a flag measuring 1.2 metres square. It was formed of a double silk which was sewn together. The flag had three vertical bands in the national colours, blue at the staff end, white then red. It was bordered with a fringe of gold between 2.5 and 1.5 centimetres in length, fixed between the two sides of the flag. The battle honours assigned to the 1811 model flag were retained. A surviving example from the Imperial Guard also includes the battle honours for La Moskowa (Borodino), Lutzen and Montmirail. The eagle was supposedly the same model as that used in 1804, but surviving examples show there were differences in newly cast models. The wings were lower than before, the beak was closed, and it was slightly lighter at 1.45 kilos. In general, the craftsmanship was poorer, perhaps indicating the speed at which the flags were issued. Following an audit of the regiments in September, almost all the eagles issued in 1815 were reclaimed by the government and melted down.

7

Notes for Re-enactors and Wargamers

Petite-guerre scenarios offer some of the best opportunities for re-enactors to replicate the operations of Napoleon's army at something approaching a realistic 1:1 scale. The formation of a *grande-garde* or picket, with outlying small posts, sentinels, patrols, and ambushes might be replicated with 60-80 infantry and a few horsemen. Opposing sides might take the opportunity to discover and probe one another's chains, or even attempt to infiltrate them at night, or to pass through woods. There is the interesting opportunity to question real 'locals' about what they have seen on the road ahead, and even to despatch spies. The fortification of the *grande-poste* offers an interesting opportunity to construct fieldworks (while respecting property) and may even provide a reasonable excuse to place a few pieces of artillery to cover a road or important position. If larger numbers and space permits it, a central camp might be formed with several pickets defending it, with regular changes of guard and patrols in force. When one adds a command team of a few mounted senior officers and aides, such a scenario can make for a dynamic and compelling event. Where skirmishes do occur, success ought to be measured in the ability to outflank, cut off and surround an enemy. The objective then is one of capturing prisoners.

An officer of voltigeurs from the 8e Ligne (1808). The uniform depicted here is wonderfully elegant. Note the plume is completely green. (Anne S.K. Brown Military Collection)

FRENCH LIGHT INFANTRY 1784-1815

The prerogatives of the avant-garde in a satirical piece named 'Arrival at Garrison'. The woman armed with a broom is exiting a house with a 'wise woman' sign above the door. (Collection Yves Martin)

Although it appears French light infantry and voltigeurs usually formed and manoeuvred in three ranks, an interpretation in two ranks is a valid interpretation for them. The commander might wish to detach a section, or even just a few files to scout ahead. If the number of files were fixed at the beginning of the exercise, it would be a simple case of using Guyard's *éclaireurs en avant* instruction to deploy them. The soldiers ought to operate in pairs and make use of natural cover as they find it. An NCO should direct them, or an officer if a significant body is deployed. When skirmishing for a larger body of infantry in close support, it is not necessary for the light infantry to maintain a reserve. The entire unit might form up in two ranks, then create an open-order chain, as described by Schèrer, opening the files by three paces, and covering the supporting unit. At larger scale events, units may wish to attempt the later period voltigeur instructions, as described by Morand, Schneider and Reille, retaining one third in a formed body, and with a 15 paces interval in the cordon. Light infantry ought to rehearse flanking and screening a column, firing during an advance and on the retreat, and loading while kneeling or in the prone position. The rehearsal of forming rally clumps is a particularly useful precaution when horses are likely to be present.

Wargamers can of course enjoy interpreting and re-fighting the grand battles of the Napoleonic Wars, although rule sets may skim over the use of skirmishers for expediency's sake. This is a great pity, because skirmish fire was arguably the principal means of delivering infantry fire by the French.

'Leaving the garrison' is the second part of this satirical study. Notice the soldiers making their excuses to the pregnant women. (Collection Yves Martin)

However, gamers might wish to create their own battalions of voltigeurs (and carabiniers/ grenadiers) at brigade or even divisional level, combining light and line voltigeurs in the same unit. Voltigeurs would have an advantage in firing, but if one attempted to use battalions of voltigeurs for shock action, their elite status ought not to cloud the fact they were the smallest men in the army, armed with shorter muskets. This physical disadvantage must be recognised. One should always remember Duhesme's assertion that light infantry always skirmished better than line infantry – that might be reflected by a weighting in the rule sets in terms of accuracy of firing, certainly before the campaigns of 1809, after which light and line infantry centre companies ought to be taken as standard.

Smaller scale, skirmish games perhaps offer better opportunities to highlight the impact of light infantry. For example, the availability of natural cover ought to provide light infantry with a weighted advantage against formed troops. Voltigeurs might also be accompanied by small units of *sapeurs* drawn from each regiment (perhaps represented by a single figure), able to cut pathways through obstacles and to remove barricades. One might also consider the effect of the rifled carbines carried by voltigeur NCOs, and some officers. In static situations, these could provide a greater level of accuracy. This might have particular use in counter-insurgency scenarios.

Gamers attempting to represent a French army in the early 1790s will find their painting skills put to the test with wonderfully outlandish costumes and soldiers reduced to rags and barefoot in equal measure. Rules should reflect the fact that swarms of tirailleurs were thrown into combat in *grande bandes*, vastly outnumbering the Austrian or Prussian skirmishers available. The fog of gunfire smoke and confusion inflicted by these skirmishers ought to prevent battalions seeing they were about to be charged by fast moving infantry columns. This might be reflected in the rules by a weighting in favour of the attack column. A light infantry demi-brigade of 1794 might include all manner of different volunteer units, along with green-coated chasseurs. An interesting feature in early 1790s games might be to improve the effect of tirailleurs by placing a young, ambitious general up in the front line directing their operations. While his presence ought to provide a weighted advantage, from time to time, it would be necessary to test if the general was 'a lucky general' or if he was among the heroes depicted by Girodet, being met by Ossian at the gates of paradise. The impact of the general's demise might be judged by the throw of the dice: it might plunge the skirmish screen into utter confusion, or enrage it to perform miracles for a round or two, such was the unpredictable nature of things in the 1790s. Again, professional chasseur battalions ought to skirmish better than levies rounded up into columns and marched off to the front. In the 1790s, particularly the Italian Campaign and those involving Massena, the line infantry battalions ought to form their own volunteer éclaireur companies in addition to the existing nine companies per battalion. Perhaps numbering around 50-70 men per battalion, these éclaireurs can be represented by a few figures in suitably dynamic poses. These should not be formed into elite battalions, but remain attached to their parent battalion and brigade, skirmishing ahead of it.

Bibliography and Further Reading

There has never been a better time to research the French army during the eighteenth century and Napoleonic Wars. Authors now have instantaneous access to an amazing array of primary and secondary sources. When I first went to study at the military archives in Vincennes in the 1990s, I would leave Paris crushed by the weight of photocopied documents, and much poorer in the bargain. I now stroll about with an electronic tablet containing all the reference books which used to occupy a massive bookshelf in the reading room. Below are the main sources used in this work and some additional titles readers may care to consult.

Andolenko, C.R., *Aigles de Napoleon contre Drapeaux du Tsar* (Paris: Eurimprim, 1969)
Avril, Jean-Baptise, *Essai Avantages d'une bonne discipline, et moyens de l'entretenir dans les corps: ouvrage suivi d'un essai historique sur l'infanterie française* (Paris: Anselin et Pochard, 1824)
Bardin, Étienne-Alexandre, *Dictionnaire de l'armée de terre, ou Recherches historiques sur l'art et les usages militaires des anciens et des modernes* (Paris: J. Corréard, 1841-1851)
Bardin, Étienne-Alexandre, *Examen de la législation sur le service en campagne et dans les place assiégés* (Paris: Magimel, 1816)
Bardin, Étienne-Alexandre, *Manuel d'infanterie, ou Résumé de tous les réglemens, décrets, usages, renseignemens propres aux sous-officiers de cette arme* (Paris: Magimel, 1813)
Bardin, Étienne-Alexandre, *Mémorial de l'officier d'infanterie* (Paris: Magimel, 1813)
Beamish, North Ludlow, *On the Uses and Application of Cavalry in War from the Text of Bismark* (London: T&W Boone, 1855)
Berriat, H., *Recueil méthodique et raisonné des lois, décrets, arrêtés, réglemens et instructions actuellement en vigueur sur toutes les branches de l'état militaire* (Alessandria: Louis Capriolo, 1812)
Brack, Antoine Fortuné de. *Avant-postes de cavalerie légère* (Breda: Broese & Comp, 1834)
Bulos, M., *Mémoires du Maréchal Ney* (Paris: H. Fournier, 1833)
Colin, Jean, *La tactique et la discipline dans les armées de la Révolution* (Paris: Chapelot et Cie, 1902)
Colin, Jean, *L'infanterie au XVIIIe siècle: la tactique* (Paris: Berger-Levrault, 1907)
Couvreur, H., *Souvenirs d'un officier de Napoléon: d'après les lettres du Capitaine Cardron, de Philippeville, 1804–1815* (Namur: Imprimerie Jacques Godenne, 1938)
Crowdy, T.E., *Incomparable: a collection of essays. The formation and early history of Napoleon's 9th Light Infantry Regiment* (Oxford: Osprey Publishing, 2012) [eBook]
Crowdy, T.E., *Incomparable: Napoleon's 9th Light Infantry Regiment* (Oxford: Osprey Publishing, 2012)
Crowdy, T.E., *Marengo: The Victory that placed the Crown of France on Napoleon's Head* (Barnsley: Pen & Sword Military, 2015)
Crowdy, T.E., *Napoleon's Infantry Handbook* (Barnsley: Pen & Sword Military, 2015)
Duhesme, Philibert-Guillaume, *Précis historique de l'infanterie légère: de ses fonctions, et de son influence dans la tactique des différens siècles* (Lyon: Bérenger, 1806)
Duhesme, Philibert-Guillaume, *Essai sur l'infanterie légère, ou Traité des petites opérations de la guerre, à l'usage des jeunes officiers: avec cartes et plans* (Paris: Michaud, 1814)
Faesch, Georg, *Instructions militaires du Roi de Prusse pour ses Généraux. Nouvelle édition augmentée avec les instructions pour la petite guerre* (London: Elemslet, 1777)

Gassendi, Jean-Jacques-Basilien de, *Aide-mémoire à l'usage des officiers d'artillerie de France* (Paris: Chez Magimel, Anselin & Pochard, 1819)

Girod de l'Ain, Félix, *Dix ans de mes souvenirs militaires de 1805 à 1815* (Paris: J. Dumaine, 1873)

Gournay, B.C., *Journal militaire* (Paris: Didot Le Jeune, then Imprimerie du Journal Militaire, 1790-1815)

Grandmaison, Thomas Auguste Le Roy de, *La Petite Guerre, ou traite du service des troupes légères en campagne* (Francfort & Leipsic: Knoch & Esslinger, 1758)

Guibert, Jacques-Antoine-Hippolyte de, *Essai général de tactique, précédé d'un discours sur l'état actuel de la politique et de la science militaire en Europe* (London: Libraries des Associes, 1772)

Guyard, Colonel, *Instruction pour le service et les manoeuvres de l'infanterie légère, en campagne*, (Paris: Magimel, An XIII)

Heusch, Waldor de, *Étude sur l'infanterie légères* (Bruxelles: Spineux & Cie, 1891)

Hollander, O., *Les Drapeaux des demi-brigades d'infanterie de 1794 à 1804: Avec un chapitre préliminaire sur les drapeaux des régiments d'infanterie de 1791 à 1794* (Paris: J. Leroy, 1913)

Hollander, O., *Nos drapeaux et étendards de 1812 à 1815* (Nancy & Paris: Berger-Levrault et Cie. 1903)

Husson, Eugène-Alexandre, *Instruction pour les voltigeurs de l'infanterie légère et de ligne* (Paris: Cordier, 1822)

Jeney, Louis Michel de, *Le Partisan ou l'art de faire la petite-guerre avec succès* (La Haye: Constapel, 1759)

Kéralio Louis-Félix de; Lacuée, Jean-Girard; Servan, Joseph, *Encyclopédie méthodique – Art Militaire* (Paris: Panckouchke, 1784-1797)

Kharkevich, V.I., *Materials of the Military-Scientific Archive of the General Staff. Patriotic War of 1812. Section II. Papers taken from the enemy. Volume I. Outgoing correspondence of Marshal Davout (from October 14 to December 31, 1811). Publication of the Military Scientific Archive of the General Staff, under the editorship of Major General V. I. Kharkevich, 1903* (St. Petersburg: Printing House Berezhlivost, 1903)

Jarry, Francis, *Instruction Concerning the Duties of Light Infantry in the Field* (London: A. Dulau, 1803)

Lafayette, Marie Joseph Paul Yves Roch Gilbert du Motier, Marquis de.,*Memoirs, Correspondence and Manuscripts of General Lafayette* (New York: Saunders & Otley Ann Street, 1837)

Marbot, Marcellin, *Remarques critiques sur l'ouvrage de M. le lieutenant-général Rogniat, intitulé: Considérations sur l'art de la guerre* (Paris: Anselin & Pochard, 1820)

Marmont, Auguste Frédéric Louis Viesse de (duc de Raguse), *Mémoires du Maréchal Marmont Duc de Raguse de 1792 à 1841* (Paris: Perrotin, 1857)

Mavidal, Jérôme; Laurent, Émile (Founders), *Archives Parlementaires de 1787 à 1860: Première Serie 1789 à 1799* (Paris: Paul Dupont, 1867-1913)

Mesnil-Durand, François Jean de Graindorge d'Orgeville de, *Fragments de tactique, ou six mémoires précédés d'un discours préliminaire* (Paris: Ant. Jombert, 1774)

Montendre de Longchamps, François Edme de; Montendre, Alexandre chevalier de; Roussel, Jacques de, *État Militaire de France* (Paris: Guillyn, then Onfroy, 1758-1793)

Napoléon I, *Correspondance de Napoléon Ier: Publiée Par Ordre de L'empereur Napoléon III* (Paris: H. Plon, J. Dumaine, 1858-1870)

Picard, Ernest; Tuetey, Louis, *Correspondance inédite de Napoléon Ier, conservée aux Archives de la guerre* (Paris: Henri Charles-Lavauzelle & Cie, 1912-1925)

Quillet, P.N., *Etat actuel de la législation sur l'administration des troupes* (Paris: Magimel, 1808)

Roche-Aymon, Antoine Charles Etienne Paul de la, *Des Troupes légères, ou réflexions sur l'organisation, l'instruction et la tactique de l'Infanterie et de la Cavalerie légères* (Paris: Magimel, Anselin & Pochard, 1817)

Rogniat, Joseph, *Considérations sur l'art de la guerre* (Paris : Magimel, 1816),

Saxe, Maurice, Comte de, *Reveries, or Memoirs concerning the art of war* (Edinburgh: Donaldson, 1759)

Schneider, Colonel Virgile, *Résumé des attributions et devoirs de l'infanterie légères en campagne* (Paris: Dondey-Dupré, 1823)

Susane, Louis, *Histoire de l'ancienne infanterie française* (Paris: Corréard, 1849-1853)

Thiébaud, Jean-Marie and Tissot-Robbe, Gérard, *Les Corps Francs de 1814 et 1815: la double agonie de l'empire: les Combattants de l'impossible* (Paris, SPM, 2011)

Varinot, Adolphe Damesme, *Cours d'administration militaire, à l'usage de MM. les élèves de l'école spéciale impériale militaire de Saint-Cyr* (Paris: Magimel, 1810)

Vernier, Jules, *Correspondance inédite de Victor-François, duc de Broglie, maréchal de France, avec le prince Xavier de Saxe, comte de Lusace, lieutenant général: pour servir à l'histoire de la guerre de Sept and campagnes de 1759 à 1761* (Paris: Albin Michel, 1903)